THE
TRUTH
TWISTERS

THE
TRUTH
TWISTERS

RICHARD DEACON

Macdonald

A Macdonald Book

Copyright © Donald McCormick 1986

First published in Great Britain in 1987
by Macdonald & Co (Publishers) Ltd
London & Sydney

British Library Cataloguing in Publication Data

Deacon, Richard, 1911–
The truth twisters.
1. Propaganda
Rn: Donald McCormick   I. Title
303.3'75

ISBN 0-356-12216-6

Photoset by Fleet Graphics, Enfield, Middlesex

Printed and bound in Great Britain by
Hazell Watson & Viney Limited,
Member of the BPCC Group,
Aylesbury, Bucks

Macdonald & Co (Publishers) Ltd
Greater London House
Hampstead Road
London NW1 7QX
A BPCC plc Company

Contents

	FOREWORD	7
1	SERVICE FIVE IS LAUNCHED	15
2	WAGING 'THE COLD WAR'	33
3	EXPLOITATION OF THE MEDIA AND BOOKS	48
4	THE TAMING OF THE CHURCHES	64
5	WHEN 'TRUTH CAN NEVER BE TOLD'	80
6	THE GREAT COMPUTER MENACE	95
7	'STAR WARS' AND OTHER NONSENSE	111
8	HOW SERIOUS IS POLLUTION?	125
9	FORGERS OF THE KGB	142
10	A WORLD OF FANTASY	159
11	PSYCHO-POLITICS: AN EASTERN OR A WESTERN INVENTION?	171
12	UFOLOGY AND THE PARANORMAL	182
13	INFORMERS OR DISINFORMERS?	196
14	SOME WESTERN WILES	208
	CHAPTER NOTES	224
	INDEX	235

Acknowledgements

Acknowledgements are gratefully made by the author for the following permissions to reproduce and quote:–
The Master, Fellows and Scholars of Churchill College in the University of Cambridge;
Mrs Margaret Godfrey for quotations from the unpublished memoirs of her husband, the late Admiral Godfrey;
The Centre for Conflict Studies, University of New Brunswick, Fredericton, for quotations from *Conflict Quarterly*.
The author is also especially grateful for much help and guidance from Mr Frederick Rubin, Dr Hugh L'Etang, the International Institute of Strategic Studies, Colonel Samuel Pope, OBE, RM, Professor Douglas Wheeler (USA) and Mr Stephen Roberts, Reference Center Director, United States Embassy in London, and countless other people who have provided evidence of disinformation at various levels.

Illustration Credits

Foreword

'Disinformation' is a word that, as yet, has not entered many dictionaries of the world and, when used, is usually garbed in inverted commas, almost as if to cast doubt on its existence.

Nevertheless, it is gradually being accepted as an increasingly important and disturbing word and in some areas of the world is used straightforwardly as a positive noun. In Soviet Russia it is called *dezinformatzia*, a word which is often on the lips of those engaged in State services. Indeed, *dezinformatzia* is an important part of Soviet policy-making. Likewise, the word is also to be found in the Hungarian *Official Dictionary of Political Terms*, published by the Central Committee of the Hungarian Socialist Workers' Party, Kossuth Publishers, of Budapest.

This is a book about disinformation in all its many forms and from now onwards the inverted commas can be dispensed with. For this sinister development in everyday life is such that it is liable to appear in the most unlikely quarters.

After much careful thought I decided to make the title of this book not *The Lie Makers* (my original choice), but The *Truth Twisters*. For, very often, disinformation is not so much a matter of blatant lies, as of concealing or twisting the truth. Sometimes such disinformation is deliberately circulated, but occasionally (perhaps more often than we should like to believe) it is an involuntary, unconscious form of deception.

In some measure the vast majority of us have at some time in our lives been disinformers, even if only to the extent of the little white lie concoted with the most benevolent of intentions, such as not wishing to make one's nearest and dearest worry needlessly. And, if we do this too often and are found out, we are liable to worry them more in future because they can never be sure we are telling the truth.

Truth-twisting on a purely domestic scale may do little real harm and sometimes a certain amount of good. One might, however, make the cynical comment that unless it is conducted with caution and great attention to detail, it will inevitably fail if practised too often. In war-time it can be justified as a method of waging battle, provided it is directed against the enemy and is not merely covering up one's own deficiencies, though sometimes it might be vital to hide these by disinforming the enemy. But when, in peacetime, truth-twisting escalates into something larger, into governmental, business and even ecological spheres, then the note of warning needs to be struck loud and clear.

Once disinformation becomes a habit in any sphere, once people become careless about the exact truth, then we are all at risk. It is not the deliberate lie which we have to fear (something that in a democracy can usually be spotted as blatant propaganda), but the half-truth, the embellished truth and the truth dressed up to appear as something quite different. If on a man's death certificate the cause of death is officially given as meningo-encephalitis, technically this may be correct. However, if the prime cause of the encephalitis was that the man was suffering from AIDS, then this is truth-twisting. If done on a large scale as a cover-up, then it could in effect be an unfortunate deterrent to pin-pointing the real horrors of this new and dreaded disease which can strike in so many different ways.

Both doctors and patients disinform, a factor which is not merely damaging to patients, but time-wasting and destructive to any health service. Dr Nicholas Rutter, senior lecturer in child health at the Nottingham University Medical School, told a British Medical Association congress in Cairo that doctors should be on the alert for cases in which mothers invented illnesses on behalf of their children. 'Fictitious epilepsy should be considered if a child is reported as having frequent fits which are never witnessed by anyone except the mother and which respond poorly to anti-convulsants.'[1]

Thus disinformation can take many forms. There is the

8

alarming but barely recognized technique of subliminal disinformation by which the truth can be twisted so that the distortion is unconsciously absorbed, something which both television and radio commentators have subtly perfected. Here the important point to bear in mind is that television and radio have an advantage over the printed word. The reader can select what he reads; he can reject instanteously what he disbelieves. Although one can switch off television or radio, psychologically one is very much more its captive.

As an author I will frankly admit that on a few occasions I have been disinformed and as a result have disinformed other people. This is a hazard which confronts us all.

Sometimes disinformation can be no more than a change of emphasis, switching from one extreme to another when the process is totally illogical. This occasionally happens in sections of the media when it is felt that a mistake has been made in presenting the news and that, to counteract this, the pendulum of emphasis needs to be swung in the opposite direction.

The London *Times*, for example, prior to World War II, had been markedly supportive of a policy of appeasement towards Nazi Germany and hostile and unenthusiastic towards any alliance with the Soviet Union, even as a defensive measure. Yet when R. McG. Barrington-Ward succeeded Geoffrey Dawson as editor during World War II there was a reversal of emphasis: the paper did not simply support the war against Germany, but suddenly became pro-Soviet, employing a fellow-travelling correspondent, Ralph Parker, in Moscow, and in the latter stages of the war was positively sympathetic to the Greek Communists when civil war was imminent in Greece.

This was not factual disinformation, but a change of policy so abrupt and exaggerated without any attempt to explain its left-about-turn that it amounted to a subtle form of manipulating the public. In retrospect the real truth lay somewhere between the pre-war attitude and the changed situation of a nation at war: the disinformation lay in the failure honestly to admit the errors of pre-war editorial policies and to show that the USSR might temporarily be an ally, but that its long-term aims were in no way changed. After all there had been the damning evidence of the Nazi-Soviet Pact of the late summer of 1939.

Most nations have practised disinformation of a deliberate

kind when they have been at war. The supreme master of this art in centuries past was undoubtedly Sun Tzu, the Chinese sage and author of the *Ping Fa,* or *Principles of War*, which is believed to have been in circulation as early as 510 BC, though this is by no means certain. Sun Tzu's theory was that 'all warfare is based on deception' and that one must 'feign incapacity when capable of being able to attack' and then 'feign disorder within and strike him'.

These principles and teachings were studiously followed by Chinese generals down the centuries and were being studied by the Japanese Army from the late nineteenth century. Those who wish for a recent simplified and summarized translation of Sun Tzu could usefully go to a comprehensive reference library and read *The Principles of War*, published during World War II by Welfare Publications, sponsored by the Royal Air Force in what is now Sri Lanka.

In his private memoirs the late Admiral J.H. Godfrey, chief of British Naval Intelligence in World War II, wrote that 'there was very little deliberate invention or twisting of intelligence in the British fighting services, but the continental systems, Russian, Austrian, Italian and German, and even the French, are never entirely free from suspicion. Deception plans and propaganda have sometimes deceived their initiators and have a way of coming back at one, through agents, prisoners-of-war, neutral capitals and foreign attachés in a form that gives them the appearance of truth.'[2]

Admiral Godfrey went on to tell how in World War I the French exaggerated their casualties to include lightly wounded in order to 'persuade the British to take over more of the line. The Germans underestimated casualty lists as they did not dare publish actual figures.'[3] The admiral admitted that in World War II 'Churchill and Pound [Admiral of the Fleet Sir Dudley Pound] trebled the U-boat casualties during the first year of the Hitler war.'

Sun Tzu's major principle of the value of capturing one's enemy and then 'turning' him against his own people was a tactic which was utilized in a highly professional manner in World War II. One of the most successful of disinformation techniques in wartime was that developed by the Double-Cross operations in Britain, Western Europe and the Middle East. The X-2, or Double-Cross, Committee in London achieved considerable successes in disinforming the enemy by capturing German agents and persuading them to radio false information to their own people. Outstanding among such 'turned' agents was Wulf Schmidt, code-named 'TATE', who tapped out thousands of words of disinformation to the Germans while under the control of the British during his captivity. Believing that Schmidt was one of the best agents they had in Britain during the war, the German authorities awarded him the Iron Cross, First Class.

However, since the end of World War II and increasingly over the past twenty years disinformation has been blatantly used as what the Soviet Union calls *aktivnyye merorpriatia* (active measures against other powers). It is still being consistently and relentlessly employed not only to deceive Western and Third World countries and the rapidly developing independent nations of the Far East, but to sow discord among allies, to try to overthrow governments and to mislead ordinary people everywhere.

It would be equally wrong to deny that some Western governments have themselves occasionally indulged in disinformation tactics, though never on the same scale or with the same fiendish purpose as the Russians. A close look will be taken at disinformation propagated by Western and democratic nations as well as by those of tightly controlled dictatorships whether of the one-man or the proletarian variety.

How successful such widescale disinformation as we have witnessed since 1945 has been is a matter of conjecture. Probably in the end it is self-defeating, but meanwhile a great deal of harm can be wrought. It is necessary to be constantly vigilant, since in searching for disinformation coming from a potential enemy one may very easily miss similar material emanating from one's own country.

A great deal of advertising, despite clap-trap about ethical codes, is sheer truth-twisting, sometimes blatantly so, at others cunningly concealed. The language of bureaucrats is riddled with double-talk, or phraseology which conceals the truth. In his book *Nineteen Eighty-Four* George Orwell provided a wonderful fictional picture of this in his 'Newspeak' with its distortion of a whole language and the perversion of former truths by such slogans as 'war is peace', 'freedom is slavery' and 'ignorance is strength'. In both the East and the West we have moved much closer to such Orwellian horrors not only in the creation of new words which are almost obscene in their fright-fulness, but in changing the meaning of old words and phrases. The Communist world has always revelled in jargon, but in many respects the Western world has been even more victimized by this process since 1945.

Orwell himself once wrote that 'the present political chaos is connected with the decay of language.' A few years ago Mr Ivor Clemitson, a Labour Member of Parliament, complained that 'politicians have started talking more gobbledegook than usual. Newspeak is moving into the House of Commons and Whitehall in a big way . . . I also think the English language is something special and ought to be regarded with respect, but it is murdered every day with death by a thousand cuts . . . All this increasingly becomes a barrier to communications.'

Using phrases which give false impressions is in itself a form of disinformation that can mislead a majority of any nation's population. Two words which are frequently on the lips of some politicians, both of the Left and the Right, and trade union leaders, are 'consensus' and 'confrontation'. Government by consensus no doubt sounds very comforting to many people, but in effect what politicians who use this phrase usually mean is: 'Don't let us do anything to upset anybody; avoid trouble and strikes at all costs; give in rather than oppose, go along with the majority even if this mean a mistaken policy.' Confron-tation is equally used to imply something different from what it is: the implication that any government or business firm which opposes unreasonable demands is in some way acting like an authoritarian tyrant. In trade union jargon confrontation means any effort made by an employer's federation, or individual firm or government, wishing to discuss an issue with a trade union without formally capitulating to its demands in advance. In short, the very people who can accurately be described as practising 'confrontation politics' are those who accuse the other side of this very thing.

The truth behind all this is quite simple. If any politician or party honestly means consensus when this word is used, then he or they should explain that such a method of government would only be logical and practical if it was conducted by holding a series of national referenda on various major issues, as they do in Switzerland. As to whether that method of government in all but a few small countries with highly civilized, educated and disciplined populations would work is another matter altogether. Similarly, to use the word confrontation when there has been no threat, but only a new proposal made, or at least an insistence on talks, is to give the impression of harsh and intransigent actions when none exist. Yet the word confrontation is today used in the wrong context as much by politicians of the soft Right as those of the hard Left.

Use the right phrase in the wrong sense and a whole nation can be slowly disinformed. What about the Nazis' *'Ein Reich, ein Volk, ein Führer*? (One nation, one people, one leader.) *Ein Volk*? What about the Jews and Christians opposed to Nazism and persecuted by this system of government? Yet within an astonishingly short time through this and similar juggling with phrases such as *Lebensraum* the German nation allowed itself to be turned from a democracy to a tyranny.

Sometimes a single individual who is a compulsive disinformer can create havoc far and wide. Quite often that individual is hailed in his or her lifetime as admirable, someone whose word is to be totally accepted. Such a person was T.E. Lawrence, more popularly known to past generations as 'Lawrence of Arabia'. He was a pathological disinformer, so much so that it was frequently impossible to tell whether he was disinforming on behalf of the British Government or for his own personal reasons. Evidence suggests it was a mixture of both. Lawrence was an example of a highly dangerous disinformer, and tragically his disinformation helped to create some of the Middle East problems of today.

Vigilance, self-questioning, the challenging of doubtful phrases are even more vital in today's society than in the past. Up to the end of the eighteenth century individuals who made extravagant claims generally needed to justify them. Much less was accepted as the truth unless it had been witnessed as such. Today, sophisticated disinformation through the media, especially on television and radio, is only too easy to disseminate.

Watchfulness on the seeming trivialities of disinformation can, or should, make us more aware of the danger of being exploited by deliberate and highly dangerous lies. This may range from some concocted plot in Moscow down to the patient who disinforms the doctor by conjuring up imaginary

13

symptoms. But the vital point to remember is that disinformation in the latter part of this century is something that is used in all walks of life, that sometimes threatens not only the security of nations, but the health and well-being of the individual.

1

SERVICE FIVE IS LAUNCHED

Within two years of the end of World War II the Soviet Union created a special disinformation service which was named Service Five.

Its innocent-sounding title was *Komitet Informatsii* (Committee of Information), but some clue as to its real purpose can perhaps be gleaned from the fact that its first chief was Colonel Grauehr, who had been head of Soviet Intelligence in Sweden and elsewhere. From 1947 onwards the art of disinformation was regularly practised by the Russians, skilfully controlled and activated until it became established policy. Its successes have been spectacular and influential and on a scale never before envisaged.

Although disinformation has been practised in various parts of the world for many centuries, politicians and leaders in all walks of life have always maintained that they respected the truth or at any rate – something with which even Machiavelli would have agreed – that they never lost sight of the truth. In most democracies it is realized that once the people learn that they have been deceived by their leaders, their faith in them is permanently destroyed, often even if the reason for deception was a good one. Admiral Godfrey put it rather less bluntly in his own private memoirs, and nobody was more aware than he of the need for deception in the sphere of naval intelligence. 'Elegant variation and tact are all very well in the proper place,' he wrote, 'but they should not obscure the truth. Deviation from what one conceives to be the truth can hardly be justified unless part of a deliberate policy or strategy.'[1]

Lenin was the first political leader positively to regard the truth as of no significance compared with the need to manipulate all information in the interests of the establishment and the triumph of Marxism-Leninism. This cynical view has prevailed in the Soviet Union ever since. It is a precept which illustrates perfectly the difference between such a system and any democratic system of government. Not to understand this is to lay oneself open to constant manipulation and disinformation by the Soviet Union.

Lenin, who regarded a final devastating battle as unavoidable if communism was to be established world-wide, actually advised his Soviet delegation to omit any reference to 'the inevitable forced *coup d'état* and bloody struggle' because such language would only frighten people.

Stalin, however, was much more of a realist in the manner in which he regarded the truth as of paramount importance. Despot though he was, suspecting the motives of all around him, he always thought an indiscriminate use of disinformation was highly dangerous. In this way he differed from Lenin, whatever view some historians may take. Rightly, he saw such tactics leading to all manner of problems, not least when it meant using Soviet agents to pose as friends of the Western powers. He realized that this could very easily lead to such agents being seduced into the Western camp.

So in the early years of Service Five those who ran it had much to contend with. Stalin had little patience with theories of any kind and Service Five was based on theories and an ancient pseudo-philosophic concept of disinformation. Links between the USSR and Communist China had led to a study of Sun Tzu, for whom disinformation was, if not a way of life, at least a vital weapon to employ against one's enemies. Yet it was not until 1950 that Sun Tzu was translated into Russian by N.I. Konrad, and sometime after this that his works were published in East Germany.

When, chiefly on Stalin's direction, an anti-Semitic campaign was waged by the USSR in the early fifties, Service Five suffered in consequence. So sudden a reversal of policy was bound to have serious repercussions for the Russians, but for a department dealing in disinformation the harm done was enormous. Originally, the USSR had supported Jewish claims for establishing their own state in the Middle East: it was one way of combating imperialism. But to reverse such a policy so quickly and to favour the Arabs, while actually persecuting Jews living in the USSR, was an incredible folly. It made nonsense of much of what Service Five had been trying to do. Not surprisingly, Colonel Grauehr had a nervous breakdown and was dismissed from his post.

Prior to this much of the disinformation that was disseminated towards the end of World War II and shortly afterwards had been aimed at enlisting Jewish allies against any possible remnants of Nazism. By today's standards much of this propagated material was naïve, yet surprisingly effective, not least in deceiving some of the Americans. One example of this was the myths perpetrated concerning the *Wehrwoelfe* (the 'Werewolves'), an organization of guerrilla fighters set up in the closing days of the war when Germany was on the verge of defeat. Their leader was *SS-Obergruppenführer* Hans Pruetzmann.

The *Wehrwoelfe* were a rather ridiculously optimistic and barbarous group who imagined they could become a powerful resistance movement which could harry the Allies from behind enemy lines and even continue to do so after Germany conceded defeat. Yet they expected to be treated as prisoners-of-war if captured. Their sponsors were the *Jagdverbaende* of the SS, the flying squads whose aim was to kill those they regarded as 'Bolshevist bandits', which included women and children. The *Wehrwoelfe*'s aim was also to intimidate the German population against dealing with the Allies when the latter arrived in their area. 'We shall punish every traitor and his entire family' was their motto. As the top Nazis realized that the end of the war was near they tried to limit the activities of the *Wehrwoelfe* in the West, but not in the Soviet-occupied territories. When Admiral Doenitz succeeded Hitler as leader of the German Reich he declared the *Wehrwoelfe* illegal, ordering them to stop all operations in Western Germany, but not in the east. These orders were obeyed.

17

Though there is scant evidence that the British took the *Wehrwoelfe* stories too seriously, they made a considerable impact upon the Americans. For the *Wehrwoelfe* had been infiltrated by Soviet agents and they had passed on to fellow agents inside Germany and Switzerland stories which suggested the *Wehrwoelfe* were far more powerful than they actually were. All this was passed on to American Military Intelligence through double-agents. There were some highly colourful and grossly exaggerated accounts of the *Wehrwoelfe* and their potentialities. It is true that the *Wehrwoelfe* regarded all supporters of Russia as their special enemies and that in areas occupied by the Russians *Wehrwoelfe* incidents continued for some time after war ended. Hans Zoeberlein, a Nazi author, organized a *Wehrwoelf* operation against Pensberg, a coal-mining village in Upper Bavaria, where the miners and the population generally had long-standing socialist and anti-Nazi traditions. Here Zoeberlein and his thugs hanged the Burgo-master and several of the inhabitants for welcoming the Americans. But generally speaking they achieved very little, nothing to substantiate the highly coloured accounts of their activities and background put out by Soviet disinformation.

These alleged that the *Wehrwoelfe* were an offspring of the *Ahnenerbe*, the Nazi Occult Bureau of the SS, that they were being strengthened by the withdrawal from Berlin of members of the Death's Head SS, the Gestapo and members of key ministries, and had stored away new rocket weapons in hideouts in the Alps. The latter were to be used against enemy targets, enabling the *Wehrwoelfe* to blot out whole cities in the United Kingdom and France. Such was the substance of the reports which Russia sought to pass on to the United States forces in Europe with a view to altering the whole course of the war.

The issue, quite simply, was this: Britain and occupied Europe might accept Russian forces pressing onwards into Europe, but for the United States any such threat would be resisted. There-fore the American military leaders must be convinced that the Nazis still posed a greater threat than the advancing Russians. Astonishingly, the colourful nonsense about Hitler comman-ding a secret army of guerrillas deep inside his mountain hideaway was not only accepted by some of the chief executives of SHAEF Intelligence (Supreme Headquarters Allied Expedi-tionary Force), but acted upon. One such report stated that:

'The rugged Alpine area of the National Redoubt is practically impenetrable. Considerable numbers of SS and other specially chosen units are now being systematically withdrawn there. Some of the more important ministries and personalities of the Nazi regime are already established there.'[2]

United States Seventh Army Intelligence informed General Eisenhower that: 'Defended by nature and by the most effective secret weapons yet invented, the powers that have hitherto guided Germany will survive to organize her resurrection. Armaments will be manufactured in bomb-proof factories, food and equipment stored in vast underground caverns and a specially selected corps of men will be trained in guerrilla warfare so that a whole underground army can be directed to liberate Germany.'

But the real threat of the *Wehrwoelfe* was directed mainly against the Russians and those areas of Germany occupied by the incoming Russians, mainly in East Prussia and Pomerania. These intrusions were easily mopped up by the Russians. Any *Wehrwoelfe* threat to the West was insignificant and hypothetical. Yet, on such disinformation as has been quoted, Eisenhower based his decision to make his main target not Berlin, but Bavaria and the National Redoubt. The *Wehrwoelfe* were swiftly destroyed and the underground runways for rocket-bombers were captured, but the defeat of Germany militarily would have ensured their downfall without any such special intervention being necessary. Eisenhower completely misread the situation and continued to do so long afterwards. Even when writing his memoirs he referred to the *Wehrwoelfe* as 'a Nazi underground army' (a gross exaggeration), going on to say that 'the way to stop this project – and such a development was always a possibility because of the passionate devotion to their *Führer* of so many young Germans – was to overrun the entire national territory before its organization could be affected.'[3]

That error of judgement – wasting time in chasing the phantom *Wehrwoelfe* – enabled the Russians under Marshal Zhukov to enter and capture Berlin and to establish their authority over a wide area of Eastern Germany. It was this particular piece of disinformation which so infuriated General George Patton, commander of the American Third Army, that he exploded with wrath against Military Intelligence. Patton had much reason to be angry in that his own views on how the war could be won satisfactorily and much more quickly were almost totally ignored. His idea of a satisfactory victory was that the Russians should never be given the chance to move far into Germany, Austria or other areas in the east of Europe and the Balkans where Hitler had held control. Therefore the Americans and British must move speedily across Germany; it was Patton's armoured thrust which contributed so richly to the Allies' victory in the West, but Patton himself considered the struggle could have been ended much earlier.

'I was, on 29 August 1944, racing for Verdun and Commercy from the Seine,' declared Patton, 'and there was no real threat against us as long as we did not allow ourselves to be stopped by imaginary enemies.' This was reported in an Associated Press telegram on that day.

Patton had even visualized using German troops after the war ended to keep the Russians at bay and prevent them from entering Europe. But that is another story.

Yet not all the disinformation towards the end of the war was being put out solely by the Soviet Union. The attitude of some of the Allies in trying to appease the USSR and hide from their respective peoples the post-war intentions of the Russians was in its way a form of deceit. If Roosevelt was a sick and dying man, as he appeared to be at Yalta, there was no excuse whatsoever for Churchill to have gone out of his way to praise the Russians and to give his Cabinet at home a highly favourable report about Stalin and Soviet intentions.

Some of the staff in the British Embassy at Moscow were appalled at the first news of the Yalta agreements. But the British Ambassador to Moscow, the pro-Soviet Archibald Clerk Kerr (later Lord Inverchapel) immediately issued orders that they should say nothing publicly about their misgivings.

At this time the Russians were being portrayed both in the world's press and by some politicians of the Allied powers as 'an ally to whom we owe much' and with whom 'we could easily and happily deal in future'. The fact that the Russians had made a pact with Nazi Germany in 1939, which was maintained until Germany invaded the Soviet Union in 1941, was completely overlooked. There never really was any unity at Yalta and Churchill's laudatory remarks were intended solely to reassure the Russians. His actual words were: 'The impression I brought back from the Crimea, and from all my other contacts, is that Marshal Stalin and the Soviet leaders wish to live in honourable friendship and equality with the Western democracies. I also feel that their word is their bond.' The chief disaster of the Yalta agreements was the Russians' failure to honour any promises to Poland.

During the Yalta talks the Russians were pressing strongly for bases in the Bosphorus and Tripolitania. Ostensibly they wanted this for their merchant ships; but the real reason was their anxiety to establish naval bases in this part of the world.

No area of the Balkans was, however, subject to so much disinformation coming from the British side as Yugoslavia both during and for several years after World War II. True, the SOE (Special Operations Executive) Balkans Section, directed from Cairo, had been infiltrated during the war with such Soviet agents as the late James Klugmann and they had manipulated a number of false reports which were passed on to London. But apart from this everything possible had been done to blacken the name of General Mihailovic, the pro-Royalist Chetnik leader, and to press forward the claims of the Russian-backed Tito. For it should always be remembered that it was not until 1948 that Tito broke with Moscow.

Tito was justifiably praised for making that break: in opposing the Stalin regime he revealed considerable personal courage. But this should not be allowed to hide the fact that during the Stalinist terror of the 1930s most of the leaders of the Yugoslav Communist Party were destroyed in Moscow and that Tito depended for his survival on his personal uncritical and abject support for Stalin in the decade when his colleagues were being wiped out one by one by that same Soviet dictator.

Only after the invasion of the Soviet Union by Germany in June 1941 did Tito's Partisans start to harass the Germans. Yet in the early part of 1944 Winston Churchill was making the wildly exaggerated statement (to be fair, based on information fed to him from Cairo) that Tito was holding down twenty-five German divisions in Yugoslavia during the war. The facts are that, once Yugoslavia was invaded by the Germans, the *Wehrmacht* never had more than seven divisions maintained in the territory. Yet during this period Mihailovic had enormous support in the Serbian areas of Yugoslavia where Tito had few allies.

If proof of this is required, then the statement of General Reinhard Gehlen, head of German Military Intelligence in Eastern Europe, made on 9 February 1943, certainly provides it. Gehlen sent a memorandum to the German General Staff stating that 'among the various resistance movements which increasingly cause trouble in the area of the former Yugoslav state, the movement of General Mihailovic remains in the first place with regard to leadership, armament, organization and activity . . . The followers of D.M. [Draza Mihailovic] come from all classes of the population and at present comprise about eighty per cent of the Serbian people . . . their number is continuously increasing.'[4]

Yet the false legend that Mihailovic was a collaborator with the Germans was sustained throughout the war by the pro-Soviet factions of the SOE in Cairo and elsewhere. In the end Mihailovic was totally disillusioned about cooperation with the Allies. He was never given credit in radio reports for such successes as the capture of Visegrad and Priboj from the enemy. The BBC, fed with the false legend and never supplied with all the facts, made no mention of these events, yet when Tito's Partisans drove out Mihailovic's forces they reported that these were successes over 'the enemy'.

For years Mihailovic's name was blackened by the Allies, long after his grossly unjust execution on Tito's orders in 1946 as a collaborator with the Germans. Even the *Encyclopaedia Britannica* was at fault: despite the fact that President Truman awarded the Chetnik leader a posthumous Legion of Merit in 1948, reference was made to Mihailovic's 'occasional collaboration with the Germans and Italians' and his abandonment by King Peter in 1944. But happily the 1985 edition of the *Encyclopaedia* omits these allegations and for the first time sets the record straight by including criticisms of Tito and mentioning the Truman award. Justice was only belatedly done to the name of Mihailovic by the personal intervention of the American Air Force General Richard Felman, who was one of some 500 Allied airmen who had been rescued by Mihailovic during the war. For a long time resistance to making such changes in the biographical entry for Mihailovic was due to fear of offending Tito or his successors.

Even as recently as 1985 a Yugoslav historian was expelled from the ruling Communist Party following a row over a book in which he re-appraised the wartime role of the royalist Chetnik movement. On 6 November 1985 the official Tanjug news agency of Yugoslavia reported that Veselin Djuretic was expelled for 'national intolerance and chauvinism', stating that his book, *The Allies and the Yugoslav War Drama*, had caused 'unprecedented anger and discontent among the Yugoslav public'. Djuretic has stated that his book was written after ten years' research from British, American, Soviet and French archive material, but unfortunately for him it challenged the official view which still asserts that the Chetniks were traitors and Nazi collaborators.

During the war some American officers were thwarted from trying to give aid to Mihailovic. Colonel Charles Sweeny, the soldier of fortune who had fought on the side of the Republicans in the Spanish Civil War and who had helped to found the Eagle Squadron for the RAF, hit upon a project for organizing a coup in Yugoslavia. Sweeny, who had fought in the Rif war in Morocco in the early 1920s, took the view that the mountains of Yugoslavia offered ideal hiding-places for guerrilla forces. He went to Washington and put up the idea of using Slav immigrants as well as American subjects for an operation inside Yugoslavia.[5]

But, while Sweeny had no difficulty in finding and signing up recruits, the State Department kept delaying giving him permission for the plan. Sweeny learned that the British Secret Service had intervened to veto him personally: ' . . . some pro-Soviet runt in Cairo had discovered that I once fought with Marshal Pilsudski of Poland against the Russians.'[6]

Doubtless in an attempt to discourage Sweeny, SOE in Cairo sent him a specially prepared map which falsely showed many areas of Yugoslavia as being held by the Partisans (Titoites) when actually they were in the control of the Chetniks. The map even purported to pin-point whole areas where Mihailovic was collaborating with the Germans. In vain did Sweeny argue back that even Tito had been forced on occasions to make expedient local deals with the German forces. Between 20 March and 5 May 1943, the Germans and Tito's forces had a tacit truce. This was a cynical move on Tito's part to enable the Germans to encircle and destroy the Chetnik forces in Montenegro, taking 5000 prisoners with their leaders as prisoners-of-war to camps in Germany and Poland. If Sweeny in the United States could acquire this kind of intelligence, it could obviously also have been made available to the SOE in Cairo.

Much of the failure to put the record straight on such matters for so very long after the war can be blamed equally on inferior or remarkably gullible historians, or on deliberate suppression of the truth. The main cause was suppression of the truth, particularly when it concerned some of the Allies' most disastrous decisions towards the end of the war and in the two subsequent years. The treatment meted out to the repatriated Russians taken prisoner during the war is a notorious example. Much of the latter part of the war was spent in helping the USSR to cover up their real intentions in demanding the forcible repatriation of more than two and a quarter million Russians from Western Europe. Hundreds of thousands of these were wanted solely that they could be liquidated, and the horrors and barbarity of this prolonged episode were as bad as anything perpetrated by the Nazis at Belsen or Buchenwald.

Count Nikolai Tolstoy has stated that 'thousands of Tsarist fugitives who had never lived in Russia under Soviet control and had fled their country in 1919 as allies of the British and Americans and who were not in consequence covered by the Yalta Agreement, were surrendered to *Smersh* in Austria under an arrangement so secret that "exceptional circumstances" are still employed to suppress the evidence.'[7]

This statement refers to File No. 383-7-14.1, which is not available to researchers at the British Public Records Office because the Ministry of Defence has withheld it on the grounds that it is 'personally sensitive'. So indeed it may be, but to whom? Mystery still surrounds this file. On 16 February 1978 Mr Fred Mulley, then Defence Minister, told the House of Commons that it had been destroyed. A copy of it was given to the US Government, but they had been asked not to release it. Challenged as to when this file vanished, the Ministry of Defence admitted that 'all three volumes were physically destroyed in 1968 or 1969 as not being worthy of permanent preservation under the Public Records Act, 1958.'

By driving these unfortunate anti-Bolshevik refugees into the hands of the Russians, by abjectly toadying to Stalin's demands and hiding the truth from the British people, all Britain's leaders and many civil servants were in effect callous co-partners in murder. The issue of the repatriation of non-Soviet Russians should be seen in the light of the handing over of 200,000 disarmed Croatian soldiers and half a million Croatian civilians to Tito's Partisans. The same pro-communist forces were at work in both operations, which led to terrible massacres in both Russia and Yugoslavia. One can perhaps make some excuse for both Roosevelt and Churchill in this period in that both were sick men. But later on Attlee and Bevin were also misled to some extent, while Eden as Foreign Secretary in the earlier period either deceived himself, or was so hell-bent on making a deal with Stalin that, as on other occasions, he ignored the evidence confronting him. Despite such excuses, it is plain that the British Government knew the fate which awaited these people.

As a result of Count Tolstoy's book, in July 1978 Foreign Office papers and other secret documents were released to the public eighteen years ahead of schedule in response to a widespread demand. Nothing like the whole truth has yet been revealed, but some of these documents show an incredible cynicism and deliberate truth-twisting in a desire to acquiesce in every Soviet demand. There was this minute written by Mr John Galsworthy, then a third secretary at the Foreign Office: 'At the meeting [with a Home Office official] . . . it was, I thought, agreed that when a Soviet deserter [sic] came into the hands of the civil police the latter should more or less assume, or pretend that the man in question was willing to return voluntarily to his camp, and hand him over to the local military authority accordingly. Any misunderstanding about the man's real wishes was, I thought, to be attributed to ''language difficulties'', etc. . . . If the deserter makes it abundantly clear that he is not willing to return, the civil police are to release him more or less into the arms of a military escort who will then bundle him away to the nearest Soviet camp. Once back in a Soviet camp the unfortunate man will have no access to any civil authorities (unless of course he escapes again) and will not, therefore, be in a position to protest against this rather rough justice.'[8]

Perhaps the hardest of the hard-liners on the question of repatriation was Geoffrey Masterman Wilson, a man with a Quaker background. It is ironical that the man who was for capitulating to Soviet demands on total repatriation, regardless of wishes or, for that matter, of nationality held, should eventually become chairman of Oxfam and the Race Relations

Board. 'When coloured people talk about fear of repatriation, that denotes a feeling of insecurity,' he has said. 'The doctrine of repatriation should not merely be condemned, but shown to be a cruel deception.' But Sir Geoffrey certainly did not take this view at the end of World War II when Russians being repatriated from HMS *Duchess of Bedford* were mown down by the machine-guns of the NKVD in nearby sheds as fast as they landed. What he said then was: 'I do not see how we can refuse to hand them back, if pressed to do so by Moscow.'

As to the myth that Tito's Yugoslavia was 'a friend of the Western democratic world', something which has been sustained for more than forty years, Tito himself, though saving his country from absolute Soviet domination, constantly served Moscow by his 'non-aligned' policy, notably in support of Arabs against Israel and for various so-called 'national liberation' movements. When Nora Beloff, the veteran British journalist, wrote her book, *Tito's Flawed Legacy*, she admitted that this was 'in part a penance for unquestionably accepting the Titoist bias shared by most of my countrymen.'[9]

In the early 1950s the Russians, after conducting a few highly successful exercises in deception, decided to develop strategic disinformation on a wide scale. True, this was not sanctioned officially until some few years after Stalin's death, but the Central Committee of the USSR had been encouraged to experiment in this direction after studying a training manual by a GRU (Soviet Military Intelligence) officer named Popov.

One of the earliest tricks employed to disinform the West was to plant Russian agents in Allied territories and to get them to persuade the relevant authorities that they were prepared to spy for the West on their return to Russia. Occasionally this was done when they wished to liquidate one of their own agents. He would be used as bait and then executed on his return.

One such case was that of a Soviet agent who claimed to the British to be a disaffected Latvian patriot, boldly asserting that if he could be safely smuggled back into Russia, he would act as a spy for the West and send back messages. His story appeared to be convincing and the British agreed to use the Royal Navy to make an illicit landing on Soviet territory in order to get the agent ashore.

The commanding officer of the RN ship was the late Mark Arnold-Forster, who later became diplomatic editor of the *Guardian*. But it was not until many years later on a visit to Oslo that a friend told him that he 'had unknowingly smuggled a Russian agent into the USSR'.[10]

When Arnold-Forster returned to London, he passed this surprising information on to the authorities. 'They confirmed it,' he stated. 'They also told me, all those years after the event, that under no circumstances should I enter the Soviet Union. Then with admirable dispatch they made contact with all the surviving members of my crew, and gave them the same warning. They knew that the Russian agent would be able to identify me, and they knew that we remained wanted men for our action in landing their man on Soviet territory.'

The agent had been landed – at his own request – on a railway embankment backed by an orchard not far from Sukhumi in Georgia. It was a difficult mission because there was a very high risk of the British ship being intercepted by Soviet search vessels. Thereafter this man had transmitted disinformation back to the British, but fortunately the deception was discovered before much harm had been done.

In the late 1950s the Soviet Union developed the branch of disinformation which they now call 'Active Measures', which expanded and originated in an imaginative fashion new theories and ideas on deception. This brought into being the agent who is the hardest to catch in any democratic nation – the agent of influence. He or she is not a spy, never (or hardly ever) breaks any laws, but steadily improves the Soviet Union's image in trade union, scientific, environmental and educational circles. In effect the agent of influence is much more dangerous than the active spy, who may have to wait for years to get results, for he represents a form of secret war upon the democracies.

The policy of 'active measures' is regarded as so successful that a KGB division has been set up to organize its operation in various parts of the world. This is Service A of the First Chief Directorate, which, from Moscow, directs and analyses all such operations through the Active Measures Officer, one of whom is established in most Russian embassies.

Towards the end of the 1950s one of the main aims of the Soviet government was to discourage Western nations from treating West Germany as a partner in either an economic or a military sense. For a while even the 'werewolves' campaign (as the Russians now referred to the *Wehrwoelfe*) was revived to try to make people believe that the Nazis still existed. KGB agents daubed swastikas and Nazi emblems all over the place in an effort to give credence to this falsehood. When West German troops were temporarily based in Wales for training and exercises, swastikas and Nazi slogans were painted on tombstones by these same agents to try and vilify the West German military personnel.

For a time this diabolical plot to suggest that West Germany could not eradicate its recent past succeeded to such an extent that some newspapers actually supported an anti-German attitude. The New York *Herald-Tribune* declared that Bonn was 'unable to eliminate Nazi poison'. Eventually, however, as a result of evidence provided to the West by defectors from the Soviet Union, the plot was totally discredited. Revelations of a subtle attempt to exacerbate relations between two NATO powers were made by Major Josef Frolik, a defector who was cross-examined by the US Senate Committee. In reply to a question asking for details of operations 'conducted by the Department of Active Measures, or the so-called Department of Dirty Tricks, he replied: "In about 1962 a West German tank regiment arrived in Wales for training. At this time the Czech service prepared operations whose aim was to smear the Germans by showing that the officers of this regiment were former Nazis. The Czech agent, who was stationed in Wales, received orders to paint swastikas on Jewish graves and vandalize Jewish graveyards. Everyone was to believe that members of the West German tank regiment were responsible for these ghoulish acts. The British newspapers accused the Germans and nobody saw that the Czechs were behind that." '[11]

This was the Soviet Union's first major operation to sabotage not only NATO but West European acceptance of West Germany as an equal partner militarily and economically. Late in 1959 anti-semitic slogans had been painted on a synagogue's walls and on Jewish graves in Cologne. Similar acts occurred in London, Manchester, Milan, New York, Oslo, Stockholm and Vienna. The Soviet radio poured out propaganda suggesting that this proved that Nazism still existed and that West Germany was not to be trusted, a theme which was taken up by some sections of the press in Western Europe. Even in the United States some doubts were raised, inducing the poet, Carl Sandburg, to urge the introduction of a death penalty for anyone found painting swastikas.

Fortunately the Jews, towards whom this propaganda was also directed, though with no pro-Jewish motives, were on the whole less easily deceived than other peoples. Since the creation of Israel in 1948 there had been developed in that new country one of the most efficient intelligence services in the whole world. Neither the Mossad (Israeli Secret Service), nor any other branch of Israeli Intelligence or Counter-Intelligence was deceived by such blatant Soviet propaganda, and they were able to reassure the rest of the Western world that this was simply a ploy by the Russians.

Undeterred, the Soviet Union has continued to exploit and manipulate neo-Nazi organizations. Not so long ago there was a long article by Lev Bezimensky, political analyst of the Soviet weekly *Novoye Vremya*, entitled 'Metamorphoses of West German Neo-Nazism'. Curiously, this article fails to mention one of the chief extreme right-wing organizations operating in the Federal Republic of Germany, the *Deutsche Volksunion*. But the omission acquires a certain significance when one considers that neo-Nazi political activities are in certain cases chain-linked to or originally initiated by either the East German State Security Service or by the USSR's KGB. That significance is enhanced when one notes that the late Reuben Ainstian, an expert on East European and communist affairs, said that 'Lev Bezimensky, associate editor of *New Times* [the English edition of a Soviet paper] is a senior officer (Colonel) of the KGB's department of disinformation and is working under cover of a journalist.' Earlier in his career, Lev Bezimensky had been an interpreter in the counter-intelligence directorate of the NKVD which was assigned to interrogate high-ranking German officers after the end of World War II. John Barron, the former US Navy intelligence officer, claims that twenty per cent of *New Times* articles are written by the KGB's disinformation service. [12]

In the 1950s considerable disinformation was emanating from the Western world, principally the United States, which in effect was helpful to the Soviet cause even though its aim was to discredit all friends of the USSR. During the period in which Senator Joseph McCarthy was fulminating against communists everywhere and claiming to discover them in the most unlikely places, the sheer extravagance of his campaign actually aided his opponents. The combination of McCarthy and J. Edgar Hoover, chief of the FBI (Federal Bureau of Investigation), was little short of disastrous. Always on the lookout for easily obtained kudos, Hoover had largely ignored Soviet infiltration in America in the vital war years when it was actually stepped up. Hoover was also xenophobically critical of the British, which made him a liability to the cause of Anglo-American collaboration in the field of intelligence. Whittaker Chambers, the most literate of the apostate Soviet agents, stated in his correspondence with William Buckley, Jr, that ' . . . Senator McCarthy will one day make some irreparable blunder which will play directly into the hands of our common enemy and discredit the whole anti-communist effort for a long time to come . . . The Communists recognized at once that Senator McCarthy is a political godsend . . . for he divided the ranks of the Right.'

One of the principal victims of the anti-communist lobby's own disinformation tactics was Dr Albert Einstein, and most of the investigations into the activities of the Nobel Prize-winning physicist and author of the *Theory of Relativity* were ordered personally by Hoover himself. The dossier which the FBI compiled on Einstein started in the early 1930s and continued until the mid-1950s. In this 1500-page file it is clear that Einstein was suspected of being the mastermind behind a communist plot to 'take over Hollywood', being the leader of a spy ring and of having used his office as a 'safe house' for the passing of messages between Soviet agents, as well as having had a hand in the kidnapping of the infant son of the aviator Charles Lindbergh in the 1930s.

In 1983 Professor Richard Schwartz of Florida International University made a request to consult the Einstein FBI file through the Freedom of Information Act. His purpose was to study the Einstein material as part of his researches into the impact of politics on science. He found that the various allegations made against the world-famous scientist had been totally discredited and proved to be based on disinformation.

Most of the investigations had been made at the behest of Hoover who for years refused to admit that there was no real evidence against Einstein. One of the letters in the file was from a German woman who had asserted she could provide evidence that Einstein was a communist. What all this 'evidence' amounted to, the FBI discovered, was that Einstein had refused to stand when the German national anthem was played during a trip to America in the 1930s. It was merely a silent protest against the Nazis. [13]

One of the vital axioms of Soviet foreign policy since 1945 had been that disinformation must be subject to the needs of military strategy as well as diplomacy. For some years Marshal Georgiy Zhukov was regarded by some Western observers as a moderating influence in Russian politics and a possible future leader when Stalin died. In truth, Zhukov was just as devious and antagonistic to the West as his colleagues. It was he who outlined the principles for strategic deception at a planning conference of Warsaw Pact officials in July 1956. Zhukov insisted that there should be a campaign which would 'conceal the full extent of Soviet capabilities from the West, in order to discourage the NATO countries from making the efforts required to contain the build-up of the Russian war machine.' This candid explanation of Soviet strategic deception ended with a comment from Zhukov that 'the Soviets never show their total strength'. A Polish defector made this revelation. [14]

Meanwhile on the 'peace front' the Russians made the most intensive efforts to manipulate world opinion, to infiltrate as many peace organizations as possible throughout the Western and undeveloped areas of the globe and to use them to support the USSR. The initiative for this took place as early as November 1949, when a peace campaign was planned by the Cominform (Communist Information Bureau) at the very time when Russia was about to start a build-up of its own nuclear deterrent. Within a few months the World Peace Council was created, linking up with such bodies as the Christian Peace Conference, the World Federation of Trade Unions and the International Union of Students. The presidency of the World Peace Council eventually fell to Romesh Chandra, a member of the Indian Communist Party and one of its leaders. Significantly, most of the money used to run the World Peace Council comes directly from Moscow, while the Council itself declines to issue a detailed budget or to allow any independent auditing of its finances.

Surprisingly, one of the most effective warnings against the World Peace Council came from that prominent unilateral nuclear disarmer, E.P. Thompson, who cautioned peace campaigners to beware of the WPC, intimating that it did not necessarily improve the chances of the anti-nuclear lobby.[15]

2

WAGING THE 'COLD WAR'

It is no exaggeration to say that, once the 'cold', undeclared war between the Western world and the USSR and its satellites began, it was largely fought by disinformation tactics. Although the Soviet Union may have been the prime exploiter of this technique, the Western powers were not altogether innocent of such measures.

If an enemy uses such tactics, then it is fair enough to employ them against him. However, there should always be the proviso that if one is caught out disinforming the enemy, or if this weapon is used carelessly or foolishly, then the harm done to one's own cause may be greater than anything the enemy has inflicted. And while the USSR had developed skilful methods of exploiting disinformation by the early 1950s, the United States lagged far behind Britain in the evolution of a highly sophisticated technique in such tactics. The result was that some Western disinformation boomeranged against the West rather than deceiving the USSR.

Early on in the Cold War one American tactic was to exaggerate the Soviet threat, creating the impression that unless prompt action was taken, World War III would break out very soon. There was, of course, no such real threat at that time, for the Western world's lead in nuclear weaponry was still sufficient to call Russia's bluff. But from the American military viewpoint

33

the aim was to persuade those nations in Europe who had escaped being taken into the Russian fold that they needed to unite behind the defensive umbrella of the United States, if they were to retain their freedom – an expedient tactic, if successful.

Nevertheless some wild stories were planted in Paris, Bonn, Amsterdam, The Hague, Rome, Madrid and Lisbon. There were even totally untrue allegations of Soviet troops being moved up to the frontiers of Poland and East Germany. Such disinformation got out of hand when the Americans started employing ex-Nazis as agents to spread the propaganda. All too frequently some of these operators practised disinformation as much to protect themselves and further their interests as to attack the Russians. Sometimes, too, they were able to cover up their own wartime crimes in the process.

Notwithstanding, it was largely through forthright, insistent United States propaganda in this period that Western Europe not only survived and avoided falling into a neutralist hotch-potch of divided nations, but actually accepted the theory of economic and political union and the North Atlantic Treaty. The truth is that in the immediate postwar period and for some years afterwards (with the exception of the USA, Britain's Foreign Secretary, Ernest Bevin, and Paul-Henri Spaak of Belgium) there existed in Europe an uneasy, indecisive and sometimes anti-American majority. To win some of these indeterminate politicians to a positive pro-Western commitment a great deal of pressure and propaganda had to be used.

America had much to offer Free Europe – financial aid, the Marshall Plan, strong defence forces, opportunities for trade and the ideal of a free and democratic society. Yet too often it was the anti-communist line which was pushed forwards as propaganda, and, if one invokes fear for too long and too often, it can cause an unlooked-for reaction. On occasions that line of approach was overdone and thus in the following decade reaction came in the form of nuclear disarmament groups and a host of so-called peace societies in a variety of disguises.

For a year or two before Stalin's death and for about two years afterwards Soviet disinformation was kept comparatively low key – far lower in many respects than it was to be in the 1970s and 1980s. Yet in this same period American disinformation was more prolific, sometimes more outrageous and certainly more widespread than later. One notes a comment by

Victor Zorza, the distinguished commentator on Soviet affairs, that 'in psychological warfare the intelligence agencies of the democratic countries suffer from the grave disadvantage that in attempting to damage the adversary they must also deceive their own public.'[1]

In fairness it should be pointed out that the American Central Intelligence Agency was a postwar organization created from scratch out of the remnants of the old wartime Office of Strategic Services, and that in the haste to get it established a number of somewhat crude cowboy-type operators were recruited. Thus in the early days of the Cold War much propaganda, including disinformation, was circulated by balloons let loose over Soviet-dominated territories. Strangely enough, unsubtle though the propaganda often was, such tactics succeeded sufficiently well in the early stages to provoke angry counterattacks from Soviet and satellite sources.

Believing that this technique could be a highly rated weapon in the Cold War, the Americans decided to extend it to the People's Republic of China. This new operation was controlled and directed by what was then known as the 303 Committee of the CIA, who, when the winds were favourable, dispatched balloons packed with propaganda from a base in Taiwan to the Chinese mainland. This time the material sent out by balloon was more disinformation than propaganda: it was designed to cause confusion among the civilian population and it contained all manner of fictitious stories about the activities of the Red Guards. Proof that the balloons had reached their target and in some cases had not been picked up by the authorities was provided within a few months by the arrival in Hong Kong of refugees from China carrying copies of the material distributed.

So far Western disinformation had been kept to a minimum and used effectively. Sufficient factual information had been disseminated amongst the censorship-ridden nations of the communist empire and the People's Republic of China for those who learned of it to accept that minimum of disinformation as the truth. But eventually the quantity of disinformation increased so much as to make even the CIA's Foreign Broadcast Information Service a source of at best propaganda and at worst falsification. Consequently after a few years American broadcasts to such foreign audiences as Eastern Europe, the Middle East and the Far East began to be treated with suspicion. In the same period, however, and for many years to come, the British Broadcasting Corporation's overseas services from Bush House in London were regarded as entirely trustworthy, often by people who were otherwise hostile to the Western world. Discipline, care in preparation of programmes and an insistence on objectivity and accuracy paid off in the long run rather better than propaganda and disinformation. Bush House, the heart of Britain's overseas broadcasts, built up for itself a reputation that ought always to be the absolute answer to those who want to cut down the funding of such activities.

While the BBC remained free of any interference from intelligence services or governmental bodies, the CIA actually conducted their own campaigns through Radio Free Europe and Radio Liberty. It did not take very long before all the media in the Western and Eastern nations as well as their governments were aware of this. In due course all American news disseminated in this way was regarded with mistrust in many of the centres to which it was directed.

This might not have mattered much if the mistrust had not spread to the media of the Western world as well. But the uninspired and often grossly ill-informed attacks on various European statesmen who questioned the wisdom of proceeding too quickly towards some form of economic union and who had relatively open minds on such topics as Korea, Indo-China and the new Republic of China, tended to fan the flames of anti-Americanism rather than to dim them.

By the mid-1950s some of the disinformation put out under American auspices got right out of hand. Pierre Mendès-France, who became Prime Minister of France in 1954, overcame fierce opposition to German rearmament and by a passionate speech swung the vote by 287 to 260 in favour of West Germany's entry into NATO. It was a formidable victory which meant that Moscow had suffered its first real defeat for many months. Yet Mendès-France was constantly attacked through CIA propaganda and misrepresented as having sabotaged the concept of a European Defence Community. In Paris and in Rome a totally erroneous story was put around that Mendès-France was the enemy of Western union and that his government contained secret allies of the communists. This theme was even taken up by Mrs Margaret Biddle, wife of

General Drexel Biddle, one-time US Ambassador in Poland. A well-known hostess in Paris, Mrs Biddle, who had business interests in France and was a large shareholder in a mining company in French Morocco (as it then was), broadcast a talk on Mendès-France to America. Among her comments were the following:

'M. Mendès-France may be compared to Senator McCarthy [an incongruous and incomprehensible comparison]. Some may consider him as France's saviour, others as the man who may destroy France. It is believed by many that he did a deal with Moscow to secure peace in Indo-China at the price of killing EDC.'

In fact, the reverse was true. What Mendès-France feared was that, if any form of European union was entered into too quickly, it would be dominated by restrictive forces. When he came to power there were four possibilities for him regarding the issue of EDC. He could come out in favour of EDC, or merely put EDC to the vote in the Assembly, making it clear that his government took no sides, but agreeing to accept the majority vote. Mendès-France tried to find an alternative, or sufficient amendments to EDC to make it worthwhile putting the revised version to the vote. He did this because he was convinced that France was not ready to adopt the supranational clauses of EDC.

For the Americans to put the blame on Mendès-France was foolish. The previous April, 1953, two months before Mendès-France came to power, the US Ambassador to France, Mr Douglas Dillon, had warned Washington that there was no possible majority for EDC in the French parliament. Dillon had not been popular in making this prediction – an ambassador who tells unpopular truths to his own Foreign Office rarely is. But there is evidence that the State Department had refused to accept his judgement. They preferred the bland assurances of ex-Foreign Minister Charles Bidault that 'EDC was in the bag'.

At this time the Russians played a trump card which decisively helped to check the waverers who might at the last moment have been won over to support an amended form of EDC. This was none other than Dr Otto John, head of the West German Federal Internal Security Office, who was abducted to East Germany by a ruse on the part of KGB agents. Though this coup was partly an attempt to cover up the mass arrests of agents of General Gehlen, head of the external section of the West German Secret Service, which had been cunningly infiltrated by a Soviet agent named Felfe, it was also a serious attempt to disinform the West on the question of EDC.

The Soviet aim was to suggest that Dr John had all the time been an agent of the USSR and had willingly gone over to the Russians. All he had done initially was to accompany a medical friend to a hospital in East Berlin. Then he was produced, like a rabbit out of a hat, at a specially convened conference at which he made a statement on East German radio on the very eve of a vital Brussels conference on EDC. 'To my fellow German citizens,' he declared, 'Germany is in danger of being perpetually torn in the dispute between East and West . . . a demonstrative act is needed to call all Germans to action for reunification. For that reason I took the determined step on 20 July and took up relations with the Germans of the East.'[2]

This statement, made under pressure after being detained by the East Germans, was bad enough, but the news which East Germany put out shortly afterwards was more significant. It was suggested from East Berlin that Dr John had declared there to be secret clauses in the proposed EDC Treaty, which Dr Adenauer was trying to conceal.

Unquestionably the Otto John affair alarmed French opinion and made Mendès-France's task more difficult. The French Prime Minister was forced to warn the participants at the Brussels conference on EDC that, if he failed to go back to Paris with an acceptable compromise, it would be the end of the European Army concept. He would be defeated in parliament and the way would be open for a Popular Front government which would be a gift for Russia. He said he had only two objectives – the need to strengthen Western Europe and a wish to avoid the neutralization of Germany. But American pressure largely sabotaged the possibility of a compromise agreement with Adenauer, which, at one time, the German leader seriously considered.

That Dr John was the victim of a scurrilous plot is now undoubted. In 1955 he escaped from the East and returned to West Germany where he was most unfairly tried and sentenced to four years' imprisonment. He was released in 1958 after the remainder of his sentence was suspended. His own memoirs clear up a great deal of misunderstanding about this mysterious business and he has retained the respect and trust of his many friends in the West. Yet so effective was the disinformation scheme by the Soviet Union that at the time it was put into operation even British officialdom did not know what to think. During World War II John had worked with the German Resistance to Hitler and tried to open negotiations with the British; he had also been involved in the plot against Hitler in 1944. The British, knowing of John's background, had raised no objection when his name was submitted by the West Germans to the Allied Directors of Intelligence as a candidate for the post of first head of Internal Security; at that time it was an accepted procedure that the Allies should vet such appointments.

To save face, knowing that Dr John had fled to Britain in 1944 and had been approved by the British authorities, Britain colluded with the Adenauer government in accepting the story that John had been drugged and kidnapped by a communist agent. On 22 July 1954, the British Foreign Office received a telegram from Sir Frederick Hoyer Millar (now Lord Inchyra), the British High Commissioner in Bonn, which gave rather a different picture, presumably based on information received from West German sources. The telegram told that Dr John had visited the clinic of a Berlin friend, Dr Wolfgang Wohlgemuth, 'of known communist tendencies', after which the two men had gone to East Berlin, But 'their decision was quite unpremeditated . . . John walked normally and by his own volition . . . Although there is a possibility that John was drugged while in the clinic, it looks most probable that he went of his own accord.'[3]

Later telegrams that same day referred to Dr Adenauer's adviser, Professor Walter Hallstein. The British High Commissioner told the Foreign Office: 'Hallstein, with whom we have discussed this at length, thinks it preferable to take the line with the press that he [John] was abducted. You will, I hope, also follow this line . . . It seems desirable that we should as far as possible play down John's contacts with the Western allies, although certain facts will of course come out . . . It would be a mistake to give any indication that we or the Germans were . . . becoming increasingly doubtful of his suitability for his appointment.'[4]

There was one final comment from Sir Anthony Eden, then

British Foreign Secretary: 'I hope we shall not pretend that he has been abducted when we think he has not been.'[5]

Here was a case of disinformation from all sides on such a massive scale that it revealed both sinister manipulations on the one side and lies to cover up crass ignorance on the other.

Behind the Otto John story lies another sad tale of disinformation, beginning with General Reinhard Gehlen, head of the West German external secret service. Gehlen was an astute intelligence officer, who had been appointed head of the FHO (*Fremde Heere Ost*), German Military Intelligence, in 1942. In most of his work he was an accurate observer of what was happening, for example his comments on Yugoslavia and Mihailovic, and in his warnings of how the Soviet Union would make West Germany a primary target for espionage, subversion and agents of influence once that nation was firmly in the Western camp. But in trying to combat this very threat, by infiltrating far too many of his agents too quickly into East Germany and Russia he laid himself open to infiltration. His organization was seriously injured by the Russians and East Germans sending in men to join it and report back to Moscow. Dr John had frequently warned that Gehlen's policy could lead to disaster.

In his memoirs Gehlen revealed himself as an elusive and disinforming character, even allowing for the fact that he had at one time been a trusted senior officer of the Nazi Government and had later offered full cooperation to the Americans when they moved into Germany in 1945. In his book *The Service: The Memoirs of General Reinhard Gehlen,*[6] he stated that he did not participate in the generals' attempt on Hitler's life in 1944, but only that he was aware of the plot. He claimed that the Gestapo failed to discover his knowledge of the plot. Somehow this story does not quite ring true: it sounds very much like somebody trying to please both sides. But quite the most extraordinary allegation which Gehlen made in his memoirs was that Martin Bormann had been a Soviet spy all the time and that in May 1945 the deputy leader of the Reich simply crossed the lines and went into Russia, where he lived ever after.

No documentary or other proof was offered for this sensational statement and, while nobody has been able to disprove it, nor has anyone else come forward with anything to substantiate such an allegation. As is now well known, Martin Bormann has been 'sighted' at various times in different parts of Latin America, but never in Russia or Eastern Europe. His disappearance after the defeat of Germany in 1945 remains as much of a mystery as ever. Dr Kenneth J. Campbell of Gallaudet College in Washington, DC, a specialist in the analysis of military leadership, has suggested that Gehlen 'possibly felt he had to give the publishers a sensation to justify their large payment to him, and so he added the Bormann story. He either believed that the probable audience of intelligence operatives would accept this undocumented claim because he told it, or he had little respect for the opinions of other professionals.'[7]

Certainly the account of Bormann having been an undercover Soviet agent while serving as Hitler's deputy sounds remarkably like pure disinformation. The motive for it may have been solely the one million dollars which Gehlen was reputed to have been paid for his memoirs. Or, to be more charitable, had Gehlen professional motives for putting out such a story? It is just possible that he had a less mercenary reason for this carefully planted *canard*. There is some evidence that the entourage, or rather the private intelligence service, of Rudolf Hess was infiltrated by Russian agents, and that this is one reason why the Russians refuse to consider any requests for setting Hess free. But evidence concerning the Bormann story is totally lacking.

Gehlen's links with the CIA in the 1950s were amicable and close, and both his own organization and the CIA cooperated on a number of occasions, as well as indulging in black propaganda directed at Russia and Eastern Europe. In the early years both Radio Free Europe and Radio Liberty scored a number of successes by the encouragement their broadcasts gave to dissidents behind the Iron Curtain. Such successes were largely due to a pathetic belief by the listeners that the Americans would in some way come to their rescue and free them from the communist dictatorship. Shortly after the Hungarian uprising in 1956 some of these American broadcasts overreached themselves by their incitement to active revolt, hinting that the United States would intervene and come to the assistance of the dissidents when in fact there was no possibility of any such action. In the long term such broadcasts did a great deal of harm and made listeners behind the Iron Curtain disillusioned, cynical and mistrustful of American radio propaganda and news. It was a lesson which took a long time for the Americans to learn.

Much of this exuberant disinformation from the American side was due to optimism overcoming commonsense. The feeling was that a clarion call to revolt and enough dire warnings would make the communist leaders both East and West think again. Still not fully realized was the absolute stranglehold which Moscow had achieved in Eastern Europe, a stranglehold which killed all hope.

The novelist Graham Greene, in his fiction, revealed some of the disinformation which the CIA produced in the Far East. In his book *The Quiet American* Greene is supposed to have modelled his central figure, Alden Pyle, on Colonel Edward Lansdale, USAF, one of the CIA's covert operations agents in Vietnam, though he had extensive experience in the Philippines in the early 1950s. Maybe Lansdale's friends visualized him as the hero of *The Ugly American*, by William J. Lederer and Eugene Burdick, while his enemies compared him to Greene's anti-hero. Greene effectively and accurately depicted a certain type of idealistic American who, in certain circumstances, can be more dangerous than a straightforward rogue. It was the portrait of a man whose faith in human nature only led to men being killed. Certainly Lansdale was involved in all manner of sabotage and guerrilla operations against North Vietnam, and was also a major political manipulator in the background in South Vietnam. Earlier in his career he had indulged in psychological warfare in the Philippines, playing on the superstitions of those who believed in the existence of a particularly virulent vampire. But *The Quiet American*, while featuring CIA intrigues as part of its background, was really a plea for commonsense to be used in the Vietnam impasse before too many lives were lost and too many horrors perpetrated on either side.

Some of the Lansdale-planned operations in disinformation sound like a combination of *grand guignol* and the occult. In the Philippines he conducted an operation which was intended to alarm people who were easily scared by stories of a mythical vampire known as the *asuang*. 'A psywar squad entered the area, and planted rumours that an *asuang* lived on where the communists were based . . . after giving the rumours time to circulate among Huk sympathizers, the psysquad laid an ambush for the rebels. When a Huk patrol passed, the ambushers snatched the last man, punctured his neck vampire-fashion with two holes, hung his body until the blood drained out, and put the corpse back on the trail. As superstitious as any other Filipinos, the insurgents fled from the region.'[8]

Later on Lansdale was transferred to South Vietnam to organize psychological warfare in aid of the regime of Ngo Dinh Diem. His propaganda included engaging North Vietnamese astrologers to predict terrible catastrophes for the Vietminh leadership in their war with the south.

During the Cold War period the KGB went to great pains to hush up any discussion, publicity or speculation concerning the mysterious death of Jan Masaryk, the Czech Foreign Minister, who had aimed to keep Czechoslovakia neutral and maintain close ties with the West as well as with the Soviet Union. On 10 March 1948, Masaryk's body was found sprawled on the flagstones of the courtyard of the Czernin Palace beneath his apartment. This occurred just two weeks after the *putsch* in which the Communists had seized power in the country. The official verdict on the death was suicide: it was alleged that he threw himself out of a window. A probe into this affair was launched under Alexander Dubcek's government in 1968 and revealed many discrepancies in the evidence. It is significant that within hours of Masaryk's death at least twenty-five people who could have testified about it were arrested and put in jail. Fourteen of these were later executed. The evidence which pointed to murder was considerable. Masaryk's body was found some twelve feet away from the wall of the building; if he had jumped to his death he would hardly have landed so far away. A police guard who 'knew of midnight visitors, but kept his mouth shut', according to his wife, was finally silenced by death.

In the mid-sixties speculation about Masaryk's death was revived both in Western and Eastern Europe. An article on the subject under the pseudonym of 'Michael Rand' appeared in the West German weekly paper, *Der Spiegel*. Later this same

'Michael Rand' wrote another story in *Der Spiegel* in November 1966, about the escape from a London prison of George Blake, the former MI6 agent who had been sentenced to forty-two years' detention for betraying his country's secrets to the Russians.

'Michael Rand' was in fact a journalist named Benno Weigel, who was living in London. It was not long before the fury of the Russians was directed against him. Major Ladislas Bittman, a Czech intelligence officer who defected to the West in 1968, reported that 'the Czech disinformation department had prepared extensive material on Benno Weigel with the aim of undermining his authority and thus discrediting the contents of his articles.'[9] As a result *Izvestia*, the Soviet newspaper, stated that 'Benno Weigel (a Czech citizen), a notorious adventurer, imposter and British agent, began his career in the early thirties by defrauding an Arab sheik to whom he sold Hradcany [Prague's celebrated castle] and acquired quite a large amount of money. During the war it is said that he worked in British Intelligence as an expert on Czech affairs.'

All this material came from the Czech Disinformation Department (Department Eight of the Czech Intelligence Service). Major Bittman recalls that in Britain, as elsewhere, Czech Intelligence devoted much energy to collecting the raw materials necessary for the production of forgeries: 'signatures of high-ranking public servants, diplomats and officials of various political, religious or special interest organizations, official letter-heads . . . The Czechoslovak Intelligence Service developed a very simple and efficient method of enlarging its collection. Intelligence officers abroad . . . send out a large number of Christmas greetings to their foreign counterparts and to important people in general . . . Their greetings are duly answered, the answers signed and the signatures sometimes written on letterhead stationery. These papers are carefully sorted, supplied with explanatory remarks and sent along to the Centre [GRU Headquarters in Moscow].'[10]

Ladislas Bittman is one of the prime informants on Soviet disinformation tactics in these years. He has revealed how Department Eight of Czech Intelligence 'generally focused on forgeries, black propaganda, disinformation, rumours and intrigues . . . in the 1960s the Czech Intelligence Service directed operations of this sort against such developing nations as Egypt and Algeria. The material utilized included forged data on various anti-Arab operations and on subversive activities planned by the United States, Great Britain and other European nations.' The object was to deepen Arab distrust of the Western world, and draw the Arab states closer to Moscow and the Eastern bloc.'[11]

The phrase 'Cold War' has long since ceased to have much meaning, though it admirably summed up the whole period between the end of World War II and the end of the Cuban missiles crisis. It was throughout that period a war of words and, frequently, sometimes on both sides, a war of rather mindless and clumsy disinformation. However, having made that point, the overwhelming evidence shows that the Soviet side practised really calculated evil, sowing seeds of doubt and hate all around the globe. The more bizarre forms of planting rumours by the Americans, for example the vampire scare in the Philippines, were at least linked to putting down guerrilla actions.

Nor should one forget that during the Cold War period, though after the death of Stalin, some British and French politicians and writers actually indulged in highly imaginative speculation that ahead lay the prospect of peace and cooperation with Russia because of the succession of Georgi Malenkov. This was disinformation against the best interests of any Western nation. In fact, the KGB came into its own in this period and acquired considerable new powers. Next to Stalin, Lavrenti Beria was by far the most powerful figure in the Soviet Union, and fear of his total control over the Secret Service and police organization united the remainder of the Kremlin leaders against him. Beria was executed.

The Soviet Union needed to justify its actions after Beria's execution. Curiously enough, quite unfounded rumours about Beria being pro-Western had been circulating in parts of Europe as early as 1948. A high-ranking Spanish diplomat had put about the story that Beria belied his image, that he wanted to come to a secret understanding with the Western powers and to end the Cold War. This diplomat, who held office under the Franco régime, was certainly not an undercover agent of the Russians, yet somebody had planted this story on him. It may well have been one of those devious ploys of Soviet Intelligence which never seem to make sense at the time: they are so outrageous and sensational that some people are tempted to accept them. It is the technique of Goebbels, who always believed that the bigger the lie, the more effective it was.

But whatever the origins of this improbable tale about Beria, a propaganda campaign against him was certainly launched after his death. In December 1953, it was stated, while Beria was still under arrest, he had admitted plotting against the Soviet Government for a foreign power. The prosecutor's statement alleged that Beria's offences included joining the British counter-revolutionary movement in Baku in 1919 and for many years working 'to revive the bourgeoisie'.[12]

There was really no need for the Russians to concoct evidence about Beria working against the Soviet Union for a foreign power. He was generally hated and after his death enough evidence of his sinister habits was provided by those who previously had been too frightened to talk. Lavrenti Beria would prowl the streets of Moscow at night in his bullet-proof ZIS limousine and when he saw an attractive girl – he usually selected teenagers, but sometimes children under ten – he would have his chauffeur pull up alongside and order the terrified girl into his car. None dared disobey him. He would then be driven to his house in the cellar of which were a number of cubicles where he incarcerated the girls. Here Beria and his deputy, Abakumov, indulged their sadistic passions in private orgies after they had drugged their victims.

One of the most striking examples of disinformation disseminated by infiltration was the manipulation of the NTS (*Netsionelno-Trudovoy-Soyuz*), which, roughly translated, means the Producers' Party, embracing technicians, labourers, artists, farmers, engineers, professional men and producers of all kinds. Its aim originally was to combat communism with a constructive alternative programme. It was not a Czarist movement when it was founded in 1930, nor did it make any suggestion of restoring Czardom. Many of its members were not Russians at all, but Letts, Lithuanians, Estonians and Germans with Russian ancestry.

Little was achieved by the NTS until the outbreak of World War II. Then it was given some impetus by the assistance it received from the German secret service, though by the end of the war more than two hundred members, including some of the leaders, were incarcerated in Nazi concentration camps. After the war aid from the American CIA came through one of its members, K. Boldyrev, and cells of the NTS were set up in Yugoslavia, Hungary, Rumania, Poland and Czechoslovakia.

Yuri Andropov denounced the NTS as 'a menace to the Soviet state'. At that time Andropov was head of the KGB, yet the truth was that the NTS has long since been infiltrated by the KGB, and indeed by the NKVD prior to that. It was far more important for the USSR to tolerate the NTS and have agents inside it than to destroy it altogether.[13] Full details of Soviet infiltration of the NTS have never been revealed because the NTS will never admit that it has been penetrated and the USSR obviously has no desire to tell its own story about this subject. The first Soviet success came when their agents inside the NTS betrayed Russian monarchist organizations in Paris in the 1930s, leading to the betrayal of General Kotyepov, whose wife proved to be an NKVD agent, and the kidnapping and killing of General Eugene Miller, former chief of staff of the Czarist Fifth Army. Later, when the CIA somewhat clumsily attempted to 'take over' the NTS, the Russians found no difficulty in fore-stalling the Americans through their own agents in the NTS. Many friends of dissident Russians became increasingly worried in the 1960s about some of the information coming from some NTS members. They suspected, not without good reason, that some of it was deliberately invented by Soviet agents.

3

EXPLOITATION OF THE MEDIA AND BOOKS

In no sphere has disinformation infiltrated so effectively as in the media in the past forty years. This is not surprising when one considers that, prior to World War II, the phrase media covered only newspapers, periodicals and radio. Today, it includes the much more easily manipulated fields of television and stereo recordings.

Yet perhaps one should include both books and works of reference, because today there is an even more fertile field for disinformation in such writings – not only in factual reference books, but in fiction, too. As mentioned in an earlier chapter, relating to General Mihailovic, a certain amount of disinformation has appeared in the much respected *Encylopaedia Britannica*, which has been caustically nicknamed 'the Soviet Britannica: an intellectual obscenity'[1] by Sidney Hook, Emeritus Professor of Philosophy at New York University. Nor is this just a personal opinion unsupported by factual evidence. Professor Hook makes out his case with meticulous care, backed up by quotations.

For many years the *Encyclopaedia Britannica* has been regarded as a model of accuracy, objectivity and detailed information. In most respects this is still the case, but in one area of the *Encyclopaedia* one can seriously question not merely the accuracy of the information, but actually find deliberate disinformation. This is because those compiling the *Encyclopaedia* make use of the citizens of Soviet-bloc nations to prepare the profiles and data they publish on these countries. The result is that quite frequently an erroneous view of Soviet and Eastern European nations and people is supplied, sometimes by falsification of the facts, but also by the omission of vital material. The contributors from the Soviet bloc are bound to supply only such information as is approved by their respective governments. In East Germany, for example, legislation insists on all manuscripts written for publication in the Western world being subject to censorship and an official stamp of approval. Surely the publishers of the *Encyclopaedia Britannica* must be well aware of such rules and how they can result in suppression of the truth.

No one would deny that today both Armenia and Georgia are constituent parts of the USSR, but the *Encyclopaedia Britannica* in its fifteenth edition states that 'It ["the Communist Party of Armenia"] was founded in 1920 through the unification of Armenia's Bolshevik organizations', and that 'during the twentieth century Georgia has experienced a major transformation from an economically backward outpost of the Tsarist empire to a modernized and diversified economy.'[2]

There is no mention of the facts that both territories were invaded and occupied by Soviet forces in 1920 and that formerly Armenia was an area administered by Turkish, Russian and Iranian authorities. Similarly, in the section on the German Democratic Republic (East Germany) it is stated that the border between Poland and East Germany is marked by the Oder and Neisse rivers as 'part of the post-World War II Potsdam Agreement'. This is incorrect: what was actually agreed was that, pending the final drawing up of borders at a peace conference which has not yet been held, Poland was to administer the territory east of the Oder-Neisse. A small point, perhaps, especially as today Poland is in the Soviet bloc, but a significant omission and distortion all the same.

Then again there is the statement that 'Article 121 of the [Soviet] constitution guarantees the right of education to all Soviet citizens, and there is an elaborate, unified and well-supported network of educational bodies within the country. Expenditure on education more than doubled over the 1960s. Education is provided free, and the building of all educational institutions is at state expense, as is the payment of supplementary scholarships to students.'[3]

This is splendid propaganda for the Soviet Union, but it fails to tell the whole story. First of all, it does not mention that the Soviet government decides what is to be taught and what type of education each individual must have. This may produce far more technicians and engineers than the West can boast of, but it is dictation as to what one can learn nonetheless. Secondly, though the education may be free, there are stringent rules attached: one of these involves being directed into certain jobs, another is that every graduate can be sent on graduation to any locality the authorities choose in order to justify his education. Finally, all males up to the age of thirty who have received higher education can be mobilized as required.

In fairness, the editorial policy of the *Encyclopaedia Britannica* has been admirably defined as follows: 'Articles should be so written that they avoid expressions of bias or prejudice on any matter about which a respectable and reasonable difference of opinion exists. Further, in all areas in which the scholarly world acknowledges significant and reputable differences of opinion, diverse views concerning such differences should be fairly presented, though the majority or accepted view may be so designated.' Undoubtedly, this policy is in most respects faithfully followed out, but evidence of it is sadly lacking in all those contributions made by Soviet and other communist nationals.

Lev Navrozov, a Russian emigrant to the USA who has founded the Centre for the Survival of Western Democracies, asserts that this work, 'the main source of reference of the English-speaking countries, has become an impersonal vehicle of officially endorsed Soviet propaganda clichés.'[4]

Anti-Jewish and anti-Zionist disinformation has for more than a century constituted one of the greatest evils in this propaganda game. The tragedy is that, though started and engineered by enemies of the Jews, intent on besmirching their reputation all round the globe, the theme has occasionally been taken seriously by fundamentally decent people who have allowed themselves to be bemused by talks of Zionist plots and cliques aiming at world domination.

The anti-Jewish disinformation game first started in Czarist Russia, where the Jews were often treated with mediaeval savagery and herded into ghettos. Anti-semitism was particularly marked at court and among the ruling classes of Russia in the nineteenth century, and the legend of such nonsense as *The Protocols of the Elders of Zion* and propaganda about secret Jewish plots to rule the world all originated here. The forged material known as '*The Protocols*' was first published by Serge Nilus in Russia in 1905; he claimed to have unmasked a sinister plot to achieve a world Jewish government. It was not until 1921 that Philip Graves, the London *Times* correspondent in Constantinople, exposed the falsity of these forgeries. Yet despite this exposure and a judicial ruling confirming it in Berne in 1934, the anti-Zionist propaganda about plots to achieve world domination still persist, unfortunately far more in the supposedly civilized and well informed Western world than in the East. However, on 18 January 1985, the Soviet news agency Tass made this astonishing list of claims:

'1.   Zionists were partners of the Nazi regime;
2.   A Jewish-owned Amsterdam bank lent Hitler 10 million dollars in 1929;
3.   A Jewish Cologne bank discussed with Hitler the desirability of the anti-Jewish holocaust;
4.   Israel is an American-sponsored imperialism;
5.   Zionists are now the enemy of the Soviet Union and should be seen as such.'

These statements were made in Russia for Russian readers, and at the time some Western diplomats professed to be surprised as to why the Soviet Union had chosen this particular moment to launch an attack on the Jews, though it should have been obvious that this propaganda was all part of Russia's increasing intervention in Middle Eastern affairs.

Yet anti-Jewish propaganda also emanates from Western sources, sometimes from periodicals and organizations which claim to be anti-Soviet and markedly right-wing. For example,

Executive Intelligence Review, founded and edited by Lyndon H. LaRouche, who was a candidate for the Democratic nomination for the Presidency in the 1980 election, has called Israelis 'fascists' and alleges that 'The Soviets are holding out to Israel the ''carrot'' of mass emigration of Jews to Israel, to populate the West Bank, in return for Israel's accommodation to the ''New Yalta'' arrangement. Israel would disengage from its alliance with the United States, and join forces with Soviet client state Syria to eliminate the pro-Arafat Palestinians and Arab moderate regimes.'

The most dangerous aspect of anti-Semitic disinformation is that quite often it is not blatant propaganda, but cunningly disguised and sometimes infiltrated into newspapers, magazines, newsletters and even some television programmes which would all vigorously deny any anti-Semitic trend. Worst of all, a number of right-wing periodicals which oppose the politics of Soviet Russia defeat their own cause by printing some of this virulent nonsense against the Jews.

Perhaps one of the most successful victories over the threat of disinformation in recent times was that of Sir James Goldsmith in October 1984. He had alleged that the KGB had 'orchestrated' a magazine campaign discrediting Dr Franz Josef Strauss, former German Defence Minister. As a result of this the German weekly magazine, *Der Spiegel*, sued Sir James for libel.

In the action in the High Court in London Lord Rawlinson, QC, stated that Sir James had never intended to imply that the owners and publishers of *Der Spiegel* were 'controlled by or co-operated with Soviet Intelligence or knowingly employed any journalist who was a KGB agent.' Nevertheless, it was and remained Sir James's contention that many Western publications were unwittingly used by the Soviets in their campaigns conducted by the KGB and other Soviet organizations. 'So,' he added, 'in Sir James's view, *Der Spiegel*, in common with other Western publications, can themselves be fairly described as victims of KGB propaganda techniques.'[5]

The action arose out of a speech by Sir James to the Conservative Party Committee in the House of Commons, in January 1981. The full text of this was later published in Sir James's short-lived magazine, *Now!*, which ceased publication in April

1981. In his speech Sir James mentioned that General Jan Sejna, a high-ranking Czech Intelligence officer who defected in 1968, had admitted that the campaign by *Der Spiegel* in 1962 to discredit Dr Strauss was organized by the KGB.

Lord Rawlinson, in outlining Sir James's case, said his client believed that the Soviets in pursuit of their policies conducted 'massive and continuous propaganda campaigns. These were through overtly controlled communist media and covertly by the dissemination and planting of stories, many of which were forgeries and deliberate falsehood known as disinformation.'[6]

The Russians had decided to discredit Strauss in every possible way following a speech he made in the Bundestag calling for deployment of United States-controlled nuclear weapons on German soil. In this campaign they had decided to make use of *Der Spiegel* because it was well known for opposing Dr Strauss's political views.

Ultimately the plaintiffs in this libel action, while rightly insisting on their editorial and journalistic independence from KGB control, acknowledged the 'dangers to press freedom posed by Soviet covert propaganda', and took the view that it was unnecessary to proceed further with the action. This, Sir James Goldsmith claimed, was 'a famous victory for the defence of the West against its main enemy, Soviet imperialism.'

It has long since been realized by the Soviet Union that propaganda in the media which actively and openly support the communist bloc is largely wasted, and that the only realistic means of influencing public opinion around the world is through infiltrating the media of the centre and the right, and, where possible, such media as normally oppose Soviet policies. Quite often this is achieved almost effortlessly. Money, skill, determination, blackmail and agents of influence are all used to this end. Sometimes success is achieved by some periodicals and newspapers unwittingly printing Soviet-concocted news or views. The section of the KGB responsible for planning most of these operations is Service A.

Orders pour out from Moscow to Soviet embassies around the world suggesting courses of action in the planting of disinformation. Attempts are made to concentrate on winning over some individual writer of influence rather than a periodical or its owner. The directors of Soviet disinformation realize that it is often easier for such a person to insert a few carefully chosen sentences into his copy than for an employer to do so, because any newspaper owner or editor in a Western democracy seeming to push his own ideas too strongly can draw unwanted attention to himself.

The late Kingsley Martin, when editor of the *New Statesman* in the 1930s, gave that journal an authority and attractiveness which secured for it an influence far greater than its circulation. But, by suppression and distortion, Martin also did much harm. He gave comfort to the Stalinists by censoring criticism of their politics. This sometimes extended to sacrificing colleagues and friends alike – even to the point of refusing to help when one of them was facing a possible death sentence.

A particularly tragic example of the last unpleasant trait was the case of Rose Cohen. This vivacious girl, born in the East End of London, of Polish parents, and a devoted communist, married D. Petrovsky, then the Comintern representative in Britain. At the end of 1929 they went to live in Russia and Rose became a sub-editor on the staff of the official English language paper, the *Moscow Daily News*. In 1938 news came that Petrovsky and his wife had been sent to a Soviet prison and that Rose had been charged with 'counter-revolutionary activity'. Kingsley Martin was asked to support her editorially, but he declined on the grounds that no individual was greater than the cause. A campaign in the *New Statesman* at that time might have had some effect in Moscow, but even when very much later a petition for her release was signed by both communist and other sympathizers Martin refused to give editorial support. George Orwell was enraged when Martin rejected his articles telling the truth about Soviet execution squads in Spain during the Civil War. Such cases undoubtedly harmed the reputation of the editor of the *New Statesman*.

Nevertheless, careful attention is always paid to the publisher or newspaper proprietor who it is thought could be won over. Such people are carefully watched and analysed by the media-watchers, and occasionally invited to Moscow for exclusive interviews or entertained in sumptuous style even to the point of being encouraged to feel that they can play a vital role in world affairs.

Both *Der Spiegel* and *Der Stern*, a widely-read and popular West German magazine, have suffered from this campaign. Articles appearing in these magazines in September 1969 suggested that in the event of Russian forces invading Western Europe the United States would not hesitate to use bacteriological and nuclear warfare against the civilian populations. The source of information on which these articles was based was said to be documentary evidence of top secret American plans; subsequently it was admitted that the documents were airmailed from Rome by someone whose signature was illegible, and that they were photocopies and not originals, so that it would not be possible to apply tests to establish their falsity.

In no sphere have the Russians acquired so strong a position from which to distil falsities as by their penetration of the ranks of UNESCO (United Nations Educational, Scientific and Cultural Organization). As far as Russia is concerned UNESCO is cynically treated as the perfect operating ground for spies and recruiters of agents of influence abroad. A few years ago it was reckoned that nearly one-third of the seventy-two Soviet officials then working permanently in UNESCO were full-time members of the KGB or GRU.

One of the chief coups which the Soviets brought off inside UNESCO was back in the late 1950s, when Charles Pierre Pathé was working in UNESCO headquarters in Paris. Pathé, the son of one of the earliest and best known of French film directors, was arrested in 1979 and charged with what amounted to the 'continuous process of disseminating Russian disinformation', to cite a description of a most unusual charge and a remarkable case. Pathé was sentenced to five years' imprisonment, while his case officer, Alexandrovich Puznetsov, a permanent Soviet delegate to UNESCO, was expelled after he had claimed diplomatic immunity. For nearly twenty years Pathé had been cunningly inserting Soviet-produced material into articles he wrote for the French press, making special use of the newsletter, *Synthesis*, which he personally directed. Though *Synthesis* was only in existence for three years – 1976-79 – it was responsible for massive disinformation during that brief period. The newsletter was in receipt of Soviet funds to enable it to carry on, and included among its subscribers French senators and members of parliament and even ambassadors. It set out to create mistrust between Europe and America: Pathé's scheme was to defend Soviet actions largely under cover of attacking the United States and appearing to boost French national interests. It was all very cleverly done, the disinformation being by emphasis and allegation rather than false facts which could have been detected.

Thus one article in *Synthesis* expounded the theory that over several years the United States had exploited all European countries and regarded the whole of Europe as an American 'economic protectorate'. West Germany was called 'the milk cow of American suzerainty'.[7] During those three years I counted no fewer than forty-three similar examples.

According to a KGB training manual, it is clearly indicated that disinformation is essential 'in the execution of State tasks, and is directed at misleading the enemy concerning the basic questions of State policy, the military-economic status and the scientific-technical achievement of the Soviet Union; the policy of certain imperialist states with respect to each other and to other countries; and the specific counter-intelligence tasks of the organs of State Security.'[8]

Richard Cox, who served as a First Secretary in the British Diplomatic Service before becoming defence correspondent of the London *Daily Telegraph*, has referred to his visits to the Russian Embassy in London during the course of his duties. 'I had become friendly with the military attaché, Major-General Nemchenko, who one day invited a number of prominent journalists to dinner. We were like debutantes at a ball, each allocated to "dance" with a particular diplomat.'[9] It was Prokopy Gamov, a Second Secretary, to whom Cox was attached. 'The purpose of his meetings with me was, I think, to spread the idea that there was a Russian agent in the Cabinet Office – a sophisticated example of disinformation. However, though our overt meetings were monitored by the Security Service, even now no one will reveal to me what they thought it was all about.'[10]

The technique of spreading alarm and confusion by planting stories of traitors in high places in American, British and French services has been consistently practised by the KGB. Mainly it has been directed against the United Kingdom, but most allies of the West have been smeared in this way, thus making each of them mistrust one another. Sometimes such stories come from bogus defectors; occasionally they are subtly planted on journalists only too anxious to exploit sensational news regardless of its reliability. The methods of using this technique are constantly changing.

One unusual method was that introduced in a book entitled *Soviet Agents' Stories*, published in Moscow early in 1983. While containing true stories about Kim Philby, Donald Maclean and Guy Burgess, all of whom spied for Russia and defected to the USSR, it also alleged that 'Sir Edward Pelham Hollis, a senior Foreign Office diplomat, passed secrets to top Soviet agents working in Western Europe' in the 1930s and later. Sir Edward, the book alleged, offered to work for Moscow for money and not for any commitment or interest in communism. He was described as being a former Army captain and the third son of an earl. Another story was that 'the agent Drobrokhotov nicked his hand while photographing throughout the night Foreign Office documents passed on to him by Sir Edward. A drop of blood fell on to the documents and the Soviet agent could not remove it properly. He warned Sir Edward, who said: "Just give them back to me. It's not important. No one will notice." '[11]

Now a careful search of Diplomatic Service lists of the 1930s and 1940s reveals no trace whatsoever of any 'Sir Edward Pelham Hollis'. Nor is there any record of such a name in Foreign Office registers earlier in the century. In fact, there is no clue to the existence of this name in any reference book whatsoever. Quite obviously, this is an item of fiction.

But why, it may be asked, should an item of disinformation which can so easily and swiftly be discredited be inserted in this way? It doesn't make conventional sense. Yet in creating a mystery and confusion, what seems stupid propaganda sometimes succeeds in a subtle way. What is interesting about the fictitious name of Sir Edward Pelham Hollis is the way in which it plays around with well-known names. Pelham-Clinton-Hope is the family name of the Dukes of Newcastle. Sir George Clinton Pelham was in the Foreign Service in the 1930s-1950s period and became Ambassador to Czechoslovakia. The late Sir Roger Hollis was not only the head of MI 5 for some years, but was himself the victim of a campaign of vilification which alleged that he had worked as a Soviet agent. So here was much scope for mischief-making by innuendo, making some people think that the Russians were telling the truth in some kind of code. In the book, *Soviet Agents' Stories*, there is a reference to 'Sir Edward' attending a League of Nations conference in Geneva before World War II, implying that on this occasion he

57

passed on information to the Russians. In the thirties Amsterdam, The Hague and Geneva were the three bases from which intelligence operations into Britain were mounted by the USSR. In September 1930, Geneva was the scene of the sensational theft of the keys of Foreign Office dispatch-boxes from Mr Philip Noel-Baker, who was then Parliamentary Secretary to the British Foreign Secretary, Arthur Henderson. Noel-Baker was asleep in his hotel in Geneva when the thief slipped into his room and took the keys from his trousers' pocket. [12]

Now it could be argued that such material in *Soviet Agents' Stories* is simply intended for Russian readers and is designed solely to show how good Soviet agents are and how the USSR has cleverly subverted the West. This is a feasible answer in that most Russian readers do not have access to Western records and therefore would have no means of checking the reports. But equally it can be argued that there is a dual purpose, that of baffling Western intelligence monitors, causing them to waste time looking for hidden meanings or obscure purposes.

The game of disinformation has been played in the field of fiction just as much as in non-fiction books. On both sides, Eastern and Western, novels have been produced with the aim of worrying the other side. Prior to 1914 such novels had a somewhat different and more positive and patriotic aim – to warn against aggression from overseas and to point to threats from Germany in particular. Often, as in the case of *Riddle of the Sands*, by Erskine Childers, they were backed by the author's own observations and gathering of facts. In those days such books were nearly all by British authors.

After World War II spy fiction tended to be produced entirely for commercial reasons and, as this was the period of the Cold War, the villains in Western fiction were usually Russians. Ian Fleming's James Bond extravaganzas (they became more unrealistic with each book) were sufficiently irritating to the Russians to provoke a counterattack in the form of an ace Russian spy named Avakum Zakhov, whose main mission in life seemed to be to destroy James Bond. The man chosen to mastermind such stories was Andrei Gulyashki, a Bulgarian novelist who responded to the KGB's request for writers to glorify the deeds of Soviet espionage and to improve its own image in the early sixties. The campaign, to popularize secret agents of the Soviet Union as noble heroes who protected the fatherland, was launched in 1961 by Vladimir Semichastny, the newly appointed head of the KGB, when he contributed an article to *Izvestia* on this very subject. So Gulyashki invented Avakum Zakhov largely because the KGB felt that Ian Fleming had scored a major propaganda success in the Cold War by producing James Bond. Avakum Zakhov was, understandably, a much more proletarian figure than 007, with a predilection for large quantities of cabbage and noodles. Gulyashki's book, *Zakhov Mission* (1966), was an instant success and was serialized in *Komsomolskaya Pravda*, the Soviet youth paper, under the title of *Avakum Zakhov versus 07*. The Bulgarians were unable to get copyright permission to use Bond's name or '007', so they got around this difficulty by deleting one zero from the code name. The book was translated into English by Maurice Michael and was published in the United Kingdom in 1968.

This was a legitimate response, for the crude thugs depicted by Fleming as representing typical KGB men posted overseas were nothing remotely like the real agents. Fleming, in fact, disinformed and, worse still, did this against his own side's interests. Reality was totally different. What Fleming should have depicted was a typical KGB officer working outside his own country as described by Richard Cox – 'well educated and intelligent, more likely to pass as a university lecturer than a policeman, the sort of man in whom it might seem safe to confide. The career or "cadre" workers of the KGB are likely to be employed in a wide range of cover activities: in embassies, in trade missions, in the offices of Aeroflot, among TASS news agency reporters . . . Virtually any Russian working for a government agency abroad is liable to be made a "co-opted collaborator" of the KGB, with obvious sanctions against himself or his family, if he tries to refuse.'[13]

For this reason, and because of his realization that there appeared to be 'a great deal of reluctance on the part of the British authorities to act publicly against KGB activity' in the United Kingdom, Richard Cox decided that this 'is where the novelist who values democracy can strike a blow to defend it, dangerous as it is in literature to make political points. Conversations with various well-informed people convinced me that I should write a novel on the subject of current KGB operations in Britain.'[14]

Thus Richard Cox produced his novel *The KGB Directive*, which was published in 1981 and which included two important themes – the aim of sabotaging a new British airliner project to weaken Britain's ability to compete in the international civil aviation market and the penetration of the Labour Party machine and of the unions at local level. Here again it is important to quote Cox's explanation of this: 'The main reason I wrote a novel, rather than attempting a factual product from my research, is that the British libel laws make it difficult, if not impossible, to describe the penetration of the Labour Party as the conspiracy which many people are certain it is.'[15]

Disinformation in the literary world is not by any means confined to agents of Soviet Russia. If the USSR is cited more frequently than any other nation in this respect, it is only because the Russians have given the dissemination of such material a top priority in policy-making.

In 1978 a book called *Discovering Africa's Past* by Basil Davidson was published in London by the Longman Group. During World War II the author was a key man on the SOE desk in Cairo. The object of this book was that it should be circulated in schools and aimed at the fourteen-plus age group. It was denounced by Mr Winston Churchill, MP for Stretford, as being likely to 'increase racial prejudice and even hatred of young blacks against young whites'. He added that there was a very great danger 'in one-sided presentation of material concerning race, particularly in those parts of the country which have schools with seventy per cent or more coloured pupils, such as in my own constituency.'[16]

Even the most objective critic could hardly deny that this was at the very best a 'slanted' history of Africa. It described the Mau Mau terrorist campaign of the 1950s as 'a great African farmers' rebellion', ignored all modern atrocities and failed even to mention the regime of Idi Amin. There was great emphasis on the slave trade, the polices of the early white settlers were consistently criticized as aimed at making a fortune out of cheap black labour, with no indication of the role played by Britain in helping Africans, while the work of Dr David

Livingstone in stirring up the public conscience against the slave trade and in opening up Central Africa to Christian influences received not a single mention.

The Mau Mau terror was referred to as 'so called', and was portrayed simply as a struggle for independence; while the number of Africans killed was carefully recorded, there was no mention of the white settlers and their families slaughtered by the Mau Mau.

It can, of course, be argued that this is simply one man's viewpoint and that every man has a right to his opinion. The answer to this is twofold: first of all, that if he has a right to his opinion, others have a right to set the record straight as they see it; secondly, that a text-book designed for schools should not confine itself to one man's viewpoint, especially when it twists the truth.

Disinformation in books deliberately planned for distribution in schools is unhappily on the increase. In October 1985, Baroness Cox, a consistent campaigner against subversion in educational spheres, drew attention to a children's book which had just been published, entitled *How Racism Came to Britain*. It was the latest in a series of 'anti-racist educational books for young people' issued by the Institute of Race Relations. Baroness Cox described this work as being a typical example of the kind of anti-police propaganda with which young people are being 'bombarded. It is grotesquely dishonest and blatantly intended to stir up racial conflict.'[17]

In the book colonialism was depicted by such a picture as a bloated pig and Queen Victoria looking at India and saying: 'Who said I was not amused by anything?' Yet another picture showed a black covered in blood lying in a gutter with a policeman's torch shining on his face: the caption read 'Now then, what's all the fuss and panic about claims of an alleged racist attack, eh? Move along there in an orderly fashion, or I'll have you for obstruction.'

The Soviet Union in the past few years has launched a major propaganda campaign through UNESCO and in schools throughout Britain. In UNESCO it has found an ally in Mr Amadou Mahtar M'Bow, the Moslem head of the organization. Politically, UNESCO has promoted the Soviet concept of 'people's rights', funded the Palestinian Liberation Organization and run a New World Information Order which appears to allow only approved journalists to report in Third World countries. Even after the Pathé affair spies were found inside UNESCO: twelve of its staff were expelled by France as Soviet agents in 1982.

The Russians fully realize that the English-speaking world is one of the strongest bastions of Western defence: it applies to the whole of North America, the United Kingdom, Australia, New Zealand and many other areas. To detach the United Kingdom from commitment to Western defence and encourage it into a kind of neutralism would be a major victory, for the United Kingdom is the one European nation sharing a common language with Americans and Canadians.

In the past few years teachers have been invited to take up offers of books, offered without any question of payment, the contents of which are unmistakably Soviet propaganda. One such letter, signed by Mrs Victoria Cherneyeni with an address in south-west London, stated that: 'We are introducing a new service for schools and organizations, providing them with a free subscription to Novosti Booklets which provide information about Russia. We intend to send approximately forty booklets a year.'

In December 1985, three London teachers who were actually involved with the 'peace movement', Greta Sykes, Helen Mercer and Jan Woolf, attacked the alleged anti-Soviet bias of many established textbooks dealing with the Cold War. Their answer was to produce their own textbook, *Deadly Persuasion*, which was backed by the CND movement. This book declares: 'Soviet policy is interpreted as sinister and volatile; sudden, yet cunningly prepared. Western policy is portrayed as long-suffering and tolerant, naïve and trusting.'

Now although Russian propaganda has found its way into British schools in the past, this current campaign of theirs is much more determined and concentrated. The number of titles available now far outreaches previous figures, and, with textbooks at a premium and many schools unable to afford too many of them, the temptation to take what is free is all the greater. This policy goes hand in hand with regular attempts to criticize or smear existing home-produced textbooks.

Such textbooks as boost the Soviet image are an example of truth-twisting, if not always of positive false information. Titles include *Privileged Class, Soviet Democracy at Work, Young*

People in the USSR, Invincibility, The Liberation Movement, and *The Great Vital Force of Leninism.*

Interestingly, the last two of these books were written by Boris Ponomarev, who was the first and highly successful head of the International Department (ID) of the Communist Party of the Soviet Union, which, in effect, took over the work formerly tackled by the Comintern. The ID was closely linked to the KGB and therefore kept informed of all KGB requirements in various parts of the world. At one time Ponomarev was tipped to be a future head of the KGB. Under his direction the ID achieved a number of propaganda coups, one of the most notable of which was in 1979 when the Russian Novosti press agency published an edition of 150,000 copies of a book entitled *Belaya Kniga* (The White Knight), which contained a vicious attack on the Western world and sought to discredit both Western writers and intelligence services.

A scholarly character and the author of a number of books, Boris Ponomarev actually gave his own definition of disinformation in the *Soviet Political Dictionary*, which he edited. Indicating that it was a word of Polish origin, Ponomarev declared that disinformation was 'the intentional presentation of incorrect information with the object of leading someone astray.'

He could hardly have put it much more clearly!

4

THE TAMING
OF THE CHURCHES

Shortly after the end of World War II a determined attempt was made to disinform the clergy. This might have seemed to most people an almost impossible task, yet it was steadily achieved year by year until today there exists a powerful lobby of priests, ministers and laymen who are spokesmen for the Roman Catholic, Anglican, Greek Orthodox, Russian Orthodox, Nonconformist and other sects of the Christian religion, actively engaged in twisting the truth.

Nor is this a question of there being a small minority on the lower levels of the Church. It extends from the top down to the bottom, from cardinals and archbishops to all ranks below.

Attempts to influence and subvert other religions have not succeeded to the same extent. While the Christians give the impression of having forgotten or dismissed the Old Testament, practising Jews have never allowed themselves to be turned away from such basic teachings. Buddhists and Hindus have remained faithful to their own creeds, while the Moslems have retained their faith in many countries with an even more fanatical zeal than hitherto. Perhaps this is why little or no attempt has been made by the Soviet Union to try to influence the Moslem religion. Their requirements have often been better served by fanatical forms of this religion which usually manifest a loathing for Western tolerance and individual freedom and contempt for Western decadence.

Religion, which in Karl Marx's view was 'the opium of the people', has since his time been subjected in turn to persecution, stamped out in one area and seduced in another, and occasionally manipulated for Soviet political reasons. One of the prime factors in the courting and manipulating of the Churches has been the creation of the World Council of Churches in Amsterdam in 1948. It was, however, not until 1961 that the WCC approved an application for membership by the Russian Orthodox Church, something which could not have been made without the permission of the Communist Party of the USSR. The leader of the Russian delegation was the Archbishop Metropolitan Nikodim, who later died of a heart attack during an audience with Pope John Paul I. Nikodim became president of the so-called 'Christian' Peace Conference, a blatant front for Soviet communism which did very little to disguise its real purpose of promoting the view that Christianity and communism are one and the same thing. Founded in Czechoslovakia in 1958, this body has organized a series of world conferences to encourage Westerners – many British clergy among them – to join in the hypocritical 'theology of peace', usually no more than a justification of terrorist warfare and Marxist wars of liberation in the Third World and a condemnation of the warlike West.

Most formidable of the 'Christian communists' during the early postwar years was the Reverend Dr Hewlett Johnson, the 'Red Dean' of Canterbury, practically a 'flat-earther' in his irrational attempts to condone every lie perpetrated from the counsels of the Politburo. The most bizarre of all paradoxes occurred when his framed photograph was put on show in the anti-religious exhibition staged in Kazan Cathedral in Leningrad, a spectacle which aimed at deriding most of the major religions of the world. In the summer of 1952 the Dean created a furore when he returned with his wife from a visit to the Far East and accused the United Nations forces of using germ warfare in Korea.

His pen was a powerful influence on the side of the USSR both inside and outside Christian circles; his book, *The Socialist Sixth of the World*, about the Soviet system, sold more than three million copies and was translated into sixteen languages.

Among his other works *Soviet Strength* and *Soviet Success* were both bestsellers.

During World War II the Dean made many visits to Russia, once having a fifty-minute talk with Stalin. Yet though he was on the editorial board of the communist *Daily Worker*, he was somewhat equivocal on his communist faith; in March 1948, he wrote: 'I am not a member of any political party. I support Russian economic socialism because I think it a better economic order and nearer Christianity than the capitalist economy of the West.' He was awarded the Stalin Peace Prize in 1951.

Since his time there has emerged a less clown-like and more dangerous type of cleric, especially inside the Church of England, but none the less visible in certain circles of the Roman Catholic Church and sometimes in the ranks of nonconformity. How the USSR has subtly insinuated Soviet policies into the WCC was illustrated by the Bishop of Bristol when he revealed that the composition of the Central Committee of the organization is forty-two per cent Western (i.e. American, British, Australian, some European); twenty-eight per cent Eastern Orthodox (mainly Russian) thirty per cent African, Latin American and other Third World countries. Thus a coalition of Russian Orthodox and Third Worlders has a substantial majority over the rest, who are regarded as representatives of 'colonialism'.[1]

The effects of such a majority can be judged from the WCC's actions: the gift of £45,000 to the Patriotic Front led by Robert Mugabe and Joshua Nkomo in the days of Rhodesia's UDI government, and the fact that only one-third of the WCC Committee members could be persuaded to sign a telegram to Brezhnev appealing to him to allow Solzhenitsyn to live with his family in Moscow. This is particularly surprising in the light of Solzhenitsyn's declaration that the way back to sanity and a more civilized way of life for Russia should be through a revival of a free and unfettered Russian Orthodox Church.

Increasingly, and largely by means of determined and skilful disinformation, the WCC has become an instrument cleverly manipulated by Marxists and by the Soviet Union itself. Though the Roman Catholics have only been observers at WCC conferences, Pope Paul VI sent a personal gift of £4000 to the WCC to finance a committee on Society, Development and Peace.

What the disinformers have done is to play on the guilty conscience of some Christians, to develop the theme of black-and-white tensions, to make the individual feel he is responsible for the sins of society in such matters as colonialism and unemployment. This resulted in a Canterbury conference which accepted a mandate calling upon churches 'to become agents for radical reconstruction of society', with a special fund 'to combat racism'. Various organizations from SWAPO to the African National Congress, the Collective of African Organizations in France, the Campagne Anti-Outspan, the Indian Brotherhood of the Northwest Territories and the Puerto Rico Solidarity Committee have been given grants from the WCC. It is noteworthy that in 1978 the grant made to SWAPO, a terrorist organization, was nearly thirty per cent of the total grants for the whole year. This was to an organization which not only indulged in terrorist tactics, but practised detention without trial and sought to promote the aims of the one-party Marxist state.

The apologists for WCC grants of this nature usually make the excuse that the terrorist organizations they support are only given grants when all non-violent, constitutional means of change have been suppressed. Yet this extremely slim and dubious excuse was refuted in a letter to *The Times* by Chief Clemens Kapuuo, later to be murdered, allegedly by SWAPO agents, when he stated that FRELIMO had gained control of Mozambique without elections and that the MPLA had prevented elections taking place in Angola. 'SWAPO,' he added, thus probably signing his own death warrant, 'has boycotted elections in Namibia, while yet claiming to be the "sole representative of the people".'[2]

FRELIMO and the MPLA have both benefited from WCC grants. Another Anglican bishop, Trevor Huddleston, though claiming to be a pacifist, insists on calling African terrorists 'patriots': 'While I could never visit a guerrilla army training camp and give them my blessing, you will never get me to describe the people engaged in guerrilla activity as evil men or terrorists. They are patriots.'[3]

In July 1974, considerable controversy raged about a grant by the British Council of Churches to TRJ (Towards Racial Justice) led by Marcus Howe, the son of an Anglican clergyman and a self-confessed Marxist. Even the *Guardian*, normally devoted to all causes associated with the Third World, carried headlines about 'Churchmen Uneasy on Gift to Black Power Group.' When challenged on this, the Reverend Harry Morton, general secretary of the British Council of Churches, said that the grant was justified on the grounds of freedom of speech, though admitting that the TRJ policy 'often seemed to stir up racial hatred rather than allay it'.[4] In fact, as time showed, the aims of TRJ were to use the emotive issue of racism as a means of arousing non-white immigrants to attack white society.

Christianity has in recent years been repeatedly distorted into a kind of 'front organization' for international communism by ministers of various churches in Britain. This may not always have been their intention, but they have been seduced into such operations by false words, skilled propaganda and hospitality enjoyed when visiting the other side of the Iron Curtain. Of all the communist regimes outside Soviet Russia that of East Germany has been the harshest. The Reverend Peter Coates, the Methodist Minister at Anerley in south-east London, led the first delegation of ministers from this country to the East German Methodist conference in June 1978. On his return he told the *Beckenham Journal*: 'I couldn't help contrasting the warm, friendly hospitality in the East with coming back to the harsh realities of a capitalist society,' and, as a throw-away comment, he added that it was on the western side of the border that he saw his first armed policeman.[5]

The most skilled of all the manipulators in the WCC right up to the time of his death was the Metropolitan Nikodim, one of the youngest bishops in Christendom and a staunch ally of the Soviet government. It is true that he managed to persuade the Soviet government to drop its opposition to the ecumenical movement, but only because he convinced them that an ecumenical policy favoured the USSR. He was given charge of the Foreign Relations Department of the Moscow Patriarchate and through this became a key figure in Soviet foreign policy. He ensured that the impetus in the World Council of Churches' policy-making came from the Eastern bloc and not from the West, so that in the end it controlled WCC thinking.

Another member of the WCC executive committee who has propounded pro-Soviet bloc sentiments is the Reverend Dr Ernest Payne, a prominent Baptist minister, created a Companion of Honour in 1968. A former member of the Baptist Missionary Society and a lecturer in comparative religion and the history of modern missions at Oxford University, Dr Payne progressed from secretary of the Baptist Union to president of the WCC. On his return from a visit to Bulgaria in 1971, when the WCC ratified a further grant to African guerrilla forces, he wrote an article in the *Baptist Times* entitled 'Churchmen in Bulgaria the Beautiful'. While admitting that Baptists in Bulgaria had for many years been cut off from their co-religionists in other countries, he insisted that they were not helped by protests and intervention from outside. When a Swiss delegate proposed a resolution expressing concern about restrictions on religious liberty in the USSR and asking for effective implementation of the Helsinki Agreement, this same Dr Payne referred the whole matter back to the committee. As a result the reference to the USSR was deleted.

Perhaps much more serious has been the almost total silence throughout Christendom concerning the fate of the besieged Christians of the Lebanon facing extermination from Soviet-provided tanks and guns of the Syrian army. Only the Israelis lend them any aid, while the Christian churches have allowed the idea to gain credence that these people are Christian in name alone and in fact are corrupt fascists. Thus the KGB propaganda machine has played its part with subtly effective disinformation. Yet the Lebanese Maronite Christians have not only existed from the beginning of the second century AD, surviving all manner of persecution by the Arabs and quietly practising their faith, but they are in communion with Rome and linked with the Greek Orthodox Church.

In his 1978 Reith Lecture the Reverend Dr Edward Norman, Dean of Peterhouse, Cambridge, summed up some of the extraordinary and confusing postures by clerics today. 'They [Christian leaders] make a simple and generally innocent conflation of Christian love of neighbour with the most hardline Marxist devices to engineer radical social change. They represent the political rhetoric of Marxism as merely a succinct manner of expressing agreed moral truths about human society. And so the Marxists' liturgy of propaganda gets reproduced in the world views of Christianity,' he said.

A good deal, if not most of, this thinking stems from the misleading statistics produced by Eastern bloc countries regarding the growth of numbers of practising Christians in those areas. After a WCC meeting in Nairobi in 1975 there was a request for the pooling of resources to produce documentation on religion in Eastern Europe. This was eventually published under the title of *Religious Liberty in the Soviet Union.*[6]

One of the reports prepared by Keston College, Kent, stated that there was evidence of a religious revival in the Soviet Union, but pointed out that while the constitution laid down the separation of Church from State, in practice the Churches in Russia were quite definitely restricted and controlled by the Soviet authorities. Contrary to the views of the Reverend Peter Coates, Nonconformists have often been more harshly treated than the other religious cults. Baptists have been a constant target of the Soviet security forces: in the mid-seventies there was an assault by 300 police and KGB officers on Baptists resisting the closure of a new house of worship in the ancient town of Bryansk. Pastor Georgy Vins, a prominent Baptist leader, was sentenced in 1975 to five years in a labour camp and five years' exile.

Indeed, Keston College is today perhaps the most valuable antidote to the disinformation on world affairs which so many of the clergy seem to lap up so avidly. Fourteen miles south of London close by Hayes Common, a village green and a windmill, it was founded by the Reverend Michael Bourdeaux as a research centre and listening post for information on the state of religion in the Eastern bloc. Its reputation for collecting and analysing such intelligence is so high that this establishment is today consulted by both the British Foreign Office and the American State Department, by delegates to the Helsinki Review Conference on human rights as well as many other organizations.

When describing various Czech agents to the Sub-Committee of the US Senate investigating communist infiltration in 1975, Josef Frolik mentioned an 'Agent Smrk', a priest in Jradec Kralove, who was, he said, 'utilized to work on an American priest who was employed by the World Council of Churches.' This item of intelligence led to the naming of two British priests, one Catholic and one Church of England, who had allowed themselves to be used as agents.[7]

It has been mainly by use of disinformation to suggest that the Soviet Union cherishes its Russian Orthodox Church that priests of so many denominations in the Western World have been suborned. During the early post-World War II years there was no country which was subjected to such diligent intelligence gathering on all levels by the USSR as Italy. The ancient Russian greed for information for information's sake was still evident and a great deal of intelligence they obtained was trivial and even irrelevant by security standards. But it did enable them to practise disinformation more skilfully, especially inside the Roman Catholic Church. Not even the Vatican was immune. In May 1952, it was announced in Rome that Father Alighieri Tondi, Professor of the Gregorian Academy at the Vatican and one-time secretary to Monsignor Montini, who later became Pope Paul, had been found to be a Soviet agent, deliberately planted in the Jesuit Order.

Tondi himself touched off what became a nation-wide sensation by repudiating his faith and openly committing himself to the Communist Party. As a youth he had been a brilliant student of engineering and architecture. Later he served with Mussolini's army in Ethiopia, returning to Italy when he was twenty-eight and deciding to become a Jesuit. At what stage of his career he became a Marxist is not clear, but he had actually attended courses at the Lenin University in Moscow. When he officially became a communist in 1952 he said he had voted for the Party since 1948. After 1952 he soon put the oratory he had devoted to religious work to the cause of communist propaganda, delivering speeches at communist political rallies and making violent attacks on the Church. He was given a post in the press office of the Italian Communist Party headquarters in Rome. In 1954 he married Signorina Zanti, who had just returned from a visit to China, in a civil ceremony.

Though it may seem a digression from the subject of this book, it is important to consider the Tondi case in the light of the book's theme. For, while Tondi was excommunicated on four counts, for renouncing his religion, abandoning the priesthood, actively furthering communism and marrying outside the Church, in 1965 he was not only readmitted to the sacraments as a lay Catholic, but was given a special dispensation which allowed him to continue to live with Signorina Zanti, who refused a Church marriage and remained a communist.

The reason for this is that so cleverly organized was the Soviet campaign of disinformation inside Italy and Spain in Catholic circles that there was a sudden switch to tolerance of communism within the Vatican itself after Pope John XXIII was enthroned. So much so that on 13 May 1963, the Office of National Estimates Staff in the United States sent a memorandum to the CIA, warning about changes in Vatican policy under Pope John, mentioning 'concessions to communism, a view of Khruschev as a force for liberalization and the belief that Marxism was losing its hold.'[8]

There are countless examples of how Western observers from Church circles have been bamboozled by the Soviet Union. There is the case of the Pochaev Monastery in the Ukraine, which was linked by tradition with the Holy Trinity Monastery in Jordanville, New York State, a Russian Orthodox community. For some years the Pochaev monastery was subjected to terrible persecutions, but, to mislead Western visitors, it was allowed to reopen and the KGB used a number of priests inside the Church as guides to mislead such visitors with propaganda. A high-ranking Metropolia (member of the Orthodox Russian Church in America) visited the monastery for about an hour, escorted by KGB priests, and reported back that there was 'no persecution of the monastery at Pochaev'. Only much later did it emerge through messages smuggled out to the West that the monastery was only to be temporarily opened and that no new novices were being permitted to enter without permission from the local KGB and then on condition that they agreed to serve the KGB and report on all activities in the monastery.

The Soviet secret service has made a number of attempts to infiltrate the Catholic priesthood, mainly in Spain and parts of Latin America, where they actively aid revolutionary movements while remaining as priests. But it has been within the Jesuit priesthood that its most spectacular successes have been obtained. In the late sixties the KGB increasingly turned its attention to the Roman Catholic Church in Africa, actually setting out to win agents among native Catholic priests and, when they could not trap them into adherence to the Soviet scheme of things, manipulating them as protesters against imperialism and poverty. By the early seventies there was an unmistakable move of the Church towards Marxism in Guatemala, with half the young churchmen and even some of the bishops preaching the doctrine of the incompatibility of Christianity with capitalism. About fifteen per cent of the priesthood were positively Marxist and the COSDEGUA (Confederation of Diocesan Priests of Guatemala) is Soviet-infiltrated and aimed at revolution.

The KGB runs its own religious centres for training appropriate agents to be sent to Western and Third World countries. These are to be found in Feodosia in the Crimea, Lvov in the Ukraine, Constanza and in Lithuania. Towards the end of the 1970s leading Soviet commentators began to attribute a 'progressive' role to religious groups and urged communists everywhere to collaborate more closely with them. An example of the new kind of disinformation was contained in an article in *Pravda* by a Dr Mchledov, entitled 'Religion in the Modern World'. This argued that religious bodies of all kinds – Christian, Islamic and Buddhist (notably it did not include those of the Jewish faith) – were actively engaged in 'the struggle for peaceful co-existence and social progress'.

But perhaps the supreme instance of disinformation by the Russians towards the Christian community was that provided by a Soviet writer, B. Zabirov. A Columbian had inquired whether the Russians shared the view of some Christians that a Christian believer could not be a Marxist or a communist. Zabirov's reply was that Marxist-Leninism was completely in accord with the Christian ideals of charity and friendship and that close collaboration between Christians and communists was both possible and desirable.[9]

Some of the results of such propaganda are not difficult to find over the past twenty years. Two examples, both of which occurred in 1978, will suffice for the moment. The Church of England announced that it was proposing to hand over one of London's best-known churches, St Dunstan-in-the-West, Fleet Street, to the Rumanian Orthodox Church to be used as its headquarters in Britain, despite the fact that the Rumanian Church is directly accountable to the Rumanian state for all its activities, and that its former representatives in Britain had been removed from office for refusing to carry out 'political work' among Rumanian refugees in Britain. Secondly, the Methodist Church withdrew permission for the new anti-Marxist International Conference of Confessing Christians to use Central Hall, Westminster, for an inaugural meeting because some Methodist leaders believed that the conference speakers might attack the World Council of Churches on political grounds.

There was, too, the case in 1981 of the Catholic Council for Social Responsibility calling for a general fast and day of prayer over the British Government's cuts in public expenditure. The fast was planned jointly by the Catholic Church, the Church of England and the Methodists, again influenced by WCC and BCC thinking. This was condemned by the Moderator of the General Assembly of the Church of Scotland as being 'immoral to humanity and blasphemous in the sight of God'. An extravagantly worded piece of criticism maybe, but probably the most honest comment was that of a Catholic priest, Father Michael Clifton, who said that 'I don't like the Government's policies any more than anyone else does, but I don't think it is the Church's job to criticize them. It is the Church meddling in politics.'[10]

This truth-twisting by the Churches is typical of what is regarded by the KGB as psychological disinformation. First, priests, ministers and laymen are encouraged to open up a dialogue with the East by means of invitations, friendly letters and a certain amount of skilled propaganda. Then, at a later stage, deliberate misinformation is supplied until, finally, there is psychological manipulation, sometimes through such movements as the Christian Peace Conference, intended to show that the real peace-makers are the USSR and their allies; then through the WCC's programme to combat racism. The disinformers play on the Christian conscience to expiate the Western world's 'guilt' for the treatment of the Red Indians, the slave trade, the conflict in Vietnam and colonialism by the setting up of a Special Fund to Combat Racism and the donations of money to guerrilla groups everywhere.

The Salvation Army, which has always retained its independence, commonsense and sound practical principles in whatever work it undertakes, was one of the first to grasp how Church and Christian organizations were being exploited by the WCC. In 1981 it announced that it was withdrawing from the Geneva-based WCC because it considered the organization was 'motivated by politics rather than the Gospel'.[11]

The withdrawal of the Salvation Army was announced during a meeting of the WCC's 140-member central committee in Dresden, East Germany, the first assembly of the WCC in an Eastern European communist country.

Racism is a word which is twisted to mean almost everything

that aids the cause of world revolution and the downfall of non-communist regimes. It was the British Council of Churches which funded the 'Race Today Collective', which published a magazine offering this opinion: 'our political aim is to assist the black population to manifest its revolutionary potential for the development of the working class as a whole.' Jesus Christ is no longer pictured as the Eternal Father and Saviour, but as the Guerrilla Leader.

But those who need aid against religious persecution, the silent spokesmen of religious dissidents from the established order of communism, can expect practically no help from the WCC. They depend increasingly upon assistance from such organizations as Keston College. As long ago as 1964 the Reverend Michael Bourdeaux was shown his first *samizdat*, a letter smuggled out of the Ukraine. This told of the persecution and beating up of monks and the imprisonment of religious leaders in far-off wastelands. From this experience and a subsequent visit to Moscow he was inspired to set up his Information Section and research teams at Keston College.

Another man who produced the first documented criticism of the WCC was Bernard Smith, whose painstaking researches resulted in his work, *The Fraudulent Gospel*, one of the most powerful indictments of the subversion of the Western churches by Marxism yet made. In 1979 Mr Smith wrote to the author saying: 'over the past ten years I have encountered considerable opposition to my views and had great difficulty in getting my book published.'[12]

Disinformation regarding not only the current Pope, but most post-World War II Popes, has been extensive both on the hard right as much as the hard left. But such material disseminated in various ways has been politically rather than religiously motivated, though the various theories and explanations for the attempted assassination of Pope John-Paul belong to another chapter of this book.

Prior to the election of Pope John XXIII there was some anxiety in CIA circles that the Cardinals were more or less evenly split between those who went along with the old traditions and those who wanted a modernist approach in the Church. After the election of John XXIII the CIA were very concerned about the general trend of the Roman Catholic Church and they made an assessment on 3 May 1963 that under the new Pope's regime there was an attempt to come to terms with communism, or as their report of this date puts it: the new Pope was 'abandoning polemics against communism in an effort to preserve the Church in Eastern Europe.'

This may or may not have been a form of appeasement to be compared with previous Popes' attempts to make a deal with fascism and nazism in an effort to survive, but ever since Pope John XXIII was elected there has been a steady, marked leftward swing in the Roman Catholic Church which has percolated through to those sections of the media previously receptive to Catholic viewpoints. Following upon a CIA analysis of the United States *Ramparts* magazine in the summer of 1967, James Angleton, then Deputy Director of Plans and Operations of the CIA, sent a memorandum to J. Edgar Hoover, then Director of the FBI, noting *Ramparts*' 'change from a non-political, literary and cultural, liberal Catholic magazine to a publication devoted to dissemination of well-known communist propaganda themes.'[13]

When the Soviet invasion of Afghanistan occurred in 1979, the WCC, through its executive committee meeting in Liebfrauberg, stated that 'the military action by the USSR constituted the latest direct armed intervention in one country by another', adding that this had 'heightened the tension especially in and around the area of development'.

Yet this statement was not followed up by any positive action or decision. On the contrary, a few days after the Central Committee meeting on this subject a two-day conference of the Prague-based Christian Peace Conference was convened by its president, Bishop Dr Karoly Toth, a key member of the WCC. The consensus of opinion at this meeting was that events in Afghanistan should not be considered in isolation, but in relation to international developments threatening peace. Prior to this the CPC had actually defended the Soviet invasion of Afghanistan on the grounds that the Soviet Union had to 'honour the request' for help made by the Afghanistan Government. When the WCC's sixth assembly met in Vancouver in the late summer of 1983, Afghanistan had become a major issue and could no longer be by-passed. But it was merely decided that the WCC should support the efforts of the Secretary-

General of the United Nations to find a formula for ending the conflict. Archbishop Kyrill, the Russian representative, told a meeting in Vancouver's Christ Church Cathedral that 'the future of Afghanistan should be decided by the Afghans without outside interference.'[14]

It is perhaps easy to see how such a statement might be accepted by gullible delegates as a genuine gesture, but there is no doubt whatsoever that the Archbishop was attempting to appease those who wanted to criticize Soviet actions. Thus when it came to a drafting of a WCC resolution on Afghanistan there was no attempt at being other than ambivalent in phrasing it. The Drafting Committee merely favoured 'a peaceful resolution of the conflict', whatever that might mean, and 'withdrawal of Soviet troops from Afghanistan in the context of an overall political settlement, including agreement between Afghanistan and the USSR.'[15]

The Russians' delegation made it abundantly clear that they would accept no other proposal, despite opposition from a few members of the WCC. The most forthright objection to the proposal came from Bishop Alexander Malik of Pakistan, who urged the rejection of the document, making the criticism that 'the drafters have selected the weakest possible language. If it had been any Western country, the WCC would have jumped on it and denounced the country in the strongest possible language.'[16]

All mention of atrocities committed by Soviet troops in Afghanistan and their use of a systematic scorched earth policy was vigorously repudiated by Eastern delegates as Western propaganda. Some of the Western Church delegates even accepted that such stories were untrue and invented. Yet in November 1985 a four-man team, including Mr Michael Barry, an American observer for the International Federation of Human Rights; Dr Johan Lagerfelt, a Swedish doctor with the French group, *Médécins du Monde*; M. Pascal Maitre, a French photographer with the Gamma Agency; and M. Yvon Deleau, a cameraman with French television, travelled on foot and horseback in the provinces of Afghanistan and reported a very different state of affairs. At a press conference in the French Senate, presided over by Mr Peers Carter, the former British Ambassador to Afghanistan who is vice-president of the International Commission of Inquiry on displaced persons in

Afghanistan, they described some of the very incidents which had been so firmly denied at the WCC conference. They confirmed that Soviet troops were committing atrocities against the civilian population. At one village they were said 'to have tortured a fourteen-year-old boy before crucifying and shooting him. Soviet soldiers seized two boys in the village of Bed-Moshk in Ghazni. Mohammed Esmail, ten, was ransomed by his parents for the equivalent of less than two pounds, but Mohammed Nabi, whose parents could not afford to buy him back, was denied water, mutilated with a bayonet, crucified on a tree and executed.'[17]

Despite Bishop Malik's plea for the rejection of the WCC document, Archbishop Kyrill successfully argued that 'any changes in the text as accepted by the Drafting Committee would be politically misused', adding ominously the threat that otherwise 'our loyalty to the ecumenical movement would be challenged'.

The Soviet aim was, of course, to ensure that the supply of arms to the Afghan resistance movement should be ended, which was why the Drafting Committee had inserted into their proposal for a settlement that there should be 'an end to the supply of arms to the opposition groups from outside' (a neat piece of disinformation to describe a united resistance movement as 'opposition groups'). The outcome of the vote on the draft text was 479 in favour of it, only 21 against and 142 abstentions. Thus did the WCC toe the Soviet line on the issue of the invasion of Afghanistan. It was achieved by a massive Russian campaign of propaganda both before the conference was held and during the meetings in Vancouver. The word 'pagan' was used to describe the Afghans, asserting that their country was no part of the Christian fraternity and that therefore they were of no concern. Nor are members of the Palestine Liberation Organization, yet they have frequently received backing from some churchmen. Everything was done to play down the idea of there being any properly organized opposition to the 'Soviet allies of Afghanistan', suggesting that the main trouble came from hordes of bandits who were only out for loot.

Interestingly, this same Assembly of the WCC which declined to give aid to Afghanistan went out of its way to refer to 'the forces of historic change in El Salvador' in a praiseworthy manner, and criticized the resistance to these by the United States Government.

In 1983 ten Russian Church leaders visited Europe, including Britain, to help promote the Soviet campaign against NATO missiles in Europe. It was the first Russian multi-Church delegation to visit Britain since 1955 and meetings with a number of British clergymen were arranged. The importance attached to the visit by the Kremlin could be measured by the size and scope of the delegation led by the Metropolitan of Kiev, Archbishop Philaret, and including members of Armenian, Georgian, Roman Catholic, Baptist and Lutheran Churches. The Catholic member was Monsignor Joseph Chamaites, a Lithuanian parish priest. The Russians lunched with the Archbishop of Canterbury.

Canon Paul Oestreicher, of the Council of Churches' international department, said of the visit that 'we are wrestling with the problem of confidence building between Britain and the Soviet Union and trying to hammer out a common programme.'[18]

Has any country in the world hammered out a common programme with the Soviet Union without ultimately being completely dominated by it?

5

WHEN 'TRUTH CAN NEVER BE TOLD'

The title of this chapter is owed to William Blake, and it becomes easier to understand when one reads what exactly Blake said: 'Truth can never be told so as to be understood, and not believed.'

Blake remains one of the most magical exponents of the sudden flash of inspiration down the centuries. He also made the quip that 'a truth that's told with bad intent beats all the lies you can invent.' What Blake meant in both cases could well be applied to recent history. To turn to Blake for inspiration is always a salutary corrective influence. For, whereas in the first few chapters there has been rather more emphasis on Soviet disinformation than that of other nations, no honest observer of this growing industry (for that is what it sometimes seems to be) could deny that all parts of the world practise such deception to a greater or lesser extent. In the main the Western world may be less guilty, but one cannot effectively pillory the guilt of our enemies without admitting our own.

A very minor recent example of deliberate disinformation will perhaps best illustrate this point. On 4 November 1985, the London *Daily Telegraph* in all good faith published a hand-written letter purportedly written by a Mr D. Evans, of Torpoint, Devon. This letter claimed that the writer had recently been in South Africa and was 'appalled, but not surprised, to see a television crew encouraging a crowd of school-children to run towards them as if rioting . . . When they complied, they were told to go back and do it again, and to wave their fists and try to look ferocious.'

The letter was quoted – *on the same day that it was published* – by Mr Louis Nel, Deputy Minister of Information, on a South African television programme in which he was attempting to justify the government's latest curbs on coverage of township unrest. However, an investigation by a South African Sunday newspaper, the *Sunday Star*, disclosed that there was no 'Mr D. Evans' at the address given in the letter and that Torpoint was in fact in Cornwall and not in Devon. The newspaper traced two D. Evans in Torpoint, but both disclaimed any knowledge of the letter. The people who lived at the address given also disclaimed any knowledge of the letter, or of a D. Evans. The whole affair was described by the *Sunday Star* as 'a shocking disinformation scandal'.

The *Daily Telegraph* subsequently stated that 'it now appears that it [the letter] was intended to deceive, and we owe our readers a sincere apology.'[1]

This was perhaps one of the stupidest disinformation ploys imaginable. As those of us who have had anything to do with the media know full well, the temptation to exploit riots of any kind in the form of television exposure is always great. That such exploitation actually encourages more violence, more riots and more thuggery is undoubted. One also suspects that in some cases, in Britain and the USA, and in Europe, too, quite apart from South Africa, cameramen have actually gone out of their way to manipulate such scenes in order to create a certain prejudiced impression, when clever editing of the film distorts the true picture. In other words, police reaction to the violence has been given more prominence than the actions of the rioters. This was occasionally the case in the filming of the miners' riots in Britain in 1984.

No doubt too much attention to the coverage of such violence can contribute to the increase in violence. But this is one of those areas where it is difficult to separate fact from specula-tion, and an example of disinformation of this kind can totally destroy what might just possibly be a legitimate point.

British disinformation is often perpetrated in such a curiously low-key, offbeat manner that it is rarely identified for what it really is. One typical example was contained in the London *Times* on 15 June 1977, at a time when something approaching a witch-hunt was in full swing for the mysterious 'Fourth Man' among those who had betrayed Britain's secrets to the Soviet Union. This witch-hunt reached the apex of fantasy when *The Times* reported that 'news of the doubts attached to the name of Donald Howard Beves in security circles since the early 1950s will come as a severe shock to the Cambridge generations who knew him . . . Beves was in many ways a conventional don in outward appearance, with mildly conservative views and an easy-going manner. He kept the political extremism which the MI 5 investigation is thought to have discovered in him deeply concealed, aided, no doubt, by his consummate skills as an actor.'

The suggestion in this article in *The Times* that Donald Beves was the 'Fourth Man' created a furore in the correspondence columns of *The Times* and elsewhere for several days. But, as *Private Eye* inquired, satirically but realistically: 'Who was responsible for *The Times*'s massive boob over Donald Beves, the bumbling old Cambridge don who was stated to have recruited Philby, Maclean and Burgess on behalf of Moscow? I understand the story originated . . . over a drink at the Garrick Club.'

Undoubtedly this story was planted on *The Times*, but whether to discredit the security services or to draw attention away from the real culprits, or some other purpose, is difficult to assess. There was just one area in which Beves was vulnerable, especially if he or others were indiscreet. He was a close friend of at least three men – all from Cambridge colleges – who were working at the Bletchley station for the deciphering of enemy messages during World War II. And Bletchley was suspected of being a source of many leakages. But MI 5 would have come to the same conclusion as did *The Times* of two weeks later when it announced 'it is indeed true that Mr Beves was suspected, but we now believe the suspicions were mistaken and regret having reported them.'

At the time of this report, though I found it hard to believe that Beves could have been a Soviet agent, I decided to check and double-check. There was not a hint of any ground for suspicion.

Beves was neither of the 'Homintern' (the pro-Soviet Cambridge homosexual mafia), nor the Comintern; the only book to his name was a translation of Rabelais, which he edited. His will contained no surprises, the beneficiaries being King's College and his relatives. His foreign travels were invariably in a party, never alone, for he was an appallingly bad car driver; the trips were mainly to cathedrals and art galleries in France, with occasional diversions to Spain and Italy.

The Beves story that emanated from the Garrick Club was certainly a cunningly, if improbably, devised red herring. It was fashionable in the first few years after the resignation of Harold Wilson from the premiership to make the smearing of MI 5 and MI 6 a national hobby for journalists and politicians in unholy alliance, always looking for a British Watergate. And the very hint that MI 5 might be following the Beves trail to the cathedral at Chartres, or analysing his concoction of brandy and crème de menthe, served in punch bowls at King's, could not fail to persuade some that all was not as it should be among the ranks of those anonymous, rain-coated gentlemen whose task is to guard the security of the realm.

Was this originally a piece of disinformation to put eager journalists off the scent of the real villain, or villains? Or was it just somebody's ridiculous fantasy? It aroused considerable controversy at the time, with the historian A.J.P. Taylor posing the question in a *Sunday Express* article, 'Who was the Fourth Man?' After attacking *The Times* for naming Donald Beves, Taylor went on to inquire: 'Whose was the hidden hand which protected these three men, gave them confidential positions when they were obviously security risks, and enabled them to escape in good time?' He was, of course, referring to Burgess, Maclean and Philby.

When eventually the name of Anthony Blunt as that of a Soviet agent was confirmed in an answer at question-time in the House of Commons by the Prime Minister, there were various alibis for the Donald Beves story. The suggestion then put about was that somebody must have told *The Times* that the 'Fourth Man' was one whose name began with a 'B' and had five letters. This, of course, fitted Beves or Blunt. What was unbelievable about that alibi was that anyone should have thought it could refer to Beves.

One besetting vice of the British is an obsession with secrecy, to which most British disinformation can be linked. This book will eventually show how the obsession operates in all fields of British life, not merely in the realm of security and secret service. It is most marked in the upper reaches of British society and the Establishment, but it also operates at much lower and more trivial levels. The result is that quite often the Establishment itself becomes tangled in the secretive webs it weaves. The Beves story is a minor example, but sometimes as a result of ultra-secrecy disinformation of a compulsive kind becomes ludicrous in the extreme.

A particularly apt instance was the way in which the British Establishment (one can never be quite sure which branch of it was principally responsible, or how many branches were involved) handled the case of Commander Lionel Crabb, R.N. In April 1956 the Soviet leaders, Marshal Bulganin and Nikita Khrushchev, paid a goodwill visit to Britain, arriving at Portsmouth in the Soviet cruiser, *Ordzhonikidze*. While the ship was moored against the south-west jetty of Portsmouth harbour, on 19 April, Commander Crabb, an expert diver and authority on underwater espionage, set out a top secret mission to examine the cruiser beneath the water-line. He never reported back to duty and his disappearance caused a parliamentary storm when the Russians indignantly announced that they had discovered all about the mission and that it was an outrageous incident which marred their goodwill visit.

In fact, Crabb's mission was espionage of a type common in peace as in wartime, with all nations indulging in it to some extent. Naturally, the aim was always to conduct it without being caught in the act, but if either side was caught out the normal procedure would be to make some plausible excuses. Commander Crabb's instructions, among other things, had been to ascertain whether the *Ordzhonikidze* was fitted with a device to reduce the chances of being detected by long-range sonar scanning.

Rear-Admiral Kotov, of the Soviet Navy, reported to the British naval authorities in Portsmouth that 'at 7.30 am on 19 April sailors aboard the *Ordzhonikidze* had observed a frogman floating between the Soviet destroyers.' The implication was that he then dived beneath the surface and was not seen again.

Commander Crabb was an experienced, knowledgeable and daring diver who, during World War II, had won the George

Medal and the OBE for removing limpet mines from British warships off Gibraltar. He had the reputation of being a fearless patriot and, though then aged forty-six and somewhat out of condition, was still confidently ready to meet new challenges.

There were two possibilities which the British had to consider: first, that Crabb had drowned while on his mission, or had been killed by the Russians; second, that he had been taken prisoner. Sir Anthony Eden, then Prime Minister, was furious that such a mission should have been attempted during the so-called 'goodwill' visit by the Russian leaders, and the last thing the authorities wanted was any suggestion that the secret service was involved. Thus a cover-up was decided upon and from then on disinformation steadily flowed from all sides. The most sensible plan would have been to admit that Crabb had been diving in the vicinity of the Soviet cruiser and to have invited the Russians to join in a search for his body. That would have covered all eventualities and made sense to the British people. But not until nine days later did the Admiralty announce that the commander was missing, presumed dead, having failed to return from 'a test-dive in connection with trials of certain underwater apparatus in Stokes Bay'.

This was, of course, not only totally untrue, but a ludicrous explanation because Stokes Bay was three miles away from where Crabb had last been seen diving – not only by the Russians, but by British naval personnel and civilians as well. In June 1981, Mrs Patricia Rose, Crabb's fiancée, received a letter which stated: 'For what it is worth – I was a schoolboy visiting the [Russian] cruiser that afternoon after school and was on the main deck looking over the side next to the quay when I saw a diver (with full deep-diving headgear) being pulled beneath the surface by two frogmen. At the same time the ship's propellers were turned over, a klaxon sounded and a line of Russian sailors cleared the deck.'[2]

The lies of British officialdom caused much more trouble than the truth would have done. They were not accepted by the Russians, who knew otherwise, nor were they believed by newspapers or members of Parliament. Matters became even worse when the rumour was started that Commander Crabb was not working for British Intelligence, but that he might have been undertaking a freelance mission for the CIA. This piece of disinformation was steadily developed over the years and even exploited in the most scurrilous manner, implying that the commander might have been a double-agent, acting not only for Britain and America, but for the Russians, too.

None of this lying did the British secret service any good; the first casualty was the head of MI 6, Major-General Sinclair. But there was worse to come. Fourteen months after the Portsmouth incident a body was washed ashore on a sandbank in Chichester harbour, and at an inquest, on the flimsiest evidence, a verdict was recorded that the corpse was Commander Crabb's.

Experts argued that any body lost in Portsmouth harbour in April 1956 would have long since been washed out to sea and was unlikely to turn up on a sandbank in Chichester harbour. This is where a fisherman found the corpse which, very conveniently, was both headless and handless, as well as being badly decomposed, and encased in a frogman's outfit. As no other frogman had been reported missing, this pointed circumstantially to Commander Crabb.

Commander Crabb's ex-wife could not be sure the body was that of her husband. A companion diver and close friend of Crabb, one Sidney James Knowles, BEM, was called to the Bognor mortuary where the body was placed in order to provide evidence of identification. The object in calling Knowles was that diving mates would have detailed knowledge of one another's bodies because they were frequently together in a state of nakedness owing to the nature of their work. Yet, as soon as he saw the corpse, Knowles declared: 'It's definitely not Commander Crabb's body. Crabb had hammer toes. This body has not.'[3]

But the two security men took Knowles on one side and eventually persuaded him that 'on patriotic grounds' he should say that the body was Crabb's. He was also told 'this matter comes under the Official Secrets Act'. Knowles reluctantly agreed, but a few years later he decided that the truth must be told of his part in this affair, which was preying on his mind, so he made a tape recording to confirm that he did not believe the body was that of Crabb. In this recording he stated that one man told him: 'I know it's not Crabb's body, but you must swear to me that if you are asked in court if it's the body, you are to say it is – for Queen and country.'[4]

Knowles' insistence that Crabb had hammer toes was also borne out by the commander's ex-wife.

Why were the authorities so anxious to prove that this was Crabb's body when it was almost impossible to do so? Had the Coroner merely returned a verdict on the death of an unknown body, the fate of the gallant commander might have remained in doubt. Why was someone so anxious for him to be presumed dead so long after the incident at Portsmouth? The Admiralty had stated as much long ago and there the matter might sensibly have been left: the discovery of a body in Chichester harbour was not only irrelevant, but led to much more mischievous speculation.

Far from solving any problems, or even justifying such nonsense as 'patriotic motives', the verdict led not only to wide-spread disbelief, but even to stories from behind the Iron Curtain that Crabb was still alive. The major query remained unanswered: who put this corpse on the sandbank in Chichester harbour – the British or the Russians? Tidal experts agreed that the body could not have been there for more than twenty-four hours.

What was the reason for this rather ridiculous ploy in disinformation? Had someone tried to be too clever, failed lamentably and therefore desperately needed to cover up a disaster? Or were the British authorities suddenly convinced that Crabb was still alive, probably in Soviet hands, and that at any moment the Russians might produce him at a press conference, as they did with Burgess and Maclean? This might have stimulated the desire to provide some proof that he was dead.

Unfortunately Lieutenant-Commander Ewen Montagu had published *The Man Who Never Was* in 1953, an account of how British Naval Intelligence fooled the Germans in World War II by dropping a corpse from a submarine off the coast of Spain. The corpse was given false identity papers – those of an alleged courier – and bogus secret plans which suggested that the next Allied invasion would be in Sardinia rather than Sicily where it actually took place. The fact that the British Navy had indulged in a faked corpse once before naturally led to the conclusion that they could do it again – another example of why the Chichester harbour incident was so foolishly exploited. If it was intended to silence stories from behind the Iron Curtain that Crabb was still alive, it failed lamentably. All it did was to reinforce them.

The official story about Crabb's body having been found was

rejected on all sides. Sir Percy Sillitoe, former chief of MI 5, insisted that 'it was known that Crabb did not perish, but was intercepted by Russian frogmen who were in the water round the Soviet ship.'[5]

Commander John Kerans, hero of the HMS *Amethyst* escape from the Yangtse River, said: 'I am convinced that Crabb is alive and in Russian hands.'[6]

Mrs Patricia Rose, Crabb's fiancée, began to receive strange messages of love which were said to have come from him. 'Messages included phrases like "the old grey witch" and a certain pet name which only Crabbie used,' says Mrs Rose. 'I have had telephone messages from strangers who have been asked to pass messages on to me that Crabbie is still alive. Then I had a telephone call from a friend who said he had seen a picture of me with my brother and sister-in-law published in an East German paper. Yet there had been only three copies of this photograph, one, which I possessed, the other with a friend and the third was with Crabbie when he disappeared. I made inquiries about the other two prints and learned they were both in their respective albums. This picture, which I later learned had also been published in *Pravda*, must have been taken from Crabbie's wallet.'[7]

There is no doubt that both the British and the Russians indulged in some disinformation tactics regarding Crabb's disappearance. But when British authorities claimed on such slender and circumstantial evidence that the body found at Chichester was that of Crabb, they gave the Russians a splendid opportunity for maintaining that Crabb was still alive and so creating doubt about the whole affair. Such stories were fed through to the Western world with great persistency over the next few years. Mr Kenneth Elliot, who held a position with the firm of Lucas, told Mrs Rose in 1968 that he had just returned from a business trip to Russia; when in Sebastopol, he had observed some frogmen emerging from the sea and his guide and interpreter told him, 'Look there is your famous Commander Crabb.'[8]

Bernard Hutton, a Middle European who adopted an English name, published a book entitled *Commander Crabb is Alive* in 1968. He declared that he had been told that Captain R. Melkov, a Leningrad seaman, who often travelled to Britain, had spoken to Crabb and that the latter gave Melkov a personal message for Mrs Rose. On 8 May 1968, Captain Melkov, master of the Soviet ship *Kolpino,* then in London docks, was found shot dead in his cabin. On the following day a verdict that Melkov had 'killed himself' was recorded at Southwark Coroner's Court.

The truth about the Crabb affair may never be known, at least for several years, but it illustrates better than almost any other incident of modern times how disinformation breeds disinformation until the truth is so hidden that it can hardly ever be divined. Mrs Rose still clings to a belief that Crabb may be alive and that messages she has had to this effect from people who were quite unknown to her are true. She was shown documents obtained by Bernard Hutton which stated that her fiancé had been taken to the Soviet Union and been forced to join the Red Navy under the name of Korablov. When Anatoli Golitsin defected to the USA in 1963 and was interrogated by the Americans he stated that Soviet Naval Intelligence had been tipped off that a British frogman would make an attempt to spy on the *Ordzhonikidze*, and he was sure this was a report which came from a spy inside the British Admiralty.

Two other tragedies in the early 1960s led to a large number of grotesque stories all of which were to some extent deliberate disinformation. I refer to the assassination of President John Kennedy in Dallas in 1963 and the death in an air crash of Dag Hammarskjold, the Secretary-General of the United Nations, two years previously.

Hammarskjold had been anxious for the United Nations to play a stronger role in extending its influence for peace both in the Middle East and in Africa. On 18 September 1961 he was killed in a plane crash when flying from Leopoldville to Ndola to arrange a cease-fire between the UN and Katangan forces. Even today, a quarter of a century after the plane crashed, mystery surrounds the whole affair.

Disinformation feeds upon mystery just as mystery (or the creation of mystery where none need exist) encourages disinformation. Dag Hammarskjold's death has been linked to the assassination of President Kennedy two years later. A former member of the Northern Rhodesian Police today claims that he was one of the officers who investigated the air crash in which Hammarskjold died. He alleges that a local police officer, a South African, 'arranged that all the lights of the airport [at Ndola] went out just as the plane was about to land. The aircraft was then misdirected over a nearby forest where its landing wheels caught the tops of the trees and caused it to crash. The plane did not catch fire and the natives living in the area glimpsed white men in khaki police uniforms heading for the plane. When they arrived at the plane machine-gunfire was heard as survivors were shot.'[9]

Such an allegation is surprising enough, but the perpetrator of this fantasy goes on to say that 'the CIA had Hammarskjold assassinated as part and parcel of the conspiracy which finally resulted in John Kennedy being killed. The explanation for this is that *Hammarskjold, Kennedy and Patrice Lumumba were plotting to set up a Marxist state in what is now Zaire.*'[10]

Now, as Goebbels long ago asserted, 'the bigger the lie, the more it will be believed.' This story is so categorical, so outrageous and so detailed that it inevitably raises questions as to whether there actually *was* some attempt on Hammarskjold's life. I have gone to some trouble to check on the history of the man who circulates this story – never, to my knowledge, in print, though even that may be possible. He was born in Northern Rhodesia and educated in South Africa, served in the Royal Navy in World War II and worked in Albert Schweitzer's leper colony before joining the Northern Rhodesian Police. He also claims that in the early 1970s he was beaten and left for dead by followers of Joshua Nkomo, who took him for a South African spy. For a short time he was a doorman at the Conservative Party Central Office in London.

When news seeped into the media that President Kennedy's assassin, Lee Harvey Oswald, not only had a Russian wife, but had also visited the Soviet Union, consternation in the Kremlin ensued. Having suffered one political reverse over Cuba in 1962, the Russians had good reason to fear that the repercussions over any hint that the KGB might be responsible for Kennedy's death could be disastrous. Their reasoning was, of course, due to the fact that current policy-making in the Kremlin was to lull the United States into believing that an accommodation with the USSR was possible.

So it came about that America was confronted with a new KGB defector, Major Yuri Ivanovich Nosenko, who contacted the Americans in Switzerland in 1964. Nosenko had been deputy director of the American section of the Seventh Department of the KGB, a section which surveyed American visitors to Russia. Consequently he had dealt with Oswald's alleged application for Soviet citizenship in 1959, and he told the CIA that he had formed the opinion that Oswald was mentally unstable and was not to be recruited to work for any Soviet organization. Nosenko gave some other information concerning KGB manipulation of foreigners in Moscow, but some in the CIA still regarded it as possible that he was a false defector and had been planted by the KGB to convince the Americans that Russia had not plotted to kill Kennedy.

It is true that, as the USSR had diplomatic relations with the United States, they could have given information about Oswald and assurances on their non-involvement in the assassination through diplomatic channels. On the other hand obsessive Soviet suspicion may have taken the view that only a man who appeared to be a defector would be likely to convince the Americans. Significantly, Major Nosenko had been promoted to lieutenant-colonel just before he defected. Some in the CIA believed that Nosenko was one of their most valuable defectors of all time. Against them was ranged a formidable body of opinion which included James Angleton, probably the ablest and most brilliant counter-intelligence officer the United States ever had, and David Murphy, chief of the CIA's Soviet Division.

Nosenko's principal achievement – probably one which the Russians in their wildest dreams could never have imagined – was by his very presence to divide the CIA into two camps, leaving that organization in a state of chaos for some years. Indeed, Hugh Tovar, former chief of the CIA Covert Action Staff, described the capacity of the CIA for counter-intelligence and clandestine action at that time as being 'close to zero'.

When Lee Harvey Oswald returned to the United States from Russia in 1962, the FBI, responsible for internal security, failed totally to keep him under surveillance. This negligence appeared to be almost criminal when it began to be whispered that Oswald had been manipulated and controlled by the KGB both while he was in Russia and when he returned to the USA. Therefore J. Edgar Hoover, head of the FBI, saw in Nosenko the perfect alibi for his alleged negligence, as Nosenko insisted there was no link between Oswald and any branch of Soviet Intelligence.

One of the most valuable of defectors to the Western cause was Anatoli Golitsin, who came over in 1962 under the codename of 'Stone'. Shortly after the Kennedy assassination Golitsin told James Angleton: 'Wait and see. Very soon someone will come over to you from Moscow and try to prove that Russia was in no way involved in the killing of your President.' When Nosenko arrived with just such a story Angleton's suspicions were aroused. These suspicions grew when he listened to other information passed by Nosenko.

Ultimately Angleton lost his battle and was forced out of the CIA by the new Director, William Colby. Disinformation had played havoc in the ranks of the organization.

What of Nosenko himself? He was the son of the late Ivan I. Nosenko, Soviet Shipbuilding Minister, and had been a member of the Soviet disarmament delegation in Geneva. But he was also said to have been a staff officer at the Soviet Security Service headquarters in Moscow. [11]

What, also, of Oswald? That he was associated with Russian agents seems to be confirmed on all sides. Why did he go to the Soviet Embassy in Mexico City to obtain visas to visit the Soviet Union? Why did he use an alias when he went to Mexico City? There is also evidence that Oswald, though not a meticulous or grammatical Russian conversationalist, actually adored the Russian language and preferred speaking it to talking in English. All this adds up to nothing positive at all, but does not exclude the fact that Oswald may in some way have been exploited.

Michael Eddowes, a British solicitor who had made a reputation by obtaining a Royal Pardon for Timothy Evans who was mistakenly hanged for murders committed by the infamous John Christie, spent a great deal of time and money researching the file on Oswald. As a result he published a book entitled *The Oswald File*, suggesting that Lee Harvey Oswald had been replaced by a look-alike KGB agent when he went to the Soviet Union. [12]

Eddowes summed up his findings as follows: 'I believe there is overwhelming evidence of conspiracy in the assassination of President John Kennedy and that this evidence was suppressed in the interest of national security. I also believe there is powerful evidence that the assassin was a Soviet agent. Furthermore I believe there is persuasive evidence that the Soviet agent was an impostor.'[13]

On the whole the United States has always been much more forthcoming in admitting governmental and intelligence errors than many other Western powers. But the Kennedy family, from President to father, from father to Attorney General son, and to almost every member of that clan, was so mixed up in scandals and indiscretions that to expose all would have been to create widespread disillusionment at a time when the name of Kennedy was, however erratically, compared to the court of King Arthur at Camelot – the last word in chivalry and honour. Thus the Warren Commission which investigated the death of the President suppressed a good deal of vital evidence.

In 1965 the well-known American newspaper columnist Dorothy Kilgallen interviewed Jack Ruby at the Dallas jail where he was being held for the murder of Lee Harvey Oswald. The nightclub owner and ex-gangster told Miss Kilgallen something which, according to her conversations with close friends, 'would blow the Kennedy case sky-high'. A few days later Miss Kilgallen was found dead of a massive overdose of barbiturates and alcohol. When her apartment was closely examined there was no trace of the notes of her talk with Ruby. Her death was attributed to suicide. Even Ruby when in prison complained that he was slowly being poisoned to death, yet when he actually died it was not from the cancer which he was diagnosed as having, but from a burst blood vessel at the base of the brain.

George de Mohrenschildt, a Polish-born professor of geology, who had come to the USA in 1938, and who had known Oswald and given testimony to the Warren Commission, began writing a book on the Kennedy assassination which, according to some reports, named names that should not have been mentioned. Late in February 1977, he gave a private interview to a Dutch journalist in which he talked about the book and what had happened to it.

As to the reliability of what de Mohrenschildt told various people, much of it is a matter of conjecture. Certainly, to some, he seemed to be suffering from paranoia. One suggestion he made was that he had been given drugs and electric shock treatment to 'wipe my mind clean'. Certainly he had been suffering from psychotic depression; in March 1977 he was found dead, with a gun by his side. His daughter afterwards maintained that she had good reason to think her father shot himself following a telephone call in which he was given a hypnotic message inducing suicide.

But, as we have observed at the beginning of this chapter, sometimes the truth can never be told. When it is lost in the convolutions of disinformation and false interpretations, it occasionally becomes a total casualty. In this respect, as will have been seen, the Western democracies are sometimes just as vulnerable as the people of totalitarian regimes – indeed perhaps more so, because they are more likely to accept what they are told as the truth. In many respects the truth may be distorted with great skill by the opponents of democracy, but all of us should be vigilant for any signs of our being disinformed by our own government and intelligence organizations.

6

THE GREAT
COMPUTER MENACE

In the middle of World War II the head of the Department of Psychology at America's Colgate University informed the government in Washington that 'I can hypnotize a man – without his knowledge or consent – into committing treason against the United States.'[1]

This was one reason advanced as to why it might have been possible for the Soviet Union to recruit an agent who, under hypnotic influence, could have assassinated President Kennedy – or, for that matter, induced the suicides of Miss Kilgallen and George de Mohrenschildt.

Hypnotism, however, is not the theme of this chapter. Here we are concerned with another, if indirectly similar, mesmerizing force – that of modern technology as expressed by the computer and other such sophisticated equipment. The computer could become the most dangerous hypnotic influence of the future.

Hypnotic might seem the wrong adjective to apply in this case, and in a strictly technical sense, of course, it is wrong. But the effect of a reliance on computerology, of allowing oneself to be manipulated and controlled by it, is certainly hypnotic in that the mind allows itself to accept whatever the computer tells it.

Consider the pocket calculator: if you use one to work out a sum, the odds are you will accept without question whatever the calculator tells you, even though at the back of your mind you must know that it is possible for the operator to make a mistake. Yet if you do the same sum by mental calculation, the odds are that you will automatically double-check it afterwards.

The computer arrived to be accepted on a managerial level by people who had never been trained to understand computerology in all its aspects. In some countries, especially Japan, this defect has long since been put right by training the managers and bosses of industry, technology and banking to grasp all the problems likely to be posed by the computer. Yet, still too often, in many Western countries one hears the managerial excuse that, when things go wrong, the computer is to blame, never the people who operate it. Worse still, some bank managers occasionally make the unforgivable plea: 'If the computer says so-and-so, there is nothing one can do about it.'

With this kind of a background to the new technology it is easy to see how the disinformer can exploit it. The extent to which he has done so is not yet fully appreciated, nor in some instances will the results of such disinformation become clear for very many years.

One of the more alarming aspects of the latter half of the twentieth century has been the manner in which science and the sophisticated world of the computer, the radar button, the thermal detector and the 'harmonica bug' (a tiny transistorized eavesdropper which can be placed inside an ordinary telephone) have opened up new avenues for the trickster and the disinformer on all levels.

All this is not merely disturbing on a purely domestic level, but in the scope it provides for the trickster to invade the realms of espionage, and especially commercial espionage, as well as threatening national security. In this age of *détente* and nuclear stalemate the lurking suspicion lingers that the only way in which we could all find ourselves involved in a devastating global nuclear war would be by somebody conning his way into a scrambled telephone conversation, or by infiltration of a computer system.

If this seems far-fetched, one has only to consider some of the feats achieved by the modern, technologically-educated trickster and the wide range of inventions which has put so many devices before him. Computers have also been proved to be so careless with money on occasions that vast sums of money are lost as a result. In July 1974, for example, one computer was found to have mistakenly handed out more than three million pounds of welfare payments. It is probably true to say that computer crime was born with the machines: they pointed the way for tricksters to exploit them, for often the machines themselves were the 'criminals'.

Not surprisingly the 'white-collar conman' was first to be found in banks, where the computer still plays surprising tricks and sometimes tantalizingly refuses to stop a direct debit payment, however many times it may be ordered to do so. One simple technique was to open bank accounts, obtain paying-in slips magnetically coded with their account numbers and then to leave these around among the blank paying-in slips on the bank's counters. If other customers used them to pay in and failed to realize that the account number was different from their own, the money would go into the swindlers' accounts. Astonishingly, this ruse worked for quite a time and one man got £40,000 in such a fashion. It could almost be argued that such an exploitation of other people's carelessness did not constitute a crime, but since then there have been added precautions to check this kind of thing.

Another man used a computer model of his firm to work out how he could best embezzle money without being detected, and then compiled the books by hand according to the computer's instructions. For this con trick the accountant got ten years' imprisonment. Perhaps the most ingenious use of a computer listed in the SRI (Stanford Research Institute) of California study was the work of a New Hampshire student who managed a delayed *coup d'état* within a computer. He incorporated a new unauthorized programme that lay dormant for six months until it was triggered off by an innocent user. It then destroyed all traces of how the programme had been placed there. This points the way to the most devastating exploitation of computers, especially in those countries where electronic know-how is of a far lower grade than, for example, in the United States.

Two men were jailed at the Old Bailey in February 1971 for programming an accounts computer with fake invoices. What the computer had done was to pay out demands from Fountain

Stores of Tooting for vast quantities of scampi, lobster and salmon which never existed. How long this particular fraud might have lasted it is impossible to say. It was only discovered almost accidentally when a clerk took a look at the faked account number – 00260 – and sensed something unusual. By that time it was found that a catering firm had been defrauded by about £50,000.

At that time – such was the ignorance of people in Britain about the feeding of disinformation into computers – it was actually claimed that this was the first case of a computer being used as an accomplice in fraud. But computer frauds had been snowballing all over the world for a long time prior to this. It is now suspected that many of the astonishing rises from poverty to riches in recent years – especially where these occur in areas of high taxation, such as the United Kingdom – have been manipulated through computer cunning. Indeed, the excessive taxation has bred the crime. More and more individuals and firms are having to turn to specialists who can rescue or protect them from computer crimes and manipulation. In the early seventies the turnover of Ballard, Ltd, the computer security specialists, increased phenomentally, business going up by 800 per cent.

What happened in the 1960s, when most of the get-rich-quick operations came to fruition, was that banks, business firms and even accountants took the view that the computer was an absolute guarantee against fraud. Once again the experts were wrong: they paved the way in for the criminals and nobody did more to lure people and government departments into a false sense of security than the Institute of Chartered Accountants who blandly assured all that accountancy by computer would make for far greater accuracy and be a protection against fraud.

But computers do not possess morals: they do not discriminate between good and bad users. They may provide safeguards in some sections of accountancy, but they also unwittingly lay themselves open to exploitation in other areas. The fact is that the computer provided a far subtler and more effective method than the old time gimmick of setting fire to the accounts when in danger of being discovered in some chicanery. All the skilled computer-conman had to do with the computer was to run a magnet over the tapes, or to run them backwards. Another factor by which computer manipulation was made easier was that the frauds could only be detected by data processing managers and that accountants, having no knowledge of computerology, would not know where to start looking for errors or frauds. And in the early days of computer development in some countries experts were so scarce that, when one was recruited, any firm was glad enough to obtain his services, let alone to worry about his character, past record, or a security clearance.

Yet as firms, banks and individuals begin to catch up on the need to protect their computer systems from fraudulent exploitation, so do the conmen improve their tactics. There is no end to this war between the two sides and it is most in evidence in the relentless guerrilla warfare of computer-snoopers bent on securing commercial intelligence and lists of potential customers from rival firms. In the case of the two men jailed in the Old Bailey trial, they had almost certainly erred by inventing a new invoice number which struck the inquisitive clerk as being odd. As this case became a classic of its kind it was carefully studied by all computer conmen who immediately decided never to repeat such an error. Since then the more sophisticated perpetrators of computer frauds take the trouble to select an invoice number that has already been registered, though first carefully ascertaining that it is no longer in use. All they do is to alter the name and address of the supplier, client or what-have-you.

One American computer programmer, working for a bank, raised his overdraft limit by a mere three digits to 300,000 dollars. He only drew 180,000 dollars because he did not want interest to accrue so fast that the charges would place his account beyond the 300,000 limit, which it would if he had drawn too much. That would have attracted attention to his account. This programmer had calculated the risks carefully and worked out that his fraud could only be detected if a special request was made to the computer for it to print out a small block of names and, even then, only if his name happened to be on that particular list and somebody actually recognized it and identified him. The odds were tremendously against all this happening at one and the same time, and for someone to be sufficiently interested to take notice.

Unfortunately for the programmer, this is what actually happened. In the ordinary course of events, rigid security rules applying to computers were such that an employee would be committing an offence to examine the list of names on a print-out. An operator broke the rules and was furious to discover that a colleague had obtained such a high credit rating. Once he had gossiped to others, the fraud was soon discovered.

But, as will be seen, a system that depends on unique coincidences for fraud to be detected is extremely vulnerable. Probably it is surprising that there have not been more tricksters in this field where the pickings are so rich. On the other hand the possibility exists that there are far more such unscrupulous operators than is generally suspected and that many of them have not yet been caught. The awful truth is that when the trickster is the computer itself – a far too frequent happening in the world of inhuman machines and inefficient human operators – it is often exceedingly difficult to prove it is in the wrong. Anyone who has had an astronomically large telephone bill which makes sheer nonsense and has tried to prove he could not possibly have made so many calls, will appreciate the point. And, without doubt, the trickster can easily shelter behind the errors of the computer itself, either real or fictitious.

A remarkable example of computer sleight-of-hand tactics coupled with imaginative if irregular business practice was uncovered when a British chemical company centralized the accounts for its three main divisions. The company's chief buyer and its chief computer programmer soon detected an anomaly in that division A was selling chemicals to division B without the normal forty per cent discount for a bulk purchaser. On the strength of this discovery they launched a subsidiary company and as such claimed and secured extended credit terms and immediate payment quite apart from the forty per cent discount.

Soon they were not only selling to sixty outside companies, but also to division B, thus undercutting their own 'parent company'. They made profits (on which they actually paid tax) of £150,000 in under three years. Eventually their enterprise was discovered and both men were dismissed from the company. Yet their operation was so efficient that it was incorporated as a recognized section of the company thereafter.

Although such activities come under the heading of trickery, it can be said that not all of them are criminal or even illegal. Indeed, many individualistic exploitations of the computer system are the results of intelligent planning and a dislike of waste. The most intelligent and efficient of computer programmers or operators may get so incensed at the inefficiencies of the system which they see being ignored that they are driven to crime. Loathing waste and seeing nothing done to prevent it, they almost instinctively take advantage of the system to eliminate some of the waste for their own ends. It cannot always be said that such conduct is necessarily immoral, let alone criminal.

Computers cost big money both to install and to maintain; when their full capacity is not taken up there is an obvious economic wastage and loss to any company or organization. This is especially true of the communications industry and in those areas where computerology is linked with a company's telex network. Many companies who use telex for sending and receiving messages all over the world do not utilize anything like total capacity for communications. In other words, they have each day several hours of unused telex time, when the machines are idle and the firm is in effect paying for wasted time. They could, of course, quite easily and profitably 'sell time' by offering telex facilities to other companies.

Sometimes this wastage on telex is exploited by individuals. It is now increasingly common for data processing managers, with spare time available on the computer, to start their own computer bureau. It is very rare indeed for the chief executives of a company to know anything about computers and they could easily be in the computer room without knowing what was going on under their very eyes.

There have been many cases in America of individuals being charged with stealing company information from a computer, as well as with feeding false information into the system. In one such case the computer, which had a built-in security system, informed its owners that it was committing a robbery. More disturbingly, this appeared to be the first case of a computer actually detecting an internal crime. One wonders how many computers are not 'owning up'. It is probable that today the biggest crimes of all – at least in terms of cash and cash value – are those perpetrated by the computer system.

The main reason for the insertion of disinformation into computer systems today is still to conceal criminal activities. But there are various other causes of disinformation in computerology. One such is what is called 'programmer's revenge' that occurrs when a programmer is subjected to discipline or dismissal and subsequently interferes with computer files in vengeance. This is more prevalent than is generally believed. Then there are those engaged in research activities, or who use their employers' facilities to do their own research at their employers' expense, and again need to conceal the results in order to hide their own private activities so that the information they have acquired can be subsequently sold. Finally, there is the person who has been deliberately planted in a competing firm by first having been dismissed officially by his own firm. Once he obtains a post in the competing firm his mandate is to wreck their research by doctoring the results (held on the computer) so as to persuade the targeted company that a particular course of research is worthless and is abandoned. This kind of disinformation is today estimated to be widespread particularly in electronic, pharmaceutical and mining industries. Sometimes it is said that entire research efforts are diverted along entirely useless routes because enticing information has been planted in computers resulting in the diversion of research away from promising areas into useless ones.

There is also evidence that computer data bases have been manipulated by both financial and commodity speculators to bring about a change in the value of shares or commodities – either up or down, depending upon what the manipulators require. Significantly, many takeover battles involving rival companies are today increasingly bad-tempered and marked by mud-slinging tactics, something which is often caused by computer-bugging and computer-disinforming. One managing director of a leading British trust company, who understandably declined to be named, told me: 'Without any doubt whatsoever when we were trying to take over —— and they published an advertisement attacking us and querying our record, they had indulged in computer snooping and we were forced to sue for libel.' Now anyone reading this might well say: 'Maybe in this case the computer aided the other company from being unfairly taken over.' My reply is that once a threat of libel was posed, the other company climbed down. Either the computer was fed with false statistics, or the company in question had twisted those statistics for its own ends.

Political organizations are also suspected of having manipulated and doctored data bases so as to make figures fit required

curves. Governments and government agencies are sometimes
guilty of altering data either to discourage or encourage private
organizations and corporations in certain spheres of their own
activity. In this connection one notes that the United States
Government has used its power to restrict the security encoding
system (known as Public Key/Private Key) to a limit of 64 bit.
The original specification for the data encryption was considerably more complex and would have rendered it impossible for
information so encrypted to be decrypted by unauthorized
persons in 'real-time'; even using the largest computers it would
have taken years for any unauthorized decryption. The system
that has emerged using 64 bit encryption still makes it difficult
for anyone using a micro, mini or mainframe computer to gain
unauthorized access to data, but it is believed that it is quite easy
using a super-computer. For the most part only governments
have these very large super-computers. The reasons advanced by
the Federal Communication Commission for the United States
Government's imposition of the less difficult encryption
formula was that the government had the right to intercept and
be able to decode any exchange of information for security
reasons. This explanation is held by many to be suspect, there
being a widespread belief that its only purpose was to allow the
government to interfere with data and do with it what they
wished.

Without question governments do 'raid' data bases and
remove information for their own purposes. In South Africa,
for example, a government-sponsored outfit has been involved
in first planting information in computers which government
agents subsequently 'find' and then use to bring pressure on a
company or organization for political purposes.

Actually to locate disinformation in computerized systems is
still very difficult. Most of the victims of computer disinformation are companies. Often, even when the tampering with
their computer records has been done by perpetrators of fraud,
the companies have largely been unwilling to bring in the police,
sometimes when the identity of the culprit has been known.
Several years ago, reports an individual computer expert, 'I
discovered quite an extensive fraud in the south-west branch of
a national chain of stores which had been carefully concealed
with misinformation. All this I reported to head office, but,
apart from dismissing the company's credit controller, they did

nothing and the man went on to bigger and better computer crimes and up until 1984 was still committing them. I think the reasons for firms' reluctance to reveal these things are twofold. First, if the true cost of computer crime were to be revealed, particularly to shareholders, there would undoubtedly be a furore. The main trouble is that a large proportion of directors know nothing of computers and are completely at the mercy of the computer system analysis and programming personnel. The second reason is that the law is far behind the times; in a judgement in a fraud case of three years or so ago, the judge held that since the computer was the only entity that knew anything of the alleged crime, the case in his view could not be sustained. His argument seemed to hinge on the fact that computer data is not intelligible to any human being and as such cannot be admitted as evidence even when translated from machine-readable form (binary) into human readable form (ASCII). I am bound to say that legally things are moving slowly to bring the law up-to-date, but most efforts at present are in the field of copyright to bring protection to software whatever its form (human or machine-readable), but I guess it will be some time before the law catches up – if it ever does.'

If at a time of international tension a few key computers in a civilized state could be put out of action by a terrorist attack, or a sabotage operation, such a state would be vulnerable when faced with an ultimatum from a foreign power. This degree of vulnerability is increasing as ever more advanced computers are produced. As computerology becomes more sophisticated so it will be easier for an electronic terrorist to probe the weaknesses in a nuclear installation and even to feed into it dangerously false information. If a programmer was in league with a terrorist group and accidentally keyed into his terminal orders giving him access to security clearance and other data, the merest chance could pave the way to disaster.

Mr David Hebditch, director of Expertise International, asserted at a conference in London that 'telecommunications systems pose the biggest threat to security at present because levels of control being applied to networks do not guard against dedicated abuse . . . It is the simplest thing in the world to pass yourself off as a Post Office engineer and the limit is boundless.'[2]

Again Mr Donn Parker, of SRI International, suggests that

the computer frauds which are known are 'merely the tip of the iceberg . . . especially with the increasing involvement of organized crime.' He went on to say that worldwide figures for computer misuse, including vandalism, larceny, embezzlement and industrial espionage, were closely linked to the numbers of computers used. Not surprisingly, the United States had the highest figures – 349 cases.[3]

If some of these assertions sound like scaremongering, it is salutary to learn that the British Institute of Directors has sent out a warning to its 33,000 members in 1986, urging them to take out fidelity insurance on their staff to protect themselves against financial loss from computer fraud. It was then estimated that companies were losing up to three billion pounds a year to thieves specializing in computer fraud. Writing in the Institute's magazine *The Director*, in February 1986, Mr Brian Hall, financial risks underwriting manager of the Sun Alliance insurance company, stated that 'the increasing use of computers had increased both the opportunities for, and the complexities of, employee frauds. Fictitious accounts can be raised and paid, or imaginary employees added to wage rolls, in a fashion which is often considerably more difficult to discover than would have been the case in the absence of computerized systems.'

One reason for failure to prosecute in many of these fraud cases is that it would cause companies too much embarrassment.

There is perhaps a danger that people may be lulled into complacency about computerology by the introduction of the Data Protection Act in the United Kingdom. This was intended to protect the individual from the misuse of data held on him, whether by banks, estate agents, companies, solicitors or other representatives of officialdom. This Act ratified the Council of Europe Convention for the Protection of Individuals with regard to 'automatic processing of personal data', and it also has the support of such organizations as the Confederation of British Industries and the National Council of Civil Liberties.

Neither this act, nor any other yet introduced, helps to prevent the crime of breaking and entering computer systems and feeding them with false data. Once penetrated, a computer programme can be changed while still performing the function for which it was intended. But the data infiltrated into the system can by degrees destroy the organization using it. What makes this kind of abuse easier is that a large firm or organization can do its work with isolated computers, and its routine work must be conducted through a network of inter-connected machines. As messages between each individual terminal have to pass through a telephone line, to infiltrate that network is almost as easy as phone-tapping. By this method some banks have been robbed of millions of pounds because all the computer-crook has to do is to order the system to remove small amounts of money from hundreds or even thousands of accounts and to pay them into a false account of his own.

What makes things worse is that whereas previously this type of crime was usually perpetrated by someone inside the bank or organization concerned, now it can be carried out by someone far removed from any direct contact with it. In 1985 the US Naval Institute described how the KGB, using some disaffected young American electronics genius, could in theory penetrate that part of the naval computer network which controls the firing of missiles or ship-to-shore communications. [4]

Attempts to protect Western electronic defensive systems and networks through COCOM (Co-Ordinating Committee for Export Control) have largely failed. Computers in Russia are controlled by Elektronorgtechnika in Moscow; this controlling body has established close links with Western computer companies. It is for example a shareholder in Elorg, which has been formed as a shareholder company in a number of Western companies. Elorg is linked to the Investronic group and the International Trading Corporation in the United States. COCOM regulations have been largely evaded by smuggling of computer systems into Russia by a variety of means.

Nevertheless, the Soviet Union is probably still at a disadvantage in the field of computerology, for it is estimated that more than 41,000 of the country's industrial enterprises have no large computers while those which possess such systems use them as little as possible, with managers preferring traditional methods to report facts and figures – 'often falsified data' – to Moscow. [5] *Fortune* magazine in America went further than this, alleging that 'the overriding obstacle to rational use of computers in Russia is the managers' recurring need to falsify data.' [6]

The more computers there are and the more material they keep on record, the greater the confusion and the liability of error, and certainly the easier it is to arrive at the wrong conclusions. Disinformation leading to wrong interpretations can sometimes be caused accidentally through a plethora of confusing and contradictory information. Take the case of ELINT (electronic intelligence as distinct from HUMINT, intelligence gathered by human beings). While it has been highly successful in some instances, it has also produced some farcical failures. In the 1970s the United States Army needed to know whether the new T-72 Russian tanks mounted 122 or 125 mm cannon. At a cost of 18 million dollars, satellites, radio-listening stations and code-breaking computers failed to find an answer. [7]

Yet British Army men managed to break into a tank depot in East Germany and not only measured the gun, but also removed the tank's operating manual, which, as is the custom with driving crews, had been left in the vehicle. All this cost was a mere 400 dollars to replace the lock on the gate where the tank was housed!

As a former British SIS man told the author: 'With SIGINT [the British secret service's Signals Interception and Analysis] miles and miles of paper reel off printers every hour of the day. Even if you could read it all, how much of it is genuine? How much is a bogus text? We all play the same game of putting out dummy transmissions with genuine prefixes, and even the occasional lapse into *en clair* to get the eavesdroppers all steamed up. The young Walker lad [an American who passed material to the Russians] gives the Russians a few of the USS *Nimitz*'s telecipher key tapes. Big deal. So what do they read? Lots of bureaucratic junk about Seaman Kowloski having got AIDS and being flown home for treatment. Number Four Generator is on the blink and will need stripping down. But when the key tape runs out, that's it. Unless Master Walker can come up with another one, you can't reconstruct.'

However, these are the absurdities, the burlesque, as it were, of some forms of modern communications. Perhaps it is as well to take note of how brilliantly and imaginatively the Israelis managed to exploit the new technology in their own self-defence and to use it for some of the most successful disinformation in modern warfare. Though this took place in the late 1960s, it is important to remember how Yuval Ne'eman brought about a technological revolution which proved of almost inestimable value during the Six-Day War.

It was Dr Ne'eman who began to take a keen interest in the new science of computerology when he worked for the Israeli Intelligence Service. He stressed the need for what he called 'instant intelligence', something which, he argued, was vital to Israel because the country was surrounded by enemies. 'We can only cope with this danger,' he said, 'if we are better informed, and informed more quickly by our Military Intelligence than are the Arabs by theirs. We cannot afford to wait until someone smuggled a message through from Cairo or Damascus, useful though that undoubtedly is.'

Dr Ne'eman devoted his time to reorganizing the Amman military intelligence agency of Israel. At university, both in Haifa and London, he had been a brilliant mathematician, being nickamed 'The Brain'. He swiftly set about installing computers for analysing and documenting intelligence on a day-to-day basis and setting up electronic intelligence devices. Once the Six-Day War began the Israelis had one crucial advantage over the Egyptians in that they had broken Egyptian and Jordanian ciphers and codes, while the Arabs had not done the same with the Israeli ciphers.

The Israelis exploited their computer techniques by feeding false information by signals to the enemy. In a relay station on Sinai radio messages from Cairo to Amman were being blocked by the Israelis and, in the jargon of the intelligence world, 'cooked' before being swiftly re-routed to Amman. The Israelis aimed to give the impression that the war was going well for the Egyptians, and at the same time blacking out and jamming messages from Cairo to Amman telling King Hussein that the Israelis were gaining ground. This ploy worked to perfection because it shortened the war and reduced the chances of any other nation intervening. The major deception plan practised on Egypt and Jordan was complemented by a devastating blow against the Egyptian air force while launching land attacks. Thus Israel won one of the most brilliantly planned military victories of modern times. Never before in any war had disinformation tactics enjoyed such overwhelming and instant success.[8]

Not even the telephone has been secure from such manipulations as those described in this chapter. For example, there was the Great Telephone Robbery of the late sixties. A group of young men, some with university degrees and others with telephone engineering experience, had evolved a system for cheating the British Post Office by making calls all over the world at local rates with the use of a 'bleep', or, as they called it, a 'cheat box'. This dishonest manipulation of the world's telephone system resulted in the conviction of a number of young Britons. They had cleverly worked on the principle of obtaining their information not the hard way, but through the efforts of others. When the men were brought to trial, it was stated that they 'have used and abused the telephone system both in the United Kingdom and abroad on an increasing and important scale, advancing at the same time not only their own, but others' knowledge of the system. For that purpose they exchanged information by letter about highly technical matters. The conspiracy had been going on from 1968 until October 1970.'

A device had been developed which defeated the Post Office system by sending signals to the Post Office machinery (this was, of course, in the days before British Telecom was launched) which would act upon them, believing them to be despatched lawfully. At the other end of the scale a system of cheating flourished which consisted of a two-penny piece being attached to a fine piece of thread, thus enabling calls to be made from a public box by inserting the piece in the slot and then retrieving it. A little silver box called a 'bleep box' enabled a call to be made at a local rate to almost anywhere in the world.

It was not so much the actual fraud which the case revealed which was alarming, but the indication that the system which these young people had organized made it possible for them to obtain a whole list of top secret numbers, including some of government departments and the Special Branch of the police. If the telephone fraud racket had not been detected by the Post Office, the whole security of the country might in time have been affected, and it was stated in court that the fraud involved 360 group switch centres and would cost the Post Office £400,000 to prevent such a fraud recurring in future.

This case is not, it might be argued, strictly speaking one of disinformation. But that would be wrong in modern terms. It is positively one of disinformation in this era simply because the device developed by the plotters caused the Post Office machinery to accept the signals, *believing them to be lawfully despatched*. The fact that equipment was disinformed, not human beings, is neither here nor there; disinformation today is perhaps more easily practised through the new technologies than in mere human relationships. Worse still, this type of technological disinformation is one which not only can affect everyone, but is a constant threat to us all unless we are not merely vigilant, but technologically progressive.

In a thesis on 'Intelligence Function in Policy Decision-Making: Models, Values and Frameworks of Analysis', a member of the Catholic University of America in Washington, DC, discussed 'the importance of input information to policy decision-makers', pointing out that this involved a careful watch on 'the truth value of ostensible factual data' and 'the possibility or probability of disinformation'.[9]

It may even be necessary for governments all over the world to create Ministries of Truth, whose sole function is to check the validity of statistics and computer data as and when required by another ministry. Such a newly designed ministry might very well serve the nation far better than, for instance, the somewhat inept and time-wasting procedures of British Parliamentary Select Committees where scoring party political points often means more than fact-finding.

7

'STAR WARS'
AND OTHER NONSENSE

It is not always an enemy who creates the worst disinformation. Quite often someone of one's own side puts the ball in his own net, thus creating a massive disadvantage.

Perhaps the best illustration of this in the field of nuclear warfare and military strategy is to be found in the *New York Times* of 27 March 1983. President Reagan had just announced the beginning of 'a comprehensive and intensive effort to define a long-term research and development programme' for a new system of strategic defence. In referring to this, the *New York Times* commented: 'He [Reagan] did not raise the idea merely to warn the Soviets about the costly new competition that vigorous missile programs might invite: he challenged them to this Star Wars competition, even if in the meantime they accept his proposals for deep cuts in weaponry.'

Thus was the phrase 'Star Wars' created, ever since when the world's media have referred to the Strategic Defence Initiative by this misleading title. When I assert that the two words 'Star Wars' constitute one of the most influential disinformation gimmicks of this century, I am not, of course, attributing any devious motives to the writer of the article. No doubt, with the film *Star Wars* in mind, he thought it an apt phrase. Unfortunately it is a phrase which has lent itself to all the opponents of SDI and resulted in a massive misunderstanding all around the globe of the US President's intentions. For the Soviet Union the 'Star Wars' label for SDI was a perfect propaganda present. As to how successful it has been, one has only to consider that one opinion poll in the United Kingdom showed that more people thought Reagan's policies were likely to start a nuclear war than those who believed Russian actions would launch a holocaust.

So the idea was skilfully exploited that the President's Strategic Defence Initiative meant 'Star Wars' and therefore that SDI meant a policy of attack, not defence. The *New York Times* had unfortunately not only used the phrase 'Star Wars', but suggested that the SDI belonged to the kind of fantasy world which the film portrayed. And, just because SDI cannot easily be summed up simply for the benefit of non-experts, so this view came to be accepted not only in the Soviet empire, but in the rest of the world as well. The Soviet intelligence officers through both their own scientists and military attachés made skilful use of American and British academics with the most respectable records to encourage them to denounce SDI as a frightful step into the future. In indulging in such fantasies as SDI, it was argued that the United States was proposing new methods of war from outer space which would make life hell for those of us on earth below.

Thus the popular idea grew that somehow what Reagan was proposing was to plan war from outer space in an attempt to deter the Soviet Union from aggression. Not unnaturally, people began to see this as adding another menace to their own lives. So support for CND and all organizations opposing nuclear armaments increased, and an undercurrent of anti-Americanism swelled. The campaign to oppose SDI steadily grew, often among some of America's staunchest allies. What worried many of the latter, however, was whether the Free World could afford the cost of the SDI programme and even if it was worthwhile.

With hindsight the White House should on 28 March 1983 have launched an almighty blast against the 'Star Wars' conception, laying to rest this unhappy phrase. For, what, quite simply, did SDI mean? It was, as its name should have implied, totally concerned with defence. The whole idea of SDI was to find a way of making nuclear war impracticable, not to wage such a war. It was not a positive programme in the sense that anyone knew exactly how successful it could be, or how soon it could be implemented. It would cost a great deal of money, but if this was the price to be paid for making nuclear warfare a nonsense, then it would eventually pay off. Could CND, Monsignor Bruce Kent and all the other war-worriers really object to this? Or were they totally won over by cleverly disseminated Soviet propaganda?

The whole purpose of SDI was to evolve an entirely new defence against nuclear warfare so that it would become pointless. It is true that the cost of the research needed to produce such a system was considerable. But, from a moral viewpoint, surely the cost should not be counted too carefully. It was also true that nobody could say for certain whether SDI would be a viable policy within a given number of years. There were a great number of uncertainties, yet the failure to face up to these was not merely a confession of doubt and in some cases total incomprehension on the political side, but often directly due to the massive propaganda campaign launched against SDI. So effective was this Soviet-inspired campaign that many politicians who normally opposed the Russians began to attack SDI.

Their case was that SDI was a fantasy, it somehow threatened any possible agreement with the USSR, nobody could be sure when or whether it would work, and that the cost was phenomenal. Yet, put quite simply, what SDI really meant was that a defensive system against nuclear weapons could be built up purely by defensive weapons in outer space which would destroy any nuclear missiles not merely long before they reached their targets, *but before they left enemy air space.* In other words, at the very best, given time and patience, nuclear war could be rendered useless.

The Soviet case against SDI was from the beginning a twisting of the truth. The late Yuri Andropov's reaction was that this was an attempt by the United States to disarm the Soviet Union in the face of the US nuclear threat. Hints were dropped into the ears of European firms and capitalists that it was highly doubtful whether they would win any contracts out of SDI. Yet Britain has already been offered a share in this strategic development.

Perhaps most alarming of all was the gullibility of many Westerners in scientific and military as well as political ranks in accepting Russian viewpoints on SDI and in visualizing the programme as a monster we could not control. Thus Dr David Baker, a space scientist with more than twenty years' experience, warned of the threat posed by SDI if the American government allowed itself to be swept on by technological advances without considering the consequences. 'I think we may have thought something up this decade that threatens the survival of our planet,' he said, adding that he doubted whether the programme was purely defensive. [1]

Interestingly, until the anti-SDI campaign was launched, Dr Baker had once been a supporter of the programme. Yet he told the British Association that 'the same physics necessary to put this system into operation could, in another age, be used for offensive systems in their own right, which would irradiate a very, very large part of the earth.' He went on to describe how, in his opinion, the defensive system of SDI could be activated by accident.

Accidents will always happen in almost any system, but, generally speaking, these need not be catastrophic on a vast scale. The 'war by accident' theme regarding SDI has since been eagerly exploited by the Russians. 'Again the plans for feverish militarization of space are prevailing over common sense,' said the youth newspaper, *Komsomolskaya Pravda*. 'What would happen if a technical failure or simple accident turned into an unexpected nuclear war for the world?'

There is perhaps only one argument which possibly has some validity on the disadvantages of SDI. This is the theory put forward by Dr Bartlett, of the Lawrence Livermore National Laboratory, California. 'I think we will need deep arms reductions with the Soviet Union to make SDI work,' he claims. His explanation for this is that there is no point in perfecting a defence aimed at Soviet missiles if this simply prompts the Kremlin to build more and better missiles. [2]

But most of these doubts can only be fully resolved by further research and experimentation. Just to say: 'Stop! Don't pursue this further,' is in effect to prevent our obtaining answers to these doubts. Naturally, the queries about the enormous cost of SDI are justified: all money spent on offensive or defensive measures is wasteful in real terms as it means that other, worthier projects must be shelved or conducted on meagre and inadequate budgets. Yet it is possible, if not probable, that in time increasing costs of military budgets will force the super-powers to re-think their strategies. What has been skilfully hidden by the anti-SDI campaigners is the fact that SDI is not a totally new concept. Research into new systems of strategic defence has been conducted for many years, but while America, adhering to the ABM Treaty of 1972, has actually cut down on such research, Russia has quietly gone ahead in this very field. It is nonsense for them to pretend otherwise.

If SDI succeeds (and the major queries are just how success-ful it will be, not how unsuccessful), then at the very best it could render nuclear weapons obsolete. One American professor, Robert Jastrow, argues that SDI could by the early 1990s enable both the United States and Russia to be equipped with networks of satellites armed with computerized missiles and lasers which could destroy enemy missiles as soon as they are launched. [3]

This statement, although to one who has considered all the evidence on both sides seemingly over-optimistic, does point the way to these possibilities:

(1) that, in the failure of the West to develop a Strategic Defence Initiative programme, the Soviet Union goes ahead and creates a system which gives them total protection (more or less) and leaves America and the Western world as a whole relatively unprotected against nuclear attack;

(2) that the United States goes ahead and gains a similar advantage over the USSR;

(3) that both the USA and Russia develop equally good defensive systems at the same time.

Dismissing all the false arguments about SDI, these are the only three possibilities which can be conceived. Failure to develop any new strategic defence systems means that both sides live at the best in a state of nuclear stalemate, and at worst one of the superpowers is at a disadvantage to the other.

If the *New York Times* is to be criticized for using the phrase 'Star Wars' to describe SDI, which is, of course, non-nuclear and entirely defensive, it is to be praised for having published an admirable explanatory article on the subject by Zbiganiew Brzezinski, Robert Jastrow and Max Kampleman. [4] This in effect shows how irresponsible it is for people without technical knowledge of the subject to oppose SDI, and how the only development to cause the Russians to return to negotiations with the West was the announcement of the SDI programme.

Given a reasonable chance of success from the SDI research programme, the plan could make a Soviet first strike against the West impossible within six to seven years, so that the only type of nuclear explosive device which might operate by the end of the century would be a land-born, garage-housed terrorist weapon. While nobody can be absolutely certain as to how soon or effectively SDI as a system could come into being, it is surely one worthwhile tackling promptly. Indeed, in the light of the pessimistic report of the Scientific Committee on the Problems of the Environment under the aegis of the International Council of Scientific Unions issued in 1985, here is the probable answer to their worst fears. In that report scientists pictured the environmental consequences of an East-West nuclear exchange as causing black smoke clouds blotting out the sun, the earth cooling swiftly and a prolonged 'nuclear winter'.[5]

Throughout the 1980s the propaganda poured out that – to quote the Dalai Lama – 'the greatest single danger facing human beings is the threat of nuclear destruction.' But the threat is not the danger, only the fear and panic which the largely imaginary threat poses. If one of the superpowers suddenly came under the control of a political lunatic, then things might be different. But as the former CIA senior officer, Miles Copeland, says, one can take consolation 'from the fact that the possibility of nuclear war, except as it may be initiated by some irresponsible minor power . . . is not in the calculations of either [super] power except as an issue of political propaganda . . . The greatest dangers facing humanity are those arising from the *fear* of nuclear war and the way it is exploited for purposes of psychological warfare. Films such as *The War Game* and *The Day After*, for example, do not make people "think" about nuclear warfare. Instead they cause them to substitute panic for reason, and to put pressures on governments which force them into positions which increase the panic even more.'[6]

A single, simple error in space could cost millions of pounds quite apart from many lives if, say, somebody in a space station overreached in calculations with a laser beam procedure. But research – and this applies to SDI and other space research – to anticipate such errors and to plan for getting the programming right costs far less. To experiment in space without getting the programming right on earth first of all is to operate on a highly dangerous premise, for there is still much to be learned about the types of manual errors which can develop in prolonged spaceflight.

Soviet disinformation in the military and strategic spheres has been conducted at an ever-increasing pace since the late 1950s. On 1 December 1958 Nikita Khrushchev told Senator Hubert Humphrey that 'the Soviet Union now has a rocket that will travel 14,000 kilometres, but has no area where we can safely test it.' He added that Russia had 'so many hydrogen and atomic bombs that we are not only stopping production of fissionable material, but will soon dismantle some of our own bombs.' That information was cited in a telegram to the CIA from the American Ambassador in Moscow.[7]

Maskirovka is one of the methods of guarantee of combat activity in the USSR and is defined as consisting of 'a complex of measures directed towards *leading the enemy into error* concerning the presence and disposition of land and naval forces, of military objectives, of their condition, combat readiness and operations and also plans of the command.' *Maskirovka,* therefore, facilitates the achievement of surprise in operations of the forces, maintains their combat readiness and augments the viability of all military organizations.

In other words, disinformation is a key word in strategy and strategic tactics. After Stalin's death there was quite a long period in which the Russians were technologically behind the Western world and at a disadvantage in terms of strategy. At such times the Soviet Union makes a positive policy of exaggerating its strength. But before this policy was adopted a prolonged row took place between the forces behind Prime Minister Malenkov, Stalin's successor, and the Bulganin-Khrushchev faction which eventually came to power. Malenkov's line had been to avoid massive rearmament and to concentrate on the policy that nuclear war meant the end of mankind and that for this reason the USA should restrict its nuclear programme.

Malenkov's policy, in fact, caused many moderate Western

politicians to take the view that the Cold War had ended and that it might foreshadow a change of heart in Russia. It didn't because Malenkov himself changed his tactics somewhat in an effort to ward off the opposition. Once Khrushchev came to power and the United States had a new, young President, every attempt was made to frighten the West into believing that the USSR had the power to knock them out, or at least inflict such severe damage that they could not hope to win any war. Thus, Khrushchev, the aggressive clown of Soviet politics, boasted in January 1960 that 'we already have enough nuclear weapons – atomic and hydrogen – and the corresponding rockets to deliver these weapons to the territory of a possible aggressor . . . if some madman stirred up an attack on our state or any other socialist states, we could literally wipe from the face of the earth the country or countries that attacked us.'

Such claims did not, of course, remotely correspond to the truth. Yet they were taken seriously by some British Conservatives and it was only due to Penkovsky's defection to the British and his invaluable information that the West was slowly able to grasp the fact that the Soviet Union posed no real threat to the Western world in 1962, when the Cuban missiles crisis broke. Astonishingly, even when the final challenge was made in the autumn of 1962, when the USA's ultimatum caused the Russian ships to turn away from Cuba, there were still some sadly ill-informed editors of Western newspapers who believed we were all on the brink of World War III. Soviet propaganda had done its work exceedingly well, and, as we now know, it was a long time before the United States could be persuaded to accept Penkovsky's testimony that Russia did not possess the intercontinental-ballistic missile strength it claimed. The USSR sought and obtained missile bases in Cuba to correct this deficiency.

Once the Cuban gamble failed, the USSR had to re-think their strategic deception tactics. Having been caught out over ICBM's in the early 1960s, they needed to switch the emphasis to their defence against missile attacks. They then sought to create a picture of their impregnability against nuclear attack; in February 1963 Marshal Biryuzov asserted that 'the problem of destroying enemy rockets in flight has been successfully solved in our country.' Yet Russia was nowhere near being able to do any such thing.

All such statements made a great impact upon the CND brigade. They ignored the threats of the USSR, while harping upon how Western intransigence could bring about the need for such threats. Gradually, the picture was built up of a ruthlessly-minded United States whose threats and talk of war could bring about a 'defensive nuclear reaction' from Russia. It was always an illogical picture, yet one which was, incredibly, accepted by very many people.

In the late 1960s and early 1970s it would seem that the United States began to underestimate the Soviet ICBM build-up, possibly because of some of the Russian deception tactics. One of these Soviet schemes may well have been to disguise the purpose of the mission for their missiles and alter their flight tests to suggest inaccuracies. William Harris, one of the most astute observers of this game of deception and analysis in strategic warfare, wrote that 'during the 1960s, just as US intelligence analysts were growing confident that the Soviets over-represented capabilities, and that we could catch them every time, just the opposite happened. With an understanding of the technical indicators and methods of US estimation of ballistic missiles accuracy, the Soviets managed to under-represent the accuracy of intercontinental ballistic missiles. The earlier bluffing upward corresponded to decisions not to invest in nuclear armed rockets early, while seeking silo-killing capabilities. US Defence Secretary Harold Brown has indicated that the Soviet SS-9 ICBM was always aimed at the launch control centres of the Minuteman missiles complexes. Only systematic biasing of technical indicators would produce the apparently large errors in guidance and the actually quite limited errors needed to justify attack on so hardened a set of military targets.'

Even in the testing of weapons, deception is not only possible, but probable. Such deception was stepped up after the beginning of SALT (Strategic Arms Limitation Talks). There was a toning-down of the language of aggression towards a potential enemy, but during this period their offensive and defensive armouries started to accelerate. There was misleading, but subtly effective talk about parity between the superpowers. SALT was used as an opportunity to play down any advantages as a cover for a major drive for strategic superiority. In plain language, the Russians cynically used the SALT agreements to conduct a number of violations all under the mask of parity. To be fair to the Russians, the actual textual details of the SALT agreement could be interpreted as allowing them a measure of concealment, if this covered 'current construction, assembly, conversion or overhaul practice'. But most of the violations included a good deal of disinformation such as dummy roads and launching sites, dummy submarines and lies about the number of SSBNs being built or already built.

But these are merely examples of technical disinformation, important, of course, but not nearly as vital as the main success of Soviet disinformation in the nuclear weaponry field which has been to argue that the more each side steps up its nuclear armoury, the greater the risk of catastrophe and the more likely it is for such a catastrophe to be created through mistakes, the pressing of the right button at the wrong moment. This kind of propaganda has aided the Soviet cause and still does. The answer is that further research can help to eliminate risks of such errors.

Yet much of this propaganda is not only accepted by the fanatical CND-ites, but by a substantial part of the Western media. Grave doubts about SDI were voiced in an article in *Newsweek* by Theo Sommer, editor-in-chief of the German newspaper *Die Welt*. He describes President Reagan's view that science will find a way to render nuclear weapons 'impotent and obsolete' as 'a dream most experts consider a dubious, even dangerous chimera'. What experts? He does not say. But he goes on to state: 'Reagan's obsession with Star Wars [not SDI, note] foiled a new arms-control agreement, ruined the Geneva summit; touched off an arms competition unlimited in cost, duration and danger, and precipitated another unmitigated cold war . . . The world had better brace itself for a cold winter.'[8]

Sometimes the technically-ignorant politicians of the West forget that there is a sound basis in long-established technology for President Reagan's administration's hunch on a means of rendering nuclear warfare impossible. For a very long time decoy transponders have been used successfully for a similar, if much simpler experiment. These, towed on a raft behind a ship at a safe distance, amplifying and reflecting back missiles' radar pulses, have been able to lure the firepower of an enemy fleet away from its targets large and small. What can be achieved at sea is surely equally possible from outer space. The parallel is by no means exact, but it surely makes sense that SDI is no worse than MAD (Mutually Assured Destruction).

Yet military leaders and diplomats, who should be that much better informed, still find themselves being seduced by Soviet arguments and thus become quite unreasonably frightened. There was the crack-pot Generals for Peace, a group of former officers who had served in NATO, who produced a pamphlet entitled *The Arms Race to Armageddon*, which was almost indistinguishable from the Soviet line. Rather more disturbing has been the line taken by one who is neither pro-Soviet, nor pacifist, but who has opposed the Trident missiles programme, none other than Field Marshal Lord Carver, former Defence Staff chief. Now Lord Carver is a highly respected figure in the world of defence, yet what was his excuse for taking this line? 'I can envisage no circumstances in which it could be right, responsible or realistic for the Prime Minister of the United Kingdom to authorize the use of British nuclear weapons when the President of the United States was not prepared to authorize the use of any US nuclear weapons.'[9]

This categoric statement, reasonable enough in the right context, was, of course, no proper answer to whether or not the British should have Trident. There is a suggestion in the Carver comment that Europe should simply nestle cosily behind an American nuclear umbrella which just might be withdrawn if Europe failed to play a full role of its own. And what about the not-impossible threat to the United Kingdom from a terrorist nuclear weapon? It should be noted that Lord Carver did not even stress the one overriding objection to Trident – the cost.

Just as many scientists as military leaders have allowed themselves to be not merely critical of SDI, but positively hostile to the whole conception. 'Star Wars tests are "showy" and of little significance, according to some American experts,' wrote Ian Mather, the Defence Correspondent of the *Observer*. 'They claim that the Reagan administration is staging impressive-looking tests which purport to show major progress towards a space-based weapons system as Congress slashes into the Strategic Defence Initiative budget. "The public is getting swindled by one side that has access to classified information and can say whatever it wants, whereas we can't," says Ray Kidder, a scientist at the Lawrence Livermore Laboratory, California.'[10]

Some people may be tempted to regard this as disinformation on the part of the Americans. But naturally, while conducting experiments and research on so vital a matter as national defence, no sensible administration would reveal all the results of such work – neither the failures nor the successes. No one would dispute the fact that there must be some failures on this trail into the unknown. If one accepts this precept the verb 'swindled', used by the scientist, sounds remarkably like disinformation, albeit merely through an unfortunate slip of the tongue.

It would be wrong to deny that SDI has a very long way to go before its value can be proved – anything from five to ten years – but it must make sense that if MAD is the current unhappy and uneasy safeguard to world peace, then SDI could eventually provide a better one. Maybe there is rather more in initials and names than one is inclined to believe. SDI is at least rational, whereas 'Star Wars' is deliberately misleading. On the other hand, maybe SDI officials are themselves somewhat to blame because they have created some confusion in the initials and codenames by assigning the acronym STAR to Significant Technical Achievements and Research. This would not matter so much if STAR was not linked in the public's mind with 'Star Wars'. The film of that name has a lot to answer for.

Possibly, too, it was tactless, or at least too optimistic, to apply the codeword MIRACL to the chemical laser which was developed in the late 1970s. For in the beginning the distance between the laser and the target was only half a mile, whereas laser beams in space would have to travel thousands of miles.

Perhaps the nuclear disarmers have been luckier with their own choice of initials and codewords, some of which are more effective than any politician's speech or scientist's verdict. Take the initials SANE, adopted by the American Friends and the Committee for a Sane Nuclear Policy, a much better word than STAR.

Some indication of the effectiveness of disinformation from the Soviet side may be gleaned from recent public opinion polls in Britain. These have revealed a massive ignorance and misunderstanding among the whole population of East-West military balance, as well as an exaggerated idea of the costs of defence and nuclear weapons. Only thirty per cent of the people knew that the Warsaw Pact nations have a superiority in conventional arms, while forty-three per cent had no idea at all on the subject. Thirty-two per cent believed the cost of our nuclear weapons was between five and thirty times the real cost. Yet surprisingly sixty-eight per cent of the people polled wanted Britain to maintain an effective independent nuclear deterrent.

The truth is that whereas the best of the Western world's democratic governments are desperately trying to find the right answer to ridding the world of the threat of nuclear horrors, the Soviet Union has set out instead to put the blame on the other side. The ID of the Soviet Communist Party uses all its various research institutes attached to the Soviet Academy of Sciences to put over disinformation on SDI and much else. Georgi Arbatov, a key member of the CPSU, has a department dealing with military, political and disarmament problems, and both he and Professor Daniel Proektor have been active in pushing out peace propaganda in Western Europe. The aim is always to weaken NATO as an institution. Some of this propaganda includes the presentation of forged NATO documents to various journalists. There is one case of a forged letter purporting to have been written by General Alexander Haig, who was then Supreme Allied Commander, Europe, on 26 June 1979.

This forged document implied the possibility of NATO being the first to use nuclear weapons in an emergency, commenting that 'if argument, persuasion and impacting the media fail, we are left with no alternative but to jolt the faint-hearted in Europe through the creation of situations, country by country, as deemed necessary to convince them where their interests lie . . . To this end your authority and your active assistance, especially in the Netherlands, can hardly be overestimated.'[11]

Probably there are more of these forgeries than can possibly be identified. But there is ample evidence of the KGB infiltrating various peace organizations. In October 1981 Valentin Kuznetsov, a cultural attaché, and Vladimir Merkulov, a Second Secretary at the Soviet Embassy in Copenhagen, were expelled from Denmark because of their involvement with the Cooperative Committee for Peace and Security. The World Peace Council held a World Parliament of Peoples for Peace in Sofia in September 1980, and it was suggested that trade unionists everywhere should urge a total disarmament programme. In Sofia they urged a lining-up of all the world's trade unionists behind Soviet disarmament proposals and support for 'nuclear free zones'.

While the arguments in favour of such zones were unexceptional in many respects, the propaganda behind the scenes included a great deal of disinformation, especially on the hazards of any form of nuclear development, whether in weapons or in industry for peaceful uses.

What impact has all this disinformation really had on peoples around the world? It has been considerable and, even when forgeries or lies have been detected, there is always the harm done among the large number of people who heard the lies, but not their refutation. The French as a whole have retained their usual sense of realism and have generally accepted that they should have their own independent nuclear deterrent. A majority of the British people think likewise, despite the very large anti-nuclear lobby. But Soviet nonsense has dangerously infected the British Labour Party, so much so that Mr Richard Perle, a US Assistant-Secretary of Defence, stated on a visit to London in February 1986 that the Labour Party was 'almost unique in its potential for divergence in and destruction of the Atlantic Alliance.' He saw Labour's 'progressive unilateralism' as the only true threat to the Alliance.

But it is what he said about SDI which, I feel, makes a succinct end to this chapter. 'We got off to a bad start on the Strategic Defence Initiative,' he said. 'More consultation before the President's speech might have been a good thing. Unfortunately the American launch of SDI gave quite the wrong idea -- that of a huge dome over the United States which would divert Soviet missiles. The essence of SDI was to develop a capability to intercept Soviet missiles while they were over Russian territory, in other words, placing the dome over the Soviet Union, not America.'[12]

8

HOW SERIOUS IS POLLUTION?

In the media, pollution used to be regarded as 'a little local difficulty' which could be put right by the local authority, backed by the local medical officer of health. Today it is a worldwide problem, the extent of which is often completely hidden from the populations concerned. So vitally important is it to day-to-day existence that the Japanese, who live in relatively confined spaces, have set up a 'think-tank' to cope with it. Indeed, a great deal of their gathering of global intelligence is devoted to studying the problem of pollution in different parts of the world and what cures other nations adopt to combat it.

Pollution takes very many forms, some so strange that, as yet, they are not even regarded as pollution. It is in these spheres where the truth-twisters are most active, not disinforming so much as hiding the true facts. In the last chapter one had the task of defending the Western defence system against the falsities of Soviet propaganda. But to do this without admitting that some in the West had been less than frank and often downright dishonest on some forms of nuclear pollution would be a total failure of any claim to objectivity.

Part of the trouble is that in many areas of the world there has developed a complete neglect of the teachings of nature and an apathy towards pollution. The British Royal Commission on

Environmental Pollution complained in 1985 about the puny sentences for polluting the environment, claiming that they often left 'offenders laughing all the way to the bank'. It complained that the fines for dangerous dumping of waste on land or in water were often far less than the saving made by dumping illegally instead of on a controlled site. Professor Sir Richard Southwood, retiring chairman of the Commission, said: 'We have been given evidence of examples where the penalties have been less than the cost of disposing of a material satisfactorily.'[1]

Such criticisms should apply equally to doctors and all health organizations, in whose ranks apathy has led, sometimes deliberately, sometimes unwittingly or carelessly, to disinformation. This is especially true of the World Health Organization of the United Nations, which has been weak and feckless in dealing with international health hazards. Even when these health hazards and pollution are on the doctors' own doorsteps they have failed to point them out or condemn them. The Royal Commission in this same report of 1985 stated that hospitals' 'exclusion from clean air laws under Crown immunity should end. Many hospital incinerators belched out copious black smoke and did not meet the demands of clean air laws.'[2]

One reason for such laxity, which would almost certainly not be tolerated in many factories and private organizations, is the granting of Crown immunity to National Health Service hospitals which consequently flout hygiene regulations. Crown immunity means that such hospitals are free from any risk of prosecution, despite the fact that lives have been endangered as a result. The Prime Minister's answer to a question on the subject by Mr Jack Ashley, Labour MP for Stoke-on-Trent, was that 'it would be wrong to jump to the conclusion that abolition of Crown immunity is the only answer. Whilst this is not ruled out as an option, the Government has no immediate plans to lift Crown immunity from the NHS.'

Why not? Mr Ashley had stated that surveys showed sixty per cent of hospital kitchens fell below Government standards and that sixteen per cent would be prosecuted but for Crown immunity. In an institution such as a hospital, where strict hygiene rules should be imperative, this is far too high a percentage. Refusal to change the law instantaneously leaves the nasty suspicion that the real reason is to do with the resulting cost of such prosecutions – almost certainly too much for the Health Service to bear.

The playing-down of the hazards of nuclear fallout and pollution has, however, been much worse. The disinformation on this subject has done harm to the justifiable needs for adequate nuclear defence, and, of course, it has only led to grossly exaggerated information from the Soviet camp on those same dangers. We now know that as a result of official pretences that no hazards existed, thousands of United States military personnel were exposed to greater radiation than was previously thought possible when they took part in the two open-air test explosions of atomic weapons in 1946. A Congressional study of the whole affair, released by Senator Alan Cranston, disputed a 1984 Pentagon study which said that military personnel were exposed only to low levels of radiation. About 220,000 military personnel took part in those tests, including 42,000 at two blasts in the lagoon at Bikini Atoll in July 1946. Of that number, it is now alleged, about forty-one per cent were hit with heavier doses of radiation than was anticipated. Senator Cranston noted that 'a column of water a mile high and nearly half a mile wide threw large masses of highly radioactive water on to the decks and into the holds of the target ships, making them highly radioactive.' Water in the lagoon remained radioactive down to eight feet deep for up to two weeks after the blast, but it was still being used by nearly 2000 Navy personnel to 'scrape, scrub and wash the ships in an effort to get them down to acceptable radiological levels.' Some 500 veterans who were taking part in these tests have since made claims for injury, citing radiation exposure.[3]

There may have been some excuses for ignorance about the extent of such dangers in 1946, but today there should be constant reviewing of all such problems, with the public being kept adequately informed. It is now clear that there were just the same cover-ups over the British nuclear tests in Australia in 1952. The Royal Commission of Inquiry into the background to these tests now reveals that the twelve major test devices detonated between 1952 and 1957 *'should not have been fired in the circumstances prevailing and that the Vixen series of twelve minor trials between 1960 and 1962, involving plutonium, should never have been made at Maralinga.'*[4]

In 1953 it was revealed that the Totem I test led to 'black

mist' which contaminated the Aborigines; long afterwards Lord Penney, the British scientist in charge, admitted belatedly it should not have been fired in the conditions prevailing. The authorities responsible for the tests were condemned for 'ignorance, incompetence and cynicism' in their treatment of the Aborigines. In 1950 Clement Attlee, then British Prime Minister, had written to the Australian Premier, Robert Menzies, saying that Britain had little hope of access to US nuclear testing facilities and asking about the use of the Monte Bello islands. Menzies agreed to this and the next government, that of Winston Churchill, went ahead with the tests there.

Rather more important in the light of the world problem of pollution is the fact that the Royal Commission's report shows that Australia was at that time entirely dependent upon British scientists pertinent to its own security. Even when a step was taken to remedy this by setting up an Australian scientific body, the AWTSC (Atomic Weapons Tests Safety Committee), the situation did not improve. The Royal Commission severely criticized the British-born physicist, Sir Ernest Titterton, the head of the AWTSC, who had taken the chair of nuclear physics at the Australian National University in Canberra. The report stated that 'his background, the manner of his appointment and his own view as a member of a British and Australian team hardly ensured the detached and independent approach to what ostensibly was his primary task – a protection of the Australian public.'[5]

Worse still, the report criticized him for his 'cavalier treatment of the truth throughout his testimony' and charged that he 'played a political as well as a safety role. He was prepared to conceal information from the Australian Government and his fellow committee members, if he believed it would suit the interests of the United Kingdom Government and the testing programme.'

But, harking back again to the question of pollution, what is perhaps more disturbing than anything is the fact that the report found that, so far as the Aborigines were concerned, denial of access for thirty years to their lands 'has contributed to their emotional, social and material distress and deprivation.' The report went on to argue that it was 'appropriate and fair that the Aboriginal people be compensated. Effective compensation would enable them to re-establish their links with the land.'[6]

James Angleton, former CIA executive, who has been one of the most formidable
uncoverers of disinformation

Above: Savik Shuster and
Vincenzo Sparagna
explaining their
disinformation exercise
in Kabul

Left: a Russian
deserter reading the
faked copy of *Red Star* in
Afghanistan

Both the Western world and the Soviet empire were raining down strange and invisible poisons on all of us in the early 1950s. It is just as hypocritical for the Soviets to pretend that they were exempt from such criticism. What evidence there is suggests that they were equally guilty. Naturally, one hears much less of this because of the ruthless code of Soviet censorship. And, curiously enough, the Americans themselves kept singularly quiet about Soviet blunders in nuclear experimentation because they feared their own experiments might be jeopardized if news of nuclear accidents in Russia were publicized. Sometime in 1957 the USSR had a large-scale nuclear disaster in the Chelyabinsk area of the Southern Urals, not far from Sverdlovsk. Zhores Medvedev, a Russian biochemist who managed to get away to tell the rest of the world about it, claimed that 'the hospitals and clinics were filled with thousands of evacuated inhabitants, who were held for observation. After a time, when symptoms of radiation sickness began to appear in more distant areas, the evacuation zone was enlarged and people began to be placed not only in hospitals, but also in sanatoria and "houses of rest" which were re-equipped as hospitals. Hunting and fishing were prohibited throughout the southern and central Urals and for several years the sale of meat and fish in private markets was not permitted without special inspection for radioactivity.'[7]

Regarding the hazards created through the development of nuclear energy, there has been disinformation once again on both sides. If the Western world has played down the risks of nuclear waste dumping and accidents to nuclear plants, the Soviets have busily, brilliantly and cunningly infiltrated all manner of innocent environmental protection lobbies in the West and supplied them with false data. This infiltration has ranged from the 'Green' parties of Europe to such organizations as WISE (the World Information Service on Energy, based in Amsterdam, and linked to offices in Oxford, Brussels, Copenhagen, Helsinki, Tokyo, Verona, Barcelona and Washington, DC) and the Political Ecology Research Group in which there are active anti-nuclear campaigners often putting forward the Soviet view.

There is just as much opposition to the development of nuclear power for peaceful purposes as to that of nuclear weaponry, and a number of leading scientists from Andrei

Sakharov to Sir Fred Hoyle have asserted that Russia is playing a key role in sabotaging nuclear development for industrial purposes in the West. The Friends of the Earth and the anti-NUKES Alliance came into this category of opposition, which draws support from known communist sources. The Friends of the Earth some years ago not only joined CND in producing the broadsheet *Windscale; the Weapons Connection*, arguing that the civilian nuclear industry is dangerous, but has also opposed the mining of uranium in Australia. Sir Fred Hoyle, the distinguished astronomer and scientist, has pinpointed some of the hidden dangers caused by these ecological lobbyists – that Russia is covertly seeking to disrupt the West's sources of oil and to cut down its current nuclear superiority.

More disturbing in the late 1970s was the campaign against the fast-breeder reactor, on which up to the mid sixties Britain was technologically well ahead of the rest of the world. Yet much of this information has been handed over to the Russians and the French, with whom the USSR has a secret understanding on the subject! There was a steady increase in technological aid from the UK towards the USSR's military build-up, resulting from the agreement for cooperation in fields of applied science signed on 19 January 1968 by Anthony Wedgwood Benn and Fred Mulley. This proved a strikingly one-way bargain in favour of Russia. It was swiftly followed by the setting-up of the International Technological Collaboration Unit, sited in an atomic energy establishment, which received lists of questions from Soviet bloc representatives and supplied answers to them. A team from Culham research station visited Russia with their latest laser-measuring equipment (which the Russians did not then possess) to lend assistance.

The USSR cleverly exploited a number of anti-nuclear power lobbies, aiming not so much at checking the reprocessing of nuclear fuel, but merely at having important contracts switched to France where the nuclear industry expanded as Britain's declined. In the controversy over whether to go for a British or an American breeder-reactor, the CPRS (Central Policy Planning Review Staff) favoured American-designed reactors, Sir Kenneth Berrill, then head of the CPRS, being Whitehall's prime advocate of this policy. Despite all this Britain began to lag behind, while Russia and the Eastern bloc have increased their generating capacity at least sevenfold since 1971. Belatedly,

British Nuclear Fuels have admitted that fast-breeder reactors are essential for maintaining strategic industries.

One of the most far-reaching agreements between the UK and the USSR, barely publicized in the media, was that on Environmental Protection in May 1974. This was so widely defined that it could be extended to cover almost every aspect of Britain's domestic activities from pollution to water resources. In effect the UK gave the USSR far-ranging powers of monitoring British industries and scientific establishments. Largely in vain Sir John Hill, chairman of the UK Atomic Energy Authority, pointed out that waste uranium from Britain's power stations could provide enough electricity for 300 years if it was burnt in fast-breeder reactors. 'Attacks by conservationists will do no good for mankind,' he replied to the welter of disinformation which was then being served up. 'When the energy shortage becomes real, it will be the poor people of the world who will suffer most.'

The background to some, though obviously not all, of the conservationist campaigns is to prevent some Western countries, most notably Britain, from becoming independent in the energy field when oil starts to run out. Uranium could run out by 2010, whereas breeder reactor systems have a life of at least a thousand years.

Nevertheless there is just as much need to ensure that both sides tell the truth, and where disinformation is concerned one needs to be objective to the utmost degree. For example in 1985 dumping of radioactive waste at sea was suspended indefinitely by the London Dumping Convention despite a strong rearguard action by Britain and the United States. Twenty-five countries led by Spain, Australia and New Zealand voted for an open-ended moratorium on sea dumping. Only six countries, including Britain, the United States and France voted against. Later the British delegation stated that the resolution was not legally binding and that sea dumping remained an option. The result of this somewhat surprise vote was that it increased pressure on the nuclear industry to find suitable land sites for disposal of waste, which could be more difficult from a political viewpoint than sea dumping. The Greenpeace anti-nuclear organization's attitude to all this was that dumping of nuclear waste should be totally outlawed, which would make life impossible for all developers of nuclear power.

Disinformation on one side tends to induce it on the other. If you have extreme anti-nuclear development organizations deliberately setting out to scare the public, it must be expected that the authorities in charge of nuclear development will tend to play down fears and hide any unpleasant facts. Thus there was an allegation in 1985 that the Department of the Environment 'distorted and concealed figures on nuclear waste disposal in an attempt to get the Trades Union Congress to withdraw its objections to sea dumping.' This was contained in a report commissioned by the National Union of Seamen. [8]

This report, published to coincide with a Trades Union Congress meeting to discuss nuclear dumping, said that records of doses of radiation suffered by workers had been distorted to make sea disposal look a good option. It also claimed that costs of land storage had been grossly inflated. Large and Associates, consultant engineers, who prepared the report for the National Union of Seamen, alleged that the Department of the Environment's report, 'Best Practical Environmental Options', was 'surprisingly insensitive to practical matters, over-sensitive to cost, and indifferent to the important matter of occupational workers' exposure to radiation.' [9]

But the question arises – what was the brief given to Large and Associates when they were asked to make this report? Was a truly objective report expected, or was the request for a report which substantiated a certain point of view? The late Lord Wigg once told me that on matters of security the National Union of Seamen had caused him more trouble than any other body. Then again there was the allegation by Friends of the Earth and other bodies opposing the scheme for a nuclear fuel reprocessing plant at Dounreay in Scotland, that letters sent to planning officials expressing support for this were forgeries. Friends of the Earth claimed that of the 670 letters of support sent to the Highland Regional Council, at least fifteen had been forged and that at least 600 others were a standard, single-sentence photocopy of a declaration drawn up by the Dounreay Action Group which favoured the project.

When one gets disinformation both for and against a particular project, all one can do is to draw attention to such tactics and to allow the truth, when discoverable, to emerge quite independently. But in trying to get the right balance the writer probably suffers more than the propagandists, for he will please neither school of thought. I am prepared to admit that possibly Western authorities have sometimes kept quiet on some subjects of environmental pollution in the belief that this would make their own decisions more acceptable. But in the long run I am more positively convinced that the anti-nuclear lobby is not so much genuinely won over to the ecological cause as it is politically-minded and Soviet-orientated.

All new developments have their hazards which need to be combated or removed by careful research and experiment. To some extent, albeit a limited one, both gas and electricity services present certain hazards, both to operators and consumers alike. So, too, has coal-mining always been a hazardous operation. But these problems have never been presented to the public in the same manner and with the same political motives. Statistics show that between 1970 and 1984 death tolls in Britain's three main fuel industries were as follows: coal 783; oil and gas 121; nuclear 10. The anti-nuclear lobby may argue that it takes several years for some nuclear accidents to reveal the true death tolls, but over fourteen years surely these figures are impressive. Even if multiplied by six they would still be impressive against the other figures.

It is true that a nuclear plant such as Sellafield has rather a depressing record for accidents. It is also true that a Yorkshire Television documentary programme highlighted an allegedly abnormal incidence of leukaemia in the Sellafield district. On the other hand the Black Report, published in 1984, gave a qualified reassurance to residents that the plant's emissions were not harmful. Far too much time has been spent defending the British nuclear plants instead of trying to sell them to the public. When has one heard a politician pointing to the fact that French electricity prices are twenty per cent lower than ours because sixty per cent of their power is nuclear compared to a mere seventeen per cent for England and Wales?

Professor Sir Fred Hoyle, author of *Common Sense and Nuclear Energy*, put things in perspective when he wrote that 'the truth is that civil nuclear reactors are not nuclear bombs. And the word nuclear does not automatically mean something sinister.[10]

'Nuclear reactors have proved to be exceedingly safe in comparison with other activities that we normally take for granted,' continued Sir Fred Hoyle. 'For example, the general accident rate in coal mining is at least fifty times greater than the rate for the nuclear industry . . . Everything around us is radioactive. Soil and rocks are radioactive. Our houses are therefore radioactive. Compared to this "natural" radioactivity, leaks from nuclear reactors are small . . . It has been calculated that married couples receive more radioactivity from sleeping with each other than they get from the nuclear industry.'[11]

So much for the domestic risks of radioactivity. But Sir Fred Hoyle also points to the real problem on the long-term political outlook: 'A worse possibility is that the political disintegration in the Middle East will increase to a point where oil supplies to the West become disrupted and industry collapses in the democracies. Industry in the West is clearly very brittle, as the economic news reminds us every day. Compared to this gross and real danger, the dangers imagined by the anti-nuclear movement are trivial.'[12]

It should not be forgotten that one of the people who addressed the Windscale Inquiry in 1977 was Arthur Scargill, who was then merely the president of the Yorkshire miners. Speaking on behalf of miners generally, he opposed any extension of the nuclear plant at Windscale. When asked by Mr Justice Parker how he could possibly represent the views of 66,000 miners, he replied: 'There was unanimous support from the delegates and they took it back to their lodges.'[13]

Mr Justice Parker asked: 'Could you let me have all the minutes of the lodges which gave you unanimous support?'

Scargill: 'It could be done, but it would be a tremendous job.'

Later, in cross-examination, Scargill admitted that he had not discussed the matter with representatives of trades unions at Windscale before opposing the development.

Yet the anti-nuclear development lobby has powerful allies in all Western countries, many of their theories based on disinformation either from outside the Western bloc or from prejudice within it. An all-party House of Commons committee on energy actually recommended a heavy cutback in nuclear power station construction at the very moment of a threat of an indefinite national coal strike. This committee gave the impression of having closed its mind to the global threat to Western energy supplies. Nor did it seem to have considered the commonsense view of the French that energy supplies are a strategic resource and a defence against the imbroglios of the Eastern bloc. One of the foremost antagonists of nuclear power is Professor Joseph Rotblat, an eminent physicist, who claims that the notion that nuclear power can solve our energy problems is a myth. Professor Rotblat was a member of the British nuclear weapons team at Los Angeles during World War II, and has been involved with nuclear technology at an international level for several decades, initially with the development of nuclear power and later with the problems of safety and proliferation. [14]

Dr Josef Luns, the former NATO Secretary-General, estimated that about £6 million was spent by Russia on anti-nuclear activities in Western Europe in 1984. This money has been distributed as much in Britain as elsewhere in Western Europe, and has resulted indirectly in the setting up of such organizations as Manchester Against Missiles, Engineers Against the Bomb, Teachers Against Missiles and Journalists Against Nuclear Extermination.

Of course deception – whether wilful or otherwise – by British Nuclear Fuels and the authorities at British nuclear plants has not helped matters. On 16 February 1986, British Nuclear Fuels admitted that figures recording discharges of radioactive material around the Sellafield site in Cumbria which they gave to the Black Inquiry, set up to investigate cancer levels three years previously, were wrong. A spokesman said that the figure given to the Black Inquiry on doses of radiation received by the population over a three-year period in the 1950s was more than forty times the original figure of about half a kilogram. Even more appalling was the spokesman's admission that 'the figures originally given to the inquiry were based on old evidence because of the lack of time available in preparation for the inquiry.' [15]

Nor has Sellafield been as forthcoming as one has a right to expect over a very long period. More than once it has minimized the hazards of a leakage at the plant and then afterwards been forced to admit that it erred. This disinformation has been so serious that the EEC Commissioner responsible for nuclear safety within the Common Market countries has asked the British Government for further information on alleged discharge of radioactive waste from the plant at Sellafield.

There are many forms of pollution which persist in the world mainly because the truth about them is hidden from the public. While one hears a great deal about the dumping of nuclear waste, one learns much less of the scourge of acid rain which has wrought such havoc in West Germany, Norway, Switzerland and elsewhere. The rapid rise in damage to forests in these territories in recent years has been attributed to sulphur dioxide pollution from power plants and coal-fired factories and nitrogen oxides from motor exhausts. Damage to West German forests from acid rain and air pollution rose further during 1985 and spread to deciduous as well as coniferous trees. It was reported from Bonn that 'a sharp increase in the number of diseased oaks is a striking feature, with the figure rising to sixty-five per cent in Bavaria compared with fourteen per cent last year. In Hesse the share of badly-affected oaks has doubled to twenty-two per cent in a year, while more than half show some signs of damage.'[16]

Only belatedly is the British public beginning to learn (and then only through reports by foreign correspondents) that much of the blame for acid rain is attributable to Britain itself. European countries are seriously concerned about the cover-up by British authorities and the fact that this menace is increasing. Statistics produced by the German Alpine Society show that seventy-eight per cent of the German Alpine forest is dead or dying entirely because of acid rain. Their forecast is grim: unless immediate action is taken, they say, the Alps could become a depopulated and treeless wilderness within fifteen years. 'All this could happen within a shorter space of time than fifteen years,' said Herr Franz Speer, the Society's environmental expert. 'A long period of drought could accelerate the process.'[17]

This is a cancer which is doing as much harm in Britain as in Europe to which winds passing over the United Kingdom direct this scourge. The World Wildlife Fund states that 'more than sixty major lakes in Britain have "died" from the effects of air pollution and symptoms of forest decline are widespread in South-East England.'

Acid rain is probably a greater long-term threat than many other forms of pollution, including those of nuclear leaks. Yet, while doctors and some scientists in Britain have actually denied that the acid rain scourge is as damaging as has been suggested, the World Wildlife Fund's monitoring of the situation has revealed that the United Kingdom alone exports twenty-seven times as much sulphur dioxide as is blown across its borders from other countries, or about 4,000,000 tonnes a year. This is easily the highest figure for Western Europe as a whole, and it would seem to be confirmed by a range of five independent statistical reports.

Why has there been such a cover-up on acid rain? How is it that Britain, Poland and the United States have refused to join the nineteen countries committed to a thirty per cent reduction in sulphur dioxide emissions by 1993? The truth is that successive British governments have consistently dodged the issue because they have funked introducing the legislation which would alleviate matters more than any other – a law to ensure that only lead-free petrol was used. Unleaded petrol is more expensive to produce than leaded petrol because it needs much more refining. Politicians fear that more expensive petrol would be a vote-loser, even though the additional cost of unleaded petrol would probably be no more than four pence a gallon at current cost levels, a small price to pay in the circumstances.

Quite apart from the damage to forests, a team of West German doctors has established a link between acid rain pollution and bronchial and chest complaints. This team from Munster University 'found in a nation-wide survey that the areas where forests were most devastated by pollution were almost the same as where people suffered from bronchial and breathing problems. Bavaria and Baden-Württemberg, which includes the Black Forest, headed the list of states for those suffering from bronchial complaints as well as forest damage.'[18]

Belatedly, the British government has taken some action on this scourge, though it is still totally inadequate. The lead content of petrol was to be reduced by six per cent as from January 1986. But it has taken five years to implement even this minor improvement. Meanwhile Switzerland has become the first country in Europe to make catalytic converters which require lead-free fuel compulsory for all private cars. In addition the Swiss government has adopted strict car pollution standards similar to those in effect in the United States since 1983. Lead-free fuel is now widely available in Switzerland.

There has been more open debate in Switzerland on the acid rain crisis than in Britain. It is calculated that one-third of Swiss forests are diseased and that if this trend continues, it could force the evacuation of up to 150,000 people from mountain areas endangered by avalanches. Yet in the United Kingdom statistics on the damage done to forests and inhabitants have been withheld from the public. Indeed, in some instances damage to trees by acid rain has been attributed to Dutch Elm disease, a blatant piece of truth-twisting.

Among the governments of many so-called civilized nations apathy towards the problems of pollution has ruled, sometimes amounting to no more than indifference, but often to deliberate playing-down of these scourges. That goes just as much for the nasty habit of straw-burning as for the dumping of waste matter of all kinds. Yet the National Society for Clean Air reported in 1985 that complaints about straw burning after harvest time were 'received by 96 of the 139 local authorities which reported burning in their area.' 'Yet again,' said the society's co-author of the report, Jane Dunmore, 'local authorities told us of damage to manufactured products and newly decorated buildings, threats to wildlife and their habitats and hazards on the roads.'[19]

In 1983 a consultative meeting of the contracting parties to the convention on the prevention of marine pollution by dumping wastes agreed by a majority vote to call for a two-year moratorium on the dumping of low-level radioactive waste at sea. Sea-dumping of high-level nuclear waste had been banned totally at the beginning of 1972. It is, however, important to note that as yet there has been no positive effort to ban all such marine dumping, and that the British government does not hold itself bound by the moratorium, which is without legal effect.

One of the problems for the government and the nuclear industry is that the implacable opposition of the anti-nuclear lobbies has made it equally difficult to find suitable land sites for dumping and burying the material. Thus the need remains to keep open the options for marine dumping. What undoubtedly misleads the public on this subject is that both sides disinform to some extent, to preserve their own positions. The anti-nuclear lobbies build up an exaggerated picture of the dangers, while those in the nuclear industry and government circles, in defence of their own position, undoubtedly play down the risks and hazards. This is a vital issue which needs to be thrashed out in the interests of all: on the one side the dangers of all forms of nuclear development, on the other the prospect of a nation becoming backward and with lower living standards if it fails to develop a nuclear industry. Somewhere in between lies the truth, but to establish it requires a genuinely objective, unprejudiced approach by government, trades unions, scientists, the medical profession, industrialists and ecologists.

To pinpoint how disinformation has been used by both sides in this question of nuclear development, I will cite one instance of each lobby. Regarding the Friends of the Earth claim that of the 670 letters of support for the Dounreay plant sent to the Highland Regional Council at least fifteen were forged, a Mrs Joan Sutherland, of Wick, said she had been appalled to find that her name had been used without her permission. 'I got an acknowledgement from the regional council saying they had received my letter of support and that it was being forwarded to the Secretary of State for Scotland.'[20]

Dr Kitty Little, of Oxford, who prepared a lengthy memorandum on the subversive background to nuclear policies at the time of the Windscale Inquiry in the late 1970s, recently made the following interesting statement: 'Last year, when I attended the inquest on an Aldermaston worker who had died from a form of cancer that could not have been caused by radiation, I found that three of the four medical witnesses gave factually incorrect evidence. Yet the Ministry of Defence counsel did not know what questions to ask of these witnesses. As a result there was an open verdict that has been unscrupulously used by the pressure groups and certain MPs to suggest that workers at Aldermaston are at risk. And so the cover for both these major acts of sabotage is allegations concerning the "health and safety" of the workers and of the public. Cross-examination of the anti-nuclear medical witnesses at the Windscale Inquiry showed that their arguments were based on false premises – but this was not reported in the press.

'I suggest that the time is long overdue for a full inquiry by the police into the activities of members of the pressure group network and their political associates, and into the activities of doctors who produce false evidence to support their allegations.'[21]

I make no comment on either of these two quite separate allegations of disinformation. However, they do call for the closest and most objective possible examination of everything that is told us by both sides on the whole subject of nuclear development.

Obviously the appalling tragedy of the Chernobyl nuclear disaster in Russia in the late spring of 1986 must be taken into account. Once again it produced truth-twisting on all sides. Until this catastrophe occurred accidents in nuclear plants had been mercifully light, as has already been mentioned. Then came claim and counter-claim. A report which seemed to emanate from the World Federation of Free Latvians alleged that a Lithuanian nuclear plant of the same type as the damaged Chernobyl reactor was the subject of a catalogue of construction errors, stating that it had been built without cooling towers and water used to cool pipes carrying radioactive material fed directly into a nearby lake and on into the Dauguva river which flowed into the Baltic.

At about the same time Greenpeace and Friends of the Earth claimed that British nuclear reactors could be less safe than the Russian reactor destroyed at Chernobyl. They alleged that the British Magnox and advanced gas cooled (AGR) reactors had fewer secondary safety systems than Chernobyl. This directly contradicted the assurances given by Lord Marshall, chairman of the Central Electricity Generating Board, the previous week.

Then, possibly to try to achieve a balance between these two unconnected themes, Dr K.C. Hutchin, medical consultant of the *Daily Telegraph*, reminded us on 8 May 1986 that 'a single chest X-ray exposes the average person to ten times more radiation than exposure for a whole week to the highest level of background radiation recorded in Britain' since the Chernobyl disaster.

All these statements, and not least the wise doctor's need to be taken into account in re-assessing the risks and the advantages of developing nuclear power. Most people have probably forgotten that more than thirty years ago the late Lord ('Rab') Butler told the British people that nuclear power was going to double the living standards of Britain in our lifetime – something which nobody would suggest has happened, or is ever imminent. Neither governments nor Parliament itself have helped us to get absolutely accurate assurances about or assessments of these things. One has the recent case of an independent governmental report on nuclear waste contradicting one of the main findings published by the House of Commons Select Committee on the Environment. The MPs alleged that Britain lagged forty years behind other countries over safe disposal sites and that nuclear industries were in a 'shambles' on disposal. Whereas there is some evidence that Britain could usefully study what other nations are doing in this respect, the fact has to be faced that the United Kingdom is a grossly over-populated and in consequence over-polluted nation for its total acreage, certainly as far as England is concerned. In recent years there has been considerable evidence that House of Commons Select Committees, consisting of members of all parties, tend increasingly to use these committees for scoring party points over one another rather than for the good of the nation as a whole.

Indeed, I would go further and say that sometimes the way in which these committees phrase their questions often leads to disinformation. In short, if these tendencies continue in the workings of such committees (and there is much more such work today than in the past), they could even bring the House of Commons into disrepute. It hasn't happened yet, though it has been perilously near to it on recent occasions. Let Select Committees be warned of this very real danger.

The Royal Commission on Environmental Pollution has urged companies, councils and other public authorities to be less secretive when they look for new dumping grounds for all forms of waste. 'When sites are operating, it is important that no attempt should be made to cover up mistakes,' its report commented. Sir Richard Southwood, chairman of the Commission, added that: 'Secrecy fuels fears. The more we look at this the more convinced we are of the wisdom of that phrase.' [22]

9

FORGERS OF THE KGB

When disinformation comes in the guise of forged documents, and when that forging is most skilfully done, the dire effects can last much longer.

The art of forgery for political disinformation has, of course, been practised by Western countries in the past, though such tactics seem to have lost credence today. Perhaps two of the most notorious cases were those of a forged letter attributed to Parnell, the Irish nationalist leader, and published in *The Times* in 1887, suggesting that he condoned the Phoenix Park murders, and the Zinoviev Letter scare which was published four days before a British general election in October 1924. The Parnell case resulted in a judicial inquiry in which forgery by one Richard Pigott was established and *The Times* had to pay £250,000 in costs. The Zinoviev Letter, which purported to be signed by Zinoviev, president of the Presidium of the Third Communist International, summoning the British Communist Party to intensify its revolutionary activities and to subvert the armed forces of the Crown, was published four days before the British General Election in 1924. This letter is now believed to have been a forgery perpetrated by a group of White Russian émigrés working with members of the Conservative Party Central Office, though the whole truth is far from being established. However, since World War II the Soviet Union has made somewhat of an industry of forgery, and a highly skilled industry at that.

The CIA has claimed that the KGB spends annually at least 200 million dollars on a variety of 'dirty tricks', a high percentage of which is devoted to forgery as a political weapon. Much of this forgery has been perpetrated by Department D of the KGB, set up by the late Yuri Andropov. It took several years before the Russians perfected their new organization. Some of the earlier forgeries were easily detectable, but in the past ten years much havoc has been wrought in the Western world not only through forged documents and letters, but forged conversations on tape and individuals used for the propagating for falsehoods.

In 1980 the Subcommittee on Oversight of the Permanent Select Committee on Intelligence of the House of Representatives in the USA conducted an inquiry into the 'forgery offensive of Soviet covert action'. During this inquiry John McMahon, Deputy Director for Operations of the CIA, stated that in 1978 the entire foreign propaganda apparatus of the USSR was put into the hands of the International Information Department of the CPSU in liaison with the KGB. This had resulted in increased use of forgeries. 'Of the some 150 anti-American forgeries produced by the Soviet Union and its East European allies in the postwar period, the most damaging ones have been fabrication of official-looking government documents and communiqués. The Soviets have also manufactured personal letters which were allegedly written by US officials and which purport to contain information regarding official policy. Previous studies prepared for the Congress by the CIA documented forty-six examples of Soviet and bloc forgeries which came to our attention from 1957 to 1965.

'For a brief period in the mid-1970s the Soviets reduced and then curtailed altogether their production of anti-US forgeries. In 1976, however, they resumed forgeries as an integral part of their covert action programme, and major new forgeries have been appearing since then at the rate of four to five per year. Not only has the number of forgeries increased in recent years, but there also have been qualitative changes as well. The new spate of bogus documents includes high quality, technically sophisticated falsifications of a calibre which the Soviet and Eastern bloc intelligence services were evidently incapable of producing in the 1950s and even in the 1960s.

' . . . The suspected Soviet and bloc forgeries which have appeared since 1976 fall into three groups. A single forgery, a bogus US Army field manual, has surfaced in more than twenty countries around the world and has received substantial media attention. Soviet propagandists have exploited it repeatedly to support unfounded allegations that the US acts as the agent provocateur behind various foreign terrorists, in particular the Italian Red Brigades. A series of current forgeries, which now totals eight examples, has been aimed at compromising the United States in Western Europe and provoking discord in the NATO Alliance, especially in the context of the continuing Greek-Turkish dispute. Another current series of seven falsifications has been directed towards undermining our relations with Egypt and other countries in the Arab world. Moscow's intensified use of forgeries appears to be aimed mainly at the United States and US security relations in Europe rather than at our allies *per se* . . . The Soviets are probably trying to play upon perceived differences between the United States and the West Europeans while at the same time they wish to preserve the less damaged relations they have with the latter.' [1]

In the early 1980s the Russians purchased publicly available maps published by the CIA and used them as a basis for false and alarming stories about US policies. The first 'map operation' occurred on 20 September 1981, when an article appeared in the Austrian Communist Party newspaper, *Volksstimme*, alleging that a CIA map with code number 77706/10-70 had been found in a 'secret service' building in West Germany near the Austrian border. The article further alleged that the map depicted targets in Austria for US raids and sabotage as well as nuclear missile and neutron weapon assaults. The author of this article, Julius Mader, had published a book in 1968 entitled *Who's Who in the CIA*, a compilation of names of alleged US intelligence officers that caused considerable trouble for US personnel overseas in subsequent years. [2]

The map was, of course, genuine and provided only basic data. But the article itself, which was totally untrue, was intended to lend support to the various West European peace movements and to suggest there was a United States' threat to European security. The story was also reproduced in the Soviet press.

Similar 'map operations' were carried out in India, Ethiopia, Nicaragua, El Salvador and Argentina. On 11 November 1981 a story appeared in *The Patriot*, an Indian daily paper, together with another US government map of Afghanistan, in which it was stated that a special aeroplane had taken these maps to Pakistan to distribute among 'Afghan terrorist leaders' and that the maps indicated targets for sabotage selected by the CIA. Similar stories with maps in various other Latin American papers suggested that the Reagan government and the CIA were waging bacteriological warfare against Cuba.[3]

One of the most blatant forgeries was that of a letter from President Reagan to King Juan Carlos of Spain. In early November 1981, several Spanish journalists and all delegations (excepting that of the USA) to the Madrid Conference on Security and Cooperation in Europe received copies of a bogus letter allegedly sent by the President to the King, together with copies of a fabricated memorandum allegedly prepared by the Spanish Foreign Minister and other officials. In terms likely to offend Spanish sensitivities, the letter urged King Juan Carlos to join NATO and to crack down on such organizations as the *Opus Dei* pacifists and left-wing opposition. It was also hinted that the United States might be prepared to support Spanish efforts to regain control of Gibraltar from Britain.[4]

It was later discovered that copies of the letter and document had first been posted to various Spanish journalists, and that the approach to the delegations resulted from a failure by any of the Spanish papers to print the story. Afterwards some Madrid newspapers published stories which exposed the letter as a forgery of Soviet origin. It soon became clear that the object of this forgery was to complicate US-Spanish relations by suggesting that America was unduly interfering in Spain's affairs and to provoke opposition to Spain joining NATO.

Generally speaking, however, the most blatant and persistent efforts of Soviet disinformation are directed to the Middle East and Latin America where such stories are rather more likely to be believed. In January 1982 a forged letter and an accompanying research analysis dated 23 September 1981, from Judge William Clark, then Deputy Secretary of State, to the US Ambassador to Greece, Monteagle Stearns, was circulated in Athens. This not only indicated support for the Conservatives in the Greek elections, but alluded to a possible military coup if Socialist leader Andreas Papandreou won. On the basis that the US Embassy advised that the letter was a fake, the story was not initially published. But several weeks later the Athens daily newspaper, *Vrathini*, ran a story describing the letter as of doubtful authenticity and probably attributable to 'a Third World intelligence service'. Nevertheless some mischief had been done and some of it was believed by many.[5]

In 1979 agents of the USSR spread a false rumour that the United States was responsible for the seizure of the Grand Mosque of Mecca, while other disinformers aimed a campaign against the American-Egyptian relationship to undermine the Camp David peace negotiations. The first of these forgeries had been a purported speech by a member of the US administration in 1976, calling for a 'total change of the government and governmental system in Egypt'. A year later there was a forged document, allegedly prepared by the Secretary of State for the President, which used language insulting and offensive to President Sadat and other Arab leaders. This forgery was delivered anonymously to the Egyptian Embassy in April 1977. A forged letter from the US Ambassador to Eygpt, Herman F. Eilts, declared that because Sadat was not prepared to serve US interests, 'we must repudiate him and get rid of him without hesitation.' This forgery was reproduced in the issue of the Syrian newspaper, *Al-ba'th*, on 1 October 1979.

Sadat's moderation, his attempts to negotiate with Israel and his friendly relations with the USA did not suit Russian Middle East policies one iota. So everything possible was done to undermine the Egyptian President during the last years of his life. This was largely done through a series of forgeries, which attempted to suggest that the United States had no high regard for Sadat and that the Egyptian President was plotting to betray other Arab nations and the PLO. While the US forensic analysts were able ultimately to prove to the Egyptians that these documents were forgeries, a great deal of harm was done meanwhile, and outside of Egypt much of this 'evidence' was accepted as true.

One of the most effective of these forgeries was published in *Al-Dawa*, the Moslem Brotherhood's periodical. It was a bogus report to the CIA, detailing plans to bribe or dupe members of the Brotherhood and to destroy their religious beliefs. So effective was this single forgery that some in the intelligence services of the world believe even today that it caused the enraged and fanatical Brotherhood to organize the assassination of Sadat.

Sometimes there takes place what can only be described as swift and instantaneous forgery. An example of this came on 26 November 1981, the day after a group of mercenaries attempted to overthrow the Seychelles government; Soviet newspaper reports were immediately implying that the CIA was responsible. Despite a statement by the Seychelles President, Albert René, that his government had no indication of any foreign involvement other than South Africa, the Soviet media continued to publish this story which, in due course, was reprinted in leading newspapers in Kenya and Nigeria.

One outcome of this spate of forgeries was that in October 1981, the Danish government expelled Vladimir Merkulov, a Second Secretary in the Soviet Embassy in Copenhagen, for engaging in activities inconsistent with his diplomatic status. Later the Danes arrested a Danish journalist, Arne Herlov Petersen, and charged him with acting as Merkulov's agent. Petersen had been recruited several years earlier by another KGB officer and had indulged in all manner of subversive activities, including the distribution of Soviet-prepared forgeries. The Danish Ministry of Justice issued a statement to the effect that Petersen had sought to influence Danish public opinion by his activities. 'A single but illustrative case in point,' commented the Ministry, 'is the promise made by the Soviet Embassy in the summer of 1981 to finance the expenditure incurred in connection with the publication of a number of advertisements in which a number of Danish artists expressed support of an initiative to establish a Nordic nuclear-free zone. The collection of signatures was organized by Arne Herlov Petersen, who said in several telephone conversations that the Soviet Embassy was involved in this matter.'[6]

Petersen was also behind a calculated attack on the British Prime Minister. For the Ministry of Justice recorded that he received money to cover 'the costs of printing a pamphlet against the British Prime Minister, Margaret Thatcher, which was published at the initiative of the Soviet Embassy and contained a text supplied by the Embassy.' This was entitled 'True Blues: the Thatcher That Couldn't Mend Her Own

Roof.' It also attacked various US Senators, Joseph Luns and the West German politician, Franz Josef Strauss.

For downright hypocrisy, however, a broadcast by the Moscow World Service in English on 13 October 1982 takes some beating. This alleged that 'the Strategic Studies Institute in London stated that there is parity in the arsenals of the Warsaw Treaty Organization and NATO in nuclear weapons. Now America and some NATO officials are claiming the reverse. They alleged that the USA is lagging behind the USSR militarily. A view is being deliberately spread about unfavourable trends in the balance of strength, changing in favour of the Soviet Union and the Warsaw powers. Disinformation and the twisting of facts is not new in US propaganda practices.'

In their development of the technique of disinformation the Russians have been clever enough to educate some Third World countries in these black arts, with the result that sometimes such nations do the Soviets' work for them. During the Angolan civil war of the mid-1970s the FNLA (National Front for the Liberation of Angola) accused Portugal of aiding the MPLA (Popular Movement for the Liberation of Angola) and warned that it would march on Luanda and would attack if Portuguese troops tried to stop them. An elaborate and highly effective propaganda programme defended the MPLA taking of Luanda, including an attempt to dominate both the Portuguese and Angolan media. The FNLA were denounced as 'cannibals'. A story was circulated by the MPLA organization that human blood and organs had been discovered in FNLA headquarters in Luanda after the MPLA takeover and that this proved 'cannibalism' was being practised.[7]

There is some evidence that this 'cannibalism' campaign was partly launched from Lisbon with some assistance from both Moscow and Havana. Ironically, the Portuguese authorities in an earlier decade had also portrayed various African nationalists as cannibals, so it could be said to constitute a form of revenge. But the manner in which the FNLA manipulated the press in Lisbon and elsewhere in the world was much more effective. In July 1975, possibly seventy-five per cent of the Lisbon daily and weekly press was controlled by the Portuguese Communist Party or its allies. The story made the allegation that bottles of blood and human organs were found in refrigerators in the headquarters of the MPLA's enemies. 'This 'evidence of cannibalism' was broadcast in Lisbon and later in Havana at a Third World congress that summer. [8]

The tactics employed by the Russians in manufacturing their forgeries are usually carefully thought out, thus ensuring that at least some of the media will publish them, or some officials in other countries will believe them. The fabricated letter to try to involve the United States in the Seychelles fiasco was composed on the letterhead of a New Orleans-based company, was addressed to Lieutenant-General Muller of the South African Air Force, and referred to the recruitment of combat-trained helicopter pilots with US government encouragement. Similarly, in the campaign to upset American-Egyptian relations during the Sadat administration a forged despatch, looking positively as though it had been prepared by the US Embassy in Teheran, suggested that the Americans had acquiesced in plans by Iran and Saudi Arabia to overthrow Sadat. This forgery was sent by mail to the Egyptian Embassy in Belgrade in August 1977. The choice of embassy was in itself quite a clever ploy. [9]

Some forgeries, say officials of the State Department, 'are not designed for public dissemination, but rather are intended to circulate privately. Their purpose is to influence individual leaders and opinion-makers. The damage is harder to assess. The purported author often gets no opportunity to set the record straight.' [10]

Frequently, the forged document is transmitted with a covering letter which attempts to lend authenticity to it. Typically, the cover letter summarizes the contents of the forgery and explains the author's alleged motive for transmitting it in terms of outrage over the revelations contained in the fabrication. Frequently, the letter is unsigned, the writer explaining that he is afraid of losing his post.

In the autumn of 1982 the Northrop Corporation sent letters to prospective customers inviting them to observe flight tests of the company's F-5F 'Tiger Shark' aircraft. The forgery substituted a false addressee, the commander of the South African Air Force, an alteration easily done with reproduction equipment. The object of this forgery was to indicate that the Northrop Corporation, with the blessing of the US government, was violating the embargo on the sales of arms to South Africa.

The letter was published as authentic in *Jeune Afrique*, a weekly newspaper in Paris, and also in *The Times of Zambia*. Later, however, *Jeune Afrique* reproduced photocopies of the forgery together with a letter from the Northrop company denying its validity.[11]

Sometimes Soviet forgeries fail in their objectives because of carelessness in preparing the text. One such was a fabricated United States Department of Defense document, dated 8 February 1982. This was entitled 'Downstream Operations – Related Missions' Directives' and bore an outsized department seal and the ZIP code (20402) of the Superintendent of Documents. It was addressed to the Department's envoys in Syria, Lebanon, Saudi Arabia, Egypt and Israel, and read:

'PLEASE CONFIRM THROUGH YOUR BOYS THAT:
'Israeli attack on Eastern Front possible even before mid-April, for heavy artillery regiments have already been moved. Egypt to strengthen bargaining position in the face of a war and if there exists any secret Saudi pledge for Syria. To what extent in terms of time and power, the Palestinians plus Lebanese left can face Israeli thrust into South Lebanon.

'Considerable possibilities for South Yemeni and Libyan support to the Palestinians in the light of Israeli offensive.

'Israel still maintains that she can halt any Libyan support to the Palestinians by means of air and sea, how far Israelis are correct in this assessments.

'Earlier reports suggest that Soviet Union can't rush military support to Damascus within first few days of war. Turkish factor, Lebanese involvement and internal trouble could help in this act. Soviet-Syrian Friendship Treaty provides such loopeholes(?).

'Threat to American and Israeli interests would drastically increase in coming months particularly in Middle East and Europe.'

As will be seen, the letter is badly written in parts, containing a number of grammatical and spelling errors. It is unthinkable that such a letter would have been sent in this form to the envoys concerned. The object was to provide 'evidence' of US-Israeli collaboration in planning the invasion of Lebanon. It seems that it was not intended for publication, but to be circulated among various Arab communities in Europe.

In the early 1980s there was a sudden increase in the number of Soviet-inspired forgeries passing around the world. In December 1983 the former KGB Major Stanislav Levchenko, who defected to the United States in 1979, told the US House of Representatives Select Committee on Intelligence that the Russians were making an extensive effort to influence Japanese political and public opinion through the full panoply of active measures techniques. There were alleged rumours of a secret nuclear deal between China and Italy and a faked last political testament of the Chinese political leader, Chou En-lai. In February 1983, a fake speech by the American Ambassador to the United Nations, Jeanne Kirkpatrick, on US policy towards the Third World surfaced in India and was reprinted in communist media in the USSR, Nicaragua and elsewhere.

In the following month a forged letter from the American Federation of Labor-Congress of Industrial Relations official Irving Brown to an Italian labour official, Luigi Scricciolo, appeared in the Sicilian paper *Sette Giorno*. A cousin of one of the Red Brigade kidnappers of James Dozier, the US Army Brigadier-General in 1981, Scricciolo was taken into custody during the Dozier investigation. He then admitted he had been working as an agent for Bulgarian intelligence. The fake letter suggested that Scricciolo was a CIA agent funneling funds clandestinely from the AFL-CIO to the Polish trade union Solidarity. The forgery's purpose was presumably to undermine the credibility of Scricciolo's testimony about Bulgarian intelligence activities and to suggest secret links between Solidarity and the CIA.

Later the same year in an apparent attempt to discredit a possible Bulgarian connection with the attempt to assassinate the Pope a Rome left-wing paper, *Pace e Guerra*, published two fabricated US Embassy telegrams in its edition of 21 July 1983. The first forgery, dated 25 August 1982, proposed a large-scale disinformation effort in cooperation with Italian intelligence and friendly members of the Socialist Party to implicate the Bulgarians and the Soviets in the papal assassination attempt. The second, dated 6 December 1982, judged the campaign a success, stating: 'The European media have enthusiastically developed themes on the lines anticipated: that the gunman was directed by the Bulgarian secret police, that the Bulgarians are under the total control of the KGB, and that the KGB was headed at the time by the present Soviet leader [then Yuri Andropov].'

There has been a surfeit of disinformation on the subject of the attempt on the Pope's life, and, while much of it was Soviet-inspired, the picture is still somewhat confused by the fact that there also seem to have been some spurious stories from Italian, Mafia and other sources. A report from Rome claimed knowledge of a bizarre deal to coax a confession from the Pope's hitman Ali Agca in exchange for a Mafia chief's safety. One Giovanni Pandico said that Agca was persuaded to implicate the Bulgarians in the Pope's shooting in May 1981, in a deal struck with the Italian secret service.

But the whole question is made even more confused by the fact that Oleg Bitov, the Soviet agent who defected to the West and then went back to the USSR and repudiated both the USA and Britain, has also muddied the waters with his own comments. During what he now describes as his 'capture' in London and New York, Bitov says he met a British intelligence agent, Colonel Hartlan, a British lawyer, Mr Russell, and an Italian agent of the SISMI or SISDE named Brunel. According to Bitov, the 'Bulgarian Connection' was invented by former Bulgarian citizen and European director of *Reader's Digest*, John Dimi Panitza. Bitov was offered a large sum of money (so he claims) to write a book on the 'Bulgarian Connection' and was 'encouraged' to testify during the Italian trial concerning the assassination attempt. Now Bitov claims he is ready and willing to testify in Italy, but against the 'Bulgarian Connection' and to identify the Western intelligence agents he met during 'captivity'.

Inevitably that earlier defector, Anatoli Golitsyn, has something to say on the subject. He says he is more inclined to agree with the views of the Israeli and West German intelligence services, that implicating the KGB in the assassination affair is outright disinformation. In Golitsyn's opinion the object of the exercise was not to undermine Andropov, as suggested, but to confuse the strategic implications.[12]

It is, of course, occasionally a good ploy in the disinformation game to spread several conflicting stories: confusion can sometimes be useful. But in the case of Pope John Paul II there seem to be attempts to confuse on more than one side. There have even been allegations of some attempts at disinformation on the Vatican side, not altogether unconnected with the financial scandals which hit the Papal entourage following revelations of links between the Vatican and some Mafia bankers.

As to any theories why the Russians should, either on their own, or through such intermediaries as the Bulgarians, attempt to murder the Pope, some observers insist that this was the result of a handwritten letter which the Pope is alleged to have sent to Moscow before the attempt on his life. In this, it is said, the Pope warned the Soviet Union that he intended to return immediately to Poland, his native land, if the violent street disturbances there provoked the invasion of the country by Russian troops. The Vatican has, however, denied that any such letter was written or sent to Moscow. Yet another story, which is as far-fetched as can be imagined, is that a dramatic helicopter flight from Rome to the deck of a Soviet warship by Pope John Paul II stopped the Russian tanks from rolling into Poland. Italian journalist Luigi Forni claimed that the Pope, in a secret meeting with Brezhnev, promised to bring Lech Walesa and Solidarity to heel if the Soviet invasion was halted. [13]

To keep a dispassionate mind on this whole subject is far from easy. On balance, having studied the various reports and canards, I would say that the USSR, the Bulgarians, the Italians and the Vatican have all been guilty of some disinformation, while the CIA may have muddied the waters somewhat by using some counter-measures.

Britain's communist newspaper, *The Morning Star*, accused the United States Ambassador to Italy, Mr Maxwell Rabb, of reporting to Washington that: 'Our operations on Bulgaria's connection with the attempt on the Pope's life has led to a complete success. European mass media have enthusiastically developed the preliminary worked-out theses.' [14]

No source for this report was cited by the *Morning Star*, and it was immediately denounced as a forgery, but the British paper did not publish this denunciation.

A fake National Security Council memorandum was cited in the Madrid weekly newspaper, *Tiempo*, on 7 February 1983. This purported to come from Zbigniew Brzezinski to President Carter in 1978, identifying Poland as 'the weakest link in the chain of Soviet domination of Eastern Europe' and proposing a destabilization programme involving 'politicians, diplomats, labour unions, the mass media and covert activity'. Dr Brzezinski sent a personal letter denying he had ever sent such a memorandum and on 16 May the same year *Tiempo* published his denial.

A false report that the United States and Israel would be testing and later deploying Tomahawk cruise missiles in South Africa first appeared in Mozambique's *Noticias* on 29 November 1982. This story subsequently acquired credence in Soviet, East German, Bulgarian, Ethiopian, Zambian and Angolan newspapers. It was a piece of propaganda put out in 1982 which was still circulating two years later. In the past ten years the KGB has been intent on stirring up trouble between blacks and whites all around the world. There was the case of a forged Carter administration document on Africa suggesting that the United States was anxious about links between US blacks and black Africans. As far back as 1980 Jody Powell, the presidential press secretary, had denounced it as a forgery, but this did not stop the story reappearing in the *Nigeria Standard* in March 1983, and the following month in the Upper Volta press.

Then in late May 1983, only two weeks before the British general elections, copies of a fabricated audiotape of an alleged telephone conversation between President Reagan and Prime Minister Thatcher circulated in Holland under an anonymous cover letter. On the tape the President tried to restrain Mrs Thatcher, who was depicted as being intent on punishing the Argentinians, and at the same time blamed her for the loss of HMS *Sheffield*. But technical analysis of the tape indicated that the voices were genuine and there was some concern that opponents of the British Prime Minister had scored something of a coup. However, more detailed analysis revealed that the President's remarks were excerpted from a broadcast to Europe on 22 November 1982, and that, from a Dutch 'transcript' circulated with the tape, phrases from that speech were rearranged and taken out of context.[15]

One of the more farcical and bizarre examples of disinformation arose when the Fidel Castro regime in Cuba alleged that the resurgence of dengue fever in Cuba was caused by the

Pakistani malaria research centre in Lahore, which the Russians had charged with implementing a CIA-sponsored bacteriological warfare programme.[16]

According to Cuban media this centre was not only for breeding malarial mosquitos for Afghanistan, but also to carry dengue fever to Cuba. A former Cuban health service official, Eduardo Gomez Cabale, who defected to the USA in 1982, has stated that the Cuban government chose this explanation to divert attention from the likeliest carriers of dengue fever, Cuban troops returning from Angola. At the same time the Mexico City office of the Salvador Human Rights Commission, which has ties to various left-wing organizations, accused the US of furnishing the El Salvador military with chemical and biological weapons.[17]

The assassination of the Indian Prime Minister, Mrs Indira Gandhi, on 31 October 1984, was almost immediately followed by a Soviet Union disinformation campaign. On the very day of the assassination the Soviet bloc put out and encouraged reports that the United States was an accomplice in this crime; these reports were immediately picked up by the press of other countries, and sometimes even given credence. More reputable newspapers and television and radio media simply reported the stories, but challenged their authenticity.

It was the Radio Moscow World Service in English which first asserted that the persons responsible for the killing of Mrs Gandhi 'received their ideological inspiration' from the CIA and linked that organization with the deaths of Lumumba, Allende, Bandaranaike and Torrijos as well. All these deaths, alleged Radio Moscow, were intended to 'destabilize the situation in one or another foreign state, compromise the leadership not approved of in Washington, and clear the way for reactionaries.'

Subsequently an article by S. Bulantsec in *Moskovskaya Pravda* went even further and positively accused the CIA of responsibility for the murder, charging that 'there can be no doubt that Washington is prepared to pay any price to remove the Indian National Congress, whose leader was Indira Gandhi, from the country's helm' and characterized US policy towards developing countries as 'state terrorism'. Such items were taken up in the press of the Western world as well, especially in the leftish newspapers. In India the same charges were made in *The Patriot* and the Communist Party's Hindu daily, *Janayug*, which contended that the 'CIA and CIA-organized extremist forces' were behind the killing of Mrs Gandhi. In Greece the Communist Party newspaper, *Rizospastis,* charged the CIA with responsibility for the killing of Mrs Gandhi as well as for alleged intended assassinations of Castro, Gaddafi and de Gaulle. The paper asserted that 'the whole world and Washington knew that India is being pushed to dismemberment with the maniacal incitement of the Sikhs . . . The charitable secret agency of the USA . . . is not ashamed to say openly that whoever gets in its way is going to get it.'

However, not only the Soviet Union launched a disinformation campaign on the killing of Mrs Gandhi. One even more astonishing story appeared in the ostensibly right-wing (some would say right-upside-down) periodical, *Executive Intelligence Review*, founded by Lyndon LaRouche, a candidate for the Democratic nomination for the presidency of the USA in 1980. Immediately after the death of Mrs Gandhi LaRouche issued a statement charging that 'certain factions in British Intelligence killed Mrs Gandhi, as a favour to Moscow.'

This was no momentary aberration of Lyndon LaRouche's, for in February 1985 the *Executive Intelligence Review* published an even more fantastic story on the whole affair. This totally unsubstantiated article was by one G. Allen Douglas, and entitled 'Lord Bethell, the Queen of England and the assassination of Mrs Gandhi.' [18]

The article alleged that 'a continuing investigation by *EIR* has uncovered much more information on the precise British intelligence factions involved. The tracks of the assassins lead to the steps of the Royal Household through the person of Lord Bethell, a lord-in-waiting to the Queen in 1970-71 and a key figure in the Sikh-supporting Afghan-rebel apparatus in the United Kingdom.'

No evidence whatsoever was offered in support of this highly imaginative theory which is almost totally without any substantiation. Lord Bethell has been one of the most active supporters of persecuted dissidents in Russia and elsewhere, as well as being a Conservative European MP. Instead of evidence unconnected and irrelevant sentences abound: that the chief Sikh spokesman, Jagit Singh Chauhan, 'has enjoyed the full protection of the British government since taking residence in

London'; and 'the Afghan rebel groups for whom Bethell is the chief spokesman, Radio Free Kabul, and the Committee for a Free Afghanistan, are a key control point of day-to-day Sikh terrorist activity'; and the 'pro-Soviet British actor Peter Ustinov and his camera crew were the only scheduled appointment of Mrs Gandhi the day of her assassination.'[19]

But finding plots behind the killing of Mrs Gandhi is a subject upon which disinformation is still pouring out. In January 1986 the chief defence lawyer in the Indira Gandhi murder trial alleged that her son, Rajiv Gandhi, could have killed his mother. But Pran Nath Lekhi, representing the defendant, Satwant Singh, did not give any details to back his charges.[20]

The death sentences passed on three Sikhs for Mrs Gandhi's killing by a New Delhi court in January 1986 put an end to all these canards. But even the court hearings revealed another fanciful episode, though this time a true one. On the day Mrs Gandhi was gunned down by her own guards in October 1984, a falcon flew into her garden. The falcon is for Sikhs a good luck omen and two of the murderers saw it as a divine order to kill her.

Within the past year there have been indications that the KGB is just as likely to involve minor politicians as cabinet ministers and presidents in its disinformation tactics. Early in 1986 there came to light an example of a crude forgery based on a genuine letter bearing the signature of Sir Frederic Bennett, the Conservative MP for Torbay. It was photostatted with a bogus text substituted between the House of Commons letterhead and Sir Frederic's genuine signature. This was used as a cover note to introduce a second, much more skilful forgery of a letter supposed to be from a US general to the American Defense Secretary, Caspar Weinberger, to a Greek-Cypriot newspaper.

The letter was phrased to give the impression that the United States was planning to turn the Turkish sector of Cyprus into a major base for Middle East operations, as well as for the evacuation of US personnel from Europe in the event of a nuclear war. It also indicated that nuclear weapons would be used in support of the US strategic scheme.

The forgery was revealed when the Greek-Cypriot daily newspaper printed a report on its front page.[21] It was then that both Sir Frederic and the Americans concerned demanded a correction. The British Foreign Office confirmed that the letters were originated by the KGB with the object of stirring up enmity between the Greek and Turkish communities in Cyprus as well as misrepresenting American policy. Yet there has been no indication of any forthright and official reproach to Moscow, nor of any reprisal.

Mr Sazzas Iacoveves, editor of the Greek-Cypriot newspaper, eventually stated: 'I now accept that it is proven that these letters were forged and the story is false.'[22]

10

A WORLD OF FANTASY

In the last chapter some examples were given of what might be called the fantasy aspect of disinformation. This is a peculiar phenomenon in that it involves not only the creators of such work, but the actors who live it out (or live it up) and those of the public who like nothing better than to be lured into a world in which they can indulged themselves in wild dreams and absurd prejudices. In short, fantasy disinformation really needs a team of highly skilled psychiatrists to sort it all out and to bring its practitioners back to normality. Regrettably only sheer hard, campaigning work can destroy it, and even then the chances are loaded against the crusaders.

Fantasy disinformation can work two ways to the disadvantage of a nation subjected to it. It can cause paranoid reactions by making some intelligence services rise to the bait and see villains where they do not exist. Or it can simply lull them into complacency and apathy and ultimately into disbelief of all they are told. Admiral Stansfield Turner, a former CIA chief, has summed up the latter category when he declares: 'It became convinced that the paranoia of the CIA's counter-intelligence under Angleton's management had indeed gone too far . . . Most books and articles purporting to describe Soviet disinformation operations fall back on two kinds of substantiation. The first is guilt by association. That is usually association with an organization the author assumes is anti-American, though

it may be just that the organization's views differ from his . . .
We should not allow the success of Soviet disinformation to
make us paranoid. That is not to say we do not face real
problems . . . Rather it is to warn how difficult it is to measure
the amount of disinformation to which we are subjected and the
damage it does, and to note that we face the same kind of risk in
basing sweeping conclusions on suspicion and innuendo as we
do in uncovering spies.'[1]

Now these comments may seem admirably restrained and
commonsensical, but they miss the whole point of how disinformation techniques not only improve, but will continue to
improve unless we are all very vigilant. It is rather like the
response of many chief constables in Britain to rising crime
figures: 'Of course, we should like to do better, but we need the
cooperation of the public.' But they are paid to their job with or
without the cooperation of the public, and if they want cooperation, they should go out and seek it – on the streets,
instead of keeping large numbers of police in desk jobs, often
just goggle-eyed in front of computers which as often as not
prove too difficult for them to absorb. They, not the public, are
responsible for putting down crime, especially as any member of
the public who takes his own stand against a would-be criminal
is liable to be prosecuted for defending himself. Similarly, it is
for the intelligence services to defeat disinformation campaigns.

As in crime, so in espionage. Fortunately the Stansfield
Turner era has ended and one has every reason to hope for more
results from today's CIA after several years of indeterminate
nonsense. The point that Turner missed, and one which showed
him singularly lacking in perceptive qualities, is that he failed to
see how Soviet propaganda can sometimes appear in media
devoted to right-wing causes. Not to grasp this essential fact is
to condemn one's own capability of running an intelligence
agency.

Why should Soviet disinformers be eager to exploit right-
wing organizations and how do they do this? The answer is
quite simple: they play on the prejudices of the right-wingers
and, by doing so, they push their most forthright critics in the
wrong direction in quest of evidence against the USSR. This
tactic has played off again and again. Curiously, the right-wing
seem never to have made any plans for using the same technique
against the left-wing.

Naturally, very few people would be taken in by vicious attacks from left-wing organizations or media on established leaders of the right. But if such attacks come from media of their own persuasion, the temptation is to accept them as the truth. This is what has frequently happened in the past thirty years. Already we have seen how cleverly the Russians have exploited racialist issues. In Africa, with great success, in the Far East with much less success, they have used racialist tactics to damn Americans and Europeans alike. This has been easy among those of a left-wing persuasion and it has resulted in the general acceptance of that non-word 'racist'. But equally, and much more cleverly, this technique has been used to damn the Jews all over the world and viciously portray them as saboteurs of the Western way of life with a view to world domination. Supposedly a highly secret Jewish society was formed a hundred years ago with this aim in mind. It is a nonsense, not least because the Jews are essentially an intensely individualistic people, but nevertheless it finds a sympathetic ear among many who are otherwise opposed to Soviet tactics.

The campaign launched by Lyndon H. LaRouche, Junior, a sixty-year-old American who lives in a shotgun-guarded apartment in New York, is imbued with fantasy. He not only as mentioned earlier runs the *Executive Intelligence Review*, published from Washington, but is also linked to the European Workers Party, chaired by his German wife, Helga Zepp-LaRouche. These varying interests add up to a quite astonishing mish-mash of extreme right-wing and mild left-wing politics. To detect which element dominates is very difficult indeed. The Anti-Defamation League of B'Nai B'rith, the international authority on Jewish affairs, summed up in a 1978 report the various allegations made by LaRouche in his publications and otherwise as 'a conspiracy fantasia in which Jews and Zionists are aligned with the British monarchy, the British nobility and upper classes, the British Secret Intelligence Service, various cults and secret societies.'[2]

Nonetheless, it must be admitted that the LaRouche magazines and newspaper are professionally produced, well-written and immaculately designed. At first glance the articles give the impression of a well-researched, logical approach to the subjects covered. The problem is that they sometimes start off from a set of fantasy premises. Even B'Nai B'rith conceded that

161

the *Executive Intelligence Review* 'is read by policy-makers around the world, and not least in the United States where more than half the members of the House of Representatives and about half the Senate read it regularly.' The B'nai B'rith report goes on to say that ' . . . in the political fantasyland the LaRouchites have created, the Jews themselves are depicted as actually instigating anti-Semitism to serve the purposes of the British Crown, the British Secret Intelligence Service and other arms of the fancied London-based conspiracy whose tentacles reach round the world.'[3]

The fantasy world created by the LaRouchites is one in which Britain's United Grand Lodge of Freemasons is accused of the ritual murder of Roberto Calvi, the Italian banker found hanged under Blackfriars Bridge in London in June 1982, linking the British Royal family with masonic plots and the illegal Italian P 2 Lodge and its Grand Master, Licio Gelli, and even alleging that the Freemasons have recycled narcotics-trafficking money and funds for terrorism in Britain.

The LaRouche hate campaign has been launched against such a diverse assortment of people as Britain's Prime Minister, Margaret Thatcher, Edward Heath, Henry Kissinger, the Duke of Kent, the Duke of Gloucester, Sir Keith Joseph, Lord Bethell, Lord Chalfont, Lord Caccia, and various Jewish banks and businesses. LaRouche himself has twice run for the US Presidency without getting remotely near his objective and was in the past a Marxist, a conscientious objector and a member of the Socialist Workers' Party. He also claims to be an economist, having devised the LaRouche Riemann Economic Model, and an authority on international terrorism. His anti-British sentiments are said to derive from the fact that his second wife left him for an Englishman, but his anti-Zionist posture seems to have developed out of a degree of political opportunism. In the 1976-77 period when LaRouche was seriously considering entering the ring as a Presidential candidate he linked up with a right-wing group known as the Liberty Lobby. *Spotlight*, the Lobby's magazine, surprisingly described LaRouche's cult, the National Democratic Policy Committee, as 'the only honest Marxist group in the United States', but it also criticized LaRouche for failing to attack Zionism. It was after this that the anti-Zionist campaign started.[4]

Anything as mixed up as this muddled and often contradictory approach to international affairs would, generally speaking, condemn itself by its own illusions. But, alas, fantasies are kept alive in the Western world and perhaps nowhere do they survive and actually flourish so much as in the United States with its polyglot population. Here such wild indulgence is assisted by the relative laxity of the laws of libel. In the United Kingdom, where libel laws go to the other extreme and lend themselves to the forces of repression, it is noticeable that LaRouche and his cult have no office, nor organization.

One of the most vicious disinformation campaigns launched against any individual in the past twelve years has been that against Henry Kissinger, the former US Secretary of State. It has been waged from several quarters, a factor which has made it more difficult to track down and to analyse, and is still being relentlessly pursued in some places. I first came upon this disinformation campaign in the late 1960s when I was researching my *History of the Chinese Secret Service.* [5] The Chinese intelligence service had compiled a detailed dossier on Dr Kissinger, mindful of the fact that in 1968 he had been appointed Assistant to the President of the United States for National Security Affairs. Reports from agents in the USA, in Europe, and particularly through Chinese agents who had links with the Israeli secret service, convinced the powers-that-be in Peking that Kissinger was their man.

Suddenly the Chinese discovered that a series of smears on Kissinger had been built up by the KGB and cleverly planted in right-wing organizations in the USA and elsewhere. Where the Chinese scored initially was by being able to tip off the USA that the KGB had concocted forged documentation to the effect that the American Secretary of State, Dr Kissinger, was, under the codename of 'Bor', a member of a secret section of Soviet intelligence. The KGB believed that, if they could destroy Kissinger, they could destroy the Sino-American accord which had been achieved under the Secretary of State.

But, according to my information, the KGB campaign against Kissinger, sustained by some enemies of Kissinger within the CIA for quite a time, had been totally sabotaged by the Chinese whose detailed evidence on this affair finally baulked the Russians. Through their Swiss network the Chinese picked up – as early as 1964 – evidence that the KGB was passing on to the CIA and others, through a double-agent, disinformation that Kissinger, as 'Bor', had been an agent of the ODRA, a section of Soviet intelligence controlled from Poland. With their usual painstaking efforts the Chinese checked and double-checked and finally obtained through another double-agent the full details of the KGB smear on Kissinger. All this was passed to the Americans.

There was a curious postscript to this research of mine. In a newsletter called *The Confidential Intelligence Report*, a privately circulated American publication, the story about Kissinger being a Soviet agent named 'Bor' was repeated in rather more detail in 1974. It alleged that the 'recruitment of Henry Kissinger by Soviet intelligence reportedly goes back to World War II . . . Under the code name of "Bor" and described as an agent of ODRA was US Sergeant (and later Captain) Kissinger, counter-intelligence interrogator of the US Army.'[6]

Then in May 1978 Colonel Michal Goleniewski, the Polish intelligence officer who defected to the United States, took up the Kissinger theme. Goleniewski, having settled in the United States, suddenly announced that he was none other than Aleksei Nicholaevich Romanoff, son of the murdered Czar Nicholas of Russia, and from then on he held court in New York, claiming the title of His Royal Highness the Tsarevich and refuting the usually accepted story that the Tsarevich was murdered by the Bolsheviks along with the other members of the Russian royal family. In his newsletter *Double Eagle*, Colonel Goleniewski had this to say: 'Another promoter of British-Soviet disinformation is a certain Richard Deacon . . . a former associate of the Deputy Director of Naval Intelligence, Ian Fleming . . . His works are disinformation vehicles, elaborated by Deacon due to classic method of half-truth and half-deception. His efforts are also serving the Soviet KGB interest, and for his endeavours to discredit myself at any price in his book, titled *The Russian Secret Service* . . . '[7]

Colonel Goleniewski then went on to quote from my book my references to the KGB campaign against Dr Kissinger, and asserted that the person unnamed to whom I referred as having planted the story about 'Bor' in the United States could be none other than himself. He added that 'there is little doubt that the whole purpose of including the fictitious item about the KGB trying to frame Henry Kissinger in the book about the Chinese

Secret Service is an effort to clear him after the charges against him had been made public. It is Deacon who is disseminating disinformation.'[8]

In backing up this assertion Colonel Goleniewski cites Frank A. Capell, the editor and publisher of *The Confidential Intelligence Report.*[9]

Nobody has attacked Dr Kissinger more virulently than Lyndon H. LaRouche, who, in advertisements for the books he and his associates publish from Benjamin Franklin House in New York, describes himself as 'the man Kissinger hates the most'. In *Who Should not be Who*, another book from his publishing house, LaRouche 'documents the activities of forty-seven administration officials and private citizens who must be purged from the Reagan administration to thwart their assault on the SDI, including foreign policy adviser Henry Kissinger.'[10] Note what an incredible mixture much of LaRouche's material is, seeming to support SDI (anti-Soviet) and attacking Kissinger (in effect pro-Soviet in that it creates confusion around a sound and trusted adviser).

When Venezuelan newspapers accused LaRouche of disinformation, he hit back by asking: 'Was it "disinformation" when in August 1983 *Executive Intelligence Review* alone revealed that at a secret meeting in Vail, Colorado, Kissinger and Rockefeller had adopted a policy to force Ibero-America to pay its foreign debt with its national patrimony?' In the same article he inquired whether it was disinformation 'when in 1982 *EIR* stood alone in the United States in support of Argentina in the Malvinas War?'[11]

A week later in another attack on Kissinger in *EIR* by M.T. Upharsin, there was also an assault on the character of the highly respected General Vernon Walters, of the US Army, outrageously suggesting that Walters was 'the "fixer" for corrupt military and political factions in Brazil and Argentina . . . Walters was an inside man in the 1964 coup in Brazil and in helping design brutal austerity policies in ensuing years. During Argentina's Malvinas War with Great Britain, Walters worked with Argentine friends to sabotage the anti-British fight from the inside while helping win the United States to support of the British side.'[12]

In this kind of a fantasy world of disinformation it is often impossible to estimate, or even to guess at, the reasons behind the truly bizarre allegations which are propounded. How does the *Executive Intelligence Review* manage to present an extreme right-wing attitude on the one hand and at the same time lend itself to wild stories and disinformation that can only damage the unity of the Western world and actually promote the kind of propaganda in which the KGB would delight? Where does Colonel Goleniewski really stand in the conflict between the Western and Soviet blocs? Most defectors from the Soviet Union settle down anonymously under an assumed name in the country to which they flee: their aim is always to hide away from the long arm of the KGB, which has been known to track down defectors and kill them. Yet Colonel Goleniewski, despite the fact that he has been publicly credited with having delivered valuable intelligence to the CIA, ignored such precautions and openly describes himself as 'His Imperial Highness Aleksei Nicholaevich Romanoff, the heir to the All-Russian Imperial Throne, Tsarevich and Grand Duke of Russia, and Head of the Russian Imperial House.' When the *New York Daily Mirror* announced the exclusive publication of his reminiscences in 1971, it stated that 'Herman E. Kimsey, former Chief of Research and Analysis of the Headquarters of the US Central Intelligence Agency, in an affidavit signed 3 June 1965, said, "I am convinced, and I continue to be convinced, that the person referred to as Colonel Goleniewski is in fact the Tsarevich . . . son of Emperor Nicholai II of Russia." '[13]

In his affidavit Mr Kimsey stated that as a result of tests he was completely satisfied as to the identification. He based this on fingerprint comparison to those of the Tsarevich taken during his visit to London in 1909 and later from other sources in possession of the British government. His report also referred to comparisons with birth and medical records and later to 'dental chart records on file with the late Dr Kostrycki of Paris, formerly dentist of the imperial family; handwriting tests and recognition and confrontation with childhood friends and relatives.'[14]

What really is the truth behind the story of Colonel Goleniewski? Ultimately it may turn out to be an example of bizarre disinformation on all sides, both Russian and American. Meanwhile one has to consider the possibility that there is not just one Colonel Goleniewski, but at least two and possibly three.

There have been at least four people who have claimed to be members of the Russian Royal Family and who have somehow survived the massacre at Ekaterinberg by the Bolsheviks. None of these has established proof of any such claim. The four are Anna Anderson, a man who used the name of Alexis Gagarin, Eugenie Smith and Colonel Goleniewski. Anna Anderson arrived in the USA about 1922 and some years afterwards insisted that she was the Tsar Nicholas's daughter, the Grand Duchess Anastasia. Some time after he arrived in America Goleniewski met Mrs Eugene Smith and claimed to recognize her as Anastasia.

In August 1963, the US Senate listened to Senator Olin D. Johnston recording a lengthy list of private bills dealing with immigration cases. One was HR 5507, 'an act of relief of Michal Goleniewski'. It was quietly passed at the specific request of the CIA. Its purpose was to make Goleniewski a citizen of the United States. He had previously held the rank of colonel in the Polish intelligence service as chief of Section 6. Prior to his defection he had secretly fed tit-bits of information to the Americans, one of which led to the discovery that at least fifteen employees of the American Embassy in Warsaw had compromised themselves with women who were under the control of the Polish intelligence service. On 12 January 1961 Goleniewski was brought to America under the protection of the CIA. Unlike the Russian Yuri Nosenko, he did not publicly 'surface' at first, nor was his presence admitted. But he provided a considerable quantity of what seemed to be invaluable intelligence, especially concerning the presence of Soviet 'moles' inside various Western intelligence services, including the British SIS and the CIA.

'I'm not at all convinced that Goleniewski did as much in unmasking various double agents as he claimed,' an officer who made a report on him to the FBI told me. 'In my report to the Bureau [FBI] I was able to provide evidence that the British, Swedes and Germans already had all of the agents Goleniewski claimed to have unmasked under investigation. My own conclusion was that he fingered only those KGB agents who were already lost or in imminent danger of being lost.'[15]

In 1964 Goleniewski surfaced and began openly to allege that

Moscow had placed active 'cells' within the CIA and the State Department. 'Last week the CIA and the White House probably wished devoutly that Mr Goleniewski was anywhere but in this country,' wrote David Wise, the Washington Bureau chief in the New York *Herald-Tribune*. 'The onetime prize defector, according to published reports, has gone off like a Roman candle charging that the CIA and other American agencies were infiltrated by the KGB.'[16]

Officially, the picture which was given to American pressmen was that, while Goleniewski had provided valuable intelligence, the things he was now saying were simply not accurate. Then, two years later, the colonel announced that he was the Tsarevich and set himself up as such in Long Island, New York. On 27 August 1966 the UP press agency reported from Moscow that the Soviet newspaper, *Komsomolskaya Pravda*, had charged the CIA with 'creating' a pretender to the throne of the Romanoffs: 'this self-appointed man is nothing less than a sinister creation of American intelligence,' adding that the reason for Goleniewski's claims was that alleged Romanoff funds amounting to 400 million dollars deposited in American banks would be his, if the courts recognized him as the heir of Tsar Nicholas.

Now on the British side there are some who say that Goleniewski's information led to the arrests of Harry Houghton, the Admiralty spy, and George Blake, the MI 6 man. This, however, is quite likely to be an attempt to hide the person or persons who really provided such vital evidence. Much more interestingly, Goleniewski is said to have been originally a KGB mole placed inside Polish intelligence, which was how he knew so much about Russian plans.

What especially aroused my interest in this complicated story was information from another Polish defector that 'Goleniewski is not only *not* the Tsarevich, but not even the real Colonel Goleniewski. As to why the CIA or someone in the State Department has not stated openly once and for all who Goleniewski really is, I can only guess that the man in New York who claims to be the Polish colonel is not what he appears to be.

'It is a tangled story, but look at the facts. The norm for a genuine and valuable defector is for him to change his identity in a new country and to remain hidden away from KGB agents who would be anxious to track him down – either to lure him back to Moscow or Warsaw, or to kill him. Astonishingly, Goleniewski makes it quite clear to one and all who he is and where he is living. It doesn't make sense unless one concludes that he has ceased to be of any importance either to the Americans or the Russians, except that his claim to be a Romanoff enables the Russians to poke fun at the CIA.'[17]

However, the story turns out to be even more bizarre than this, according to a deposition made by another Pole whose real identity must be guarded under the codename of GRODZISK. I cannot confirm the absolute authenticity of GRODZISK's statement, but it tallies with information from other sources on both sides of the Atlantic. GRODZISK worked in the Polish intelligence service prior to his defecting and he knew Goleniewski well. 'I knew that he had made a number of trips to West Germany where he had established contact with members of the Free Poland movement and the Americans. In November 1960, he was planning another visit to West Germany when two of his fellow officers in Warsaw insisted that he must return at once to Moscow before making his trip to West Germany. Goleniewski obeyed their instructions, went to Moscow and never returned.

'It was another "Goleniewski" altogether who took a plane to East Berlin that very night – another officer of the Polish intelligence masquerading as Goleniewski. It was he who defected to the Americans and claimed that he was Aleksei Nicholaevich Romanoff, Tsarevich of Russia. He, with his girl-friend, were taken by the CIA to Frankfurt and after debriefing brought to the United States.'[18]

GRODZISK then makes the claim that Eugenie Smith (who says she is the Grand Duchess Anastasia) was taken to meet Goleniewski No. 2 and that she immediately claimed to recognize him as her brother. From another source I have learned that this mutual recognition and friendship did not last very long.

But the most sensational of GRODZISK's statements is that in which he insists that there is a third Colonel Goleniewski. This substitution was made in Frankfurt when Goleniewski No. 2 arrived; Goleniewski No. 3 was a nominee of the CIA. 'From then on Goleniewski No. 3 had to play the CIA's game and follow their instructions that he should act as Goleniewski No. 2 would have done, thus deceiving the Russians. I cannot say for certain what happened to Goleniewski No. 2, or No. 1 for that matter. But No. 1 is almost certainly dead. Goleniewski No. 3 was wanted as a witness before the Senate Intelligence Committee hearings, but when he was on his way to Washington he was taken off the train at Baltimore and he never has testified before any of the committees who wanted to question him.'[19]

While I should risk laying myself open to a charge of disinformation if I supported GRODZISK's story one hundred per cent, I must admit that a large part of his statement makes sense. If it is true, then all one can say is that by now the Russians would almost certainly have learned or guessed that Goleniewski No. 3 is not their 'No. 2.' Which would render him no longer useful either to the Americans or the Russians.

Just one final quotation from Goleniewski's article on 'The Deadly Weapon of the Secret World: Disinformation': 'Various forms of deception based on disinformation are practised by the Eastern and Western Intelligence Agencies, and especially on the part of the key enemies of this country [the United States]: the Soviet KGB, *the British SIS* and the Red Chinese Secret Service.'[20] The italics are mine!

I cannot bring myself to believe that any of us are even near to learning the whole truth about Colonel Goleniewski, or the stories surrounding him. To end on another bizarre note, it is perhaps worth comment that, in introducing his newsletter, *Double Eagle*, the editor wrote: 'An incisive perspective on history, current events and intelligence matters by the son of the last reigning Emperor and Tsar of All the Russias . . . dedicated to the national independence and security of the United States and the survival of Christian civilization . . . *Double Eagle* is . . . the only self-edited publication issued under the auspices of HIH the Heir to the All-Russian Imperial Throne, Tsarevich and Grand Duke Aleksei Nicholaevich Romanoff of Russia, the August Ataman and Head of the Russian Imperial House of Romanoff, also known under the cover identity of Colonel Michal M. Goleniewski, renowned for his support for the national security of the United States and its Western allies.'[21]

11

PSYCHO-POLITICS:
AN EASTERN OR
A WESTERN INVENTION?

I have in my possession a printed booklet, edited by one Charles
Stickley, which was purchased at the Tottenham Court Road
offices of the Scientology Organization. It has also been sold
together with another tract called *Brain-Washing* by the
Victorian League of Rights of Melbourne, Australia.

The most fascinating item in the first pamphlet is a verbatim
account of what is supposedly an address by the late Lavrenti
Beria, head of the dreaded NKVD, which he is alleged to have
given to 'American students at the Lenin University'. It is hard
to believe that Beria ever gave such an address, but here is what
he is claimed to have said:

'American students at the Lenin University, I welcome your
attendance at these classes on psycho-politics. Psycho-politics is
an important if less known division of geo-politics. It is less
known because it must necessarily deal with highly educated
personnel, the very top strata of "mental healing". By psycho-
politics our chief goals are effectively carried forward. To
produce a maximum of chaos in the culture of the enemy is our
first most important step. Our fruits are grown in chaos,

distrust, economic depression and scientific turmoil. At least a weary populace can seek peace only in our offered Communist State, at last only Communism can resolve the problems of the masses.'

The address went on to assert that 'a psycho-politician must work hard to produce the maximum chaos in the fields of "mental healing" . . . until the entire field of mental science is entirely dominated by Communist principles and desires.' To achieve these goals the psycho-politician 'must crush every homegrown variety of mental healing in America. Actual teachings of Freud, James, Eddy and others amongst your misguided people must be swept away . . . You must work until every teacher of psychology unknowingly or knowingly teaches only Communist doctrine under the guide of "psychology". You must labour until every doctor and psychiatrist is either a psycho-politician or an unwitting assistant to our aims.'

There was worse to come: 'You must achieve such disrepute for the state of insanity and such authority over its pronounce-ment that not one statesman so labelled could again be given credence by his people. You must work until suicide arising from mental imbalance is common and calls forth no general investigation or remark. With the institutions for the insane you have in your country prisons which can hold a million persons and can hold them without civil rights or any hope of freedom. And upon these people can be practised shock and surgery so that never again will they draw a sane breath . . . Psycho-politics is a solemn charge. With it you can erase our enemies as insects. You can cripple the efficiency of leaders by striking insanity into their families through the use of drugs. You can wipe them away by testimony as to their insanity. You can change their loyalties by psycho-politics.'

The sales assistant who sold this book denied that it was published by the Church of Scientology, but he was unable to tell me where and when it was published. The rest of the book is devoted to the history and definition of psycho-politics and how this is put into practice – e.g. 'in order to be conquered, a nation must be degraded, either by acts of war, by being overrun, by being forced into humiliating treaties of peace, or by the treatment of her populace under the armies of the conqueror . . . Defamation is the best and foremost weapon of psycho-politics . . . continual and constant degradation of national leaders, national institutions . . . must be systematically carried out, but this is the chief function of Communist Party members, in general, not the psycho-politician.'

Now the literary and ideological style of this so-called speech by Beria is completely unlike the Marxist-Leninist style of language, although the basic principles of the Pavlovian philosophy about animal and human organisms and their behaviour are more or less correctly interpreted. Nonetheless it must be suspected as a deliberate piece of anti-communist propaganda, something no serious student of international politics would be likely to see as other than a piece of fiction. But the reasons for this disinformation may not be simply to damage the reputation of the Soviet Union and communist ideology, as it seems to be aimed at the student class generally and those who belong to the Church of Scientology in particular. This Church's hostility towards traditional psychiatry is well known and the publication seems to have a dual objective of denouncing both what is known as behaviourism in psychiatry and the Church's hostility to communism.

The extract from the book purporting to be Beria's speech is on Congressional record in the USA, a fact of which the Scientologists' leadership make much. What they do not add – and what may not be known to many people – is that any document can be 'read into the record' in the United States by any Congressman who says he wants it to be, if none of his colleagues object. Its mere appearance in the Congressional Records is therefore no indication by itself of the authenticity of the document, or the truth of its contents.

The Church of Scientology's quasi-philosophical creed, as proclaimed by the late L. Ron Hubbard, aims at achieving a dramatic improvement in the mental and physical well-being of its members. Hubbard, a native of Nebraska and a little-known science-fiction writer, was during his career a journalist, a singer and gold-miner, according to his own account. All that was changed when he founded scientology and produced his best-seller, *Dianetics: the Modern Science of Mental Health*, in 1950. He was once described by a British High Court judge as 'a charlatan and worse' during a child custody case. Mr Justice Latey, when ordering a scientologist father to hand over his two children to their mother, described practices of the sect as 'both immoral and socially obnoxious'.

It may well be that the springing up of a number of strange cults such as scientology spurred the USSR's Academy of Sciences to develop a special study group known as the Scientific Council on Foreign Ideological Trends. All anti-Soviet religious sects or pseudo-scientific organizations are carefully studied there. There is a similar body in the University of Debrecen in Hungary.

Brain-Washing: A synthesis of the Communist Textbook on Psychopolitics, a similar pamphlet to that just cited, also contained the so-called 'Beria address'. More importantly it launched a violent attack on orthodox American psychiatrists, sometimes hinting that they often played the communist game either deliberately or unconsciously. In one article Charles Stickley asserted that there were only two American groups which were entirely above suspicion in this respect: 'the Christian Scientists and the Dianeticists (Scientologists) . . . Knowing from my information sources that Dianetics and Christian Science and their people have experienced years of mauling and defamation at communist hands, I am submitting to these organizations this work. I wish to express my appreciation for their bold resistance to communism through the years.'[1]

The rest of the pamphlet claims to present what it calls 'a synthesis of the communist textbook on psycho-politics', suggesting that it is a summary of such a textbook published by the Russians. There is, of course, not the slightest evidence for this claim, and indeed the book is so blatantly outrageous in its assertions that it defeats its own objective, unless that objective is very different from what it seems to be.

Yet the authors or editors of this pamphlet should be aware of the dangers of their McCarthy-style exaggerations boomeranging against them, because, in referring to Soviet tactics, they state: 'One of the first and foremost missions of the psycho-politician is to make an attack upon communism and insanity synonymous. It should become the definition of insanity, of the paranoid variety, that "a paranoid believes he is being attacked by communists." Thus, at once the support of the individual so attacking communism will fall away and wither.'[2]

This is, of course, abundantly true; it is a tactic which the Soviets have often cleverly exploited and, doubtless, will continue to do so. It is a ploy which can cause many liberals to become fellow-travellers. What is surprising is that the Scientologists and some of their spokesmen do not realize how they themselves have fallen into this trap. But Hubbard succeeded in his mission by brain-washing his followers and disinforming his converts by a mixture of bogus psychotherapy and truth-twisting. Sometimes converts were won over by a subtle campaign of disinformation against their parents, brothers and sisters. Certainly this was the opinion of Mr Justice Latey in that High Court case when he condemned the Scientology movement as being 'corrupt, sinister and dangerous' and 'grimly reminiscent of the ranting and bullying of Hitler and his henchmen'.[3]

Perhaps the clue to all this lies in the advice which Hubbard gave to a gathering of authors shortly before he founded his new religion in 1952: 'Writing for a penny a word is ridiculous. If a man wants to make a million dollars, the best way would be to start a new religion.'[4]

Followers of the cult paid more than £200 an hour for courses in some cases; many spent thousands of pounds over the years simply to erase painful images which the Scientologists called 'engrams' in their own jargon. At one time Scientology was said to be earning £65 million a year with a membership of six million.

Just as Hubbard was fascinated by the psycho-political theories of the Russians, so were other philosophers in the 1950s encouraged to look for new philosophies and cults in violence and destruction. Hubbard's obsession with psycho-politics probably arose because he found it could be woven into his own creed. The leader of Scientology who denounced brain-washing in communist circles and 'mental healing' (his phrase) among psychiatrists unashamedly practised both himself, but for 'mental healing' one should read mind-bending.

Again and again in history the fallacy has been promulgated that indiscriminate violence is an essential stepping stone to revolution. This belief was subtly adapted and modified shortly after World War II by Jean-Paul Sartre, who sought to develop the theory that violence was a means of self-liberation. It was a theory (delusion might be a better word) which was propounded in his own writings and those of Franz Fanon, the fanatical black psychiatrist who proved to be the inspiration for Andreas Baader, the founder of the Baader-Meinhof organization.[5]

The doctrine of violence as a means to self-liberation gained ground very easily among various liberation-seeking organizations all over the world from the Justice Commandos of the Armenian Genocide to the IRA and the PLO. Various liberation organizations which in the past only used violence against specifically military targets suddenly indulged in indiscriminate violence – i.e. against the innocent as much as the so-called guilty. The aim was to make terrorism respectable, to define acts of terrorism as positive duties to a cause, and to argue that only when the innocent were made to suffer as well as the guilty would the great mass of the people be won over. In other words, the proponents of 'liberating terrorism' relied upon that adage held by many people in Europe that, if it came to a choice, it was 'better to be Red than dead'.

The real lesson of psycho-politics as the Soviets have exploited it is an adaptation of Lenin's precept: 'Communism will be constructed by its enemies.' This precept is put into practice in a variety of ways, not simply by infiltrating the enemy camp, but by manipulating the enemy into doing its propaganda for the ultimate cause of world communism. Para-academic bodies like Arbatov's American Institute, established in 1968 to manipulate perceptions in the Western world of Soviet Union policies and practices, have played their part. The Arbatov Institute promotes exchanges with various academic bodies in America, all of which are subjected to some deception.

However, if any Western or neutral nation sets up a study group on the subject of intelligence services and the techniques of espionage, it is immediately subjected to hostile reactions from Moscow, even though these may appear under other guises from Rome, Brussels or Paris. In the mid-1970s Professor Stefan Dedijer, a brother of the Yugoslav partisan leader, Vladimir Dedijer, started what claimed to be the world's first university course for studying the intelligence services at the oldest university in Sweden. A small independent institute attached to the Lund University's faculty of social sciences, it is officially known as the Research Policy Programme, but has been widely nicknamed the 'Lund Spy School'.

Professor Dedijer studied at Princeton University in the

USA, became a journalist on the American *Daily Worker* and subsequently was imprisoned for some months for his communist activities. He returned to his native Yugoslavia and during the war was a parachutist with the American forces. He freely admits that at various times he has worked for the Yugoslav, Soviet and US intelligence services. After World War II he was editor of the communist newspaper, *Borba*, and then director of Yugoslavia's atomic physics institute before quarrelling with the régime, emigrating and becoming a Swedish citizen.

Dedijer calls himself an 'élitist individualist egalitarian', describing his creed as 'the search for the holy Socialist grail. My first "scientific love", Marxism, turned out to be helpful as a personal religion under war conditions, disastrous nonsense as a "science of development" and hateful reactionary oppression when institutionalized as state religion in a dozen countries.'[6]

He believes that Sweden is 'the model country in Europe, once again the most civilized part of the world'.[7] Yugoslavia, in his opinion, is still 'blinded by the belief that democracy and deviation are capitalist luxuries', while the United States 'during the last two generations and still today is the most creative and innovative society in human history'.

Dedijer's institute deals with all kinds of intelligence operations – business, industrial and social as well as military and political. 'Two hundred countries have intelligence organizations,' he says, 'yet nobody studies them. These services know enormously more about each other than the public know about any of them. I think it is time that politicians and ordinary citizens learn how these things function.'[8]

Having sent announcements of his course to places all over the world, including academies of social science in China and the USSR as well as in the West, Dedijer insists that he treats his study of intelligence, 'just as if it was a traditional subject like chemistry or physics'. Not surprisingly Lund's institute has been smeared by an extensive disinformation campaign from the USSR, just as St Antony's College, Oxford, became known as a 'spy shop' by both KGB and CIA watchers.

St Antony's was founded as a centre for European studies in 1950 with money donated by Antonin Besse, a businessman from France with headquarters in Aden, who, during World War II, had had secret dealings with MI 6 and the SOE at the same time as he was trading with the enemy, Japan. Perhaps this was one reason for the attention which foreign intelligence services paid to the college in the 1950s-1970s. Ever since its formation the college tended to have ex-intelligence officers appointed to the staff. Throughout the fifties the Foreign Office sent people to write confidential papers on particular political subjects at St Antony's. George Blake was briefed there before being sent to the Middle East, and, more surprisingly, Mrs Ludmila Zhivkova, daughter of the Bulgarian President, was given a place there in 1970, with backing from the Foreign Office.

Dedijer has cleverly confounded his critics and enemies by being absolutely open about his aims and methods, whereas St Antony's in the 1960s probably suffered by being totally unforthcoming.

One of the earliest attacks on Dedijer's institute came from the pen of Dr Julius Mader in an East German magazine. He dubbed it the 'Agent Academy', implying that it was a training ground for secret agents, adding that the course had been 'offered to 21,000 undergraduate and post-graduate students as well as practitioners of the intelligence services . . . A number of these taking the course have been recruited from the circles of the notorious Anglo-American intelligence services. The numerous participants, for obvious reasons, have joined under the cover of the list of the matriculated of this part of the world [Sweden] . . . It is officially not yet clear in what proportion the centre of Sweden's secret service, the so-called Information Bureau, supports the internationally emerged course. There is no doubt of the usage of academic possibilities to qualify its agents in order to come out of its crisis of 1973. At that time the left-orientated magazine, *Volk in Bild*, exposed the Information Bureau's cooperation with the espionage services of the NATO countries and also that of the aggressor state of Israel.' [9]

Dr Mader added that the foundation of the faculty had 'received considerable support from the Swedish state and also from foreign intelligence agencies'. [10]

Among those who have lectured at Professor Dedijer's institute are Professor R.V. Jones, of Aberdeen University, one-time Director of Scientific Intelligence in the United Kingdom; Cy Sulzberger, of the *New York Times*, who spoke on 'Intelligence and the Press'; Colonel P.H.J. Borberg,

Defence Intelligence, Denmark; Anders Clason, a member of the Swedish Government 1974 Committee; Dhirendra Sharma, of the Centre for Studies in Science Policy, Nehru University, New Delhi; and L. Toure, Senegal and Lund, who spoke on 'National Intelligence Problems of Black Africa countries.'

Professor Dedijer believes that a study of intelligence techniques and new methods of disinformation could be greatly helped if this included an analysis not only of factual historical works in various countries, but in the sphere of spy novels, too. The earliest attempts at spy fiction behind the Iron Curtain have on the whole been somewhat mediocre, but this is not to deny that they may have contained effective disinformation and played a positive role in the intelligence game.

Meanwhile spy novels of the Western world, while becoming increasingly a mixture of fact and fiction, favour subtler ways of exploiting the enemy. Sometimes this is done at the request, or suggestion, of the intelligence services. This may range from cleverly devised disinformation to what one could call fiction forecasting possible enemy moves. If that sounds an obscure observation, perhaps the simplest example to give would be a recent novel by Frederick Forsyth, *The Fourth Protocol*. The setting for this book is the late 1980s with the fictional Kim Philby giving advice to the General Secretary of the Communist Party of the Soviet Union on how to manipulate a Labour victory at the British polls so that Neil Kinnock could be overthrown shortly afterwards and a hard-left Marxist-Leninist man put in as Prime Minister.

Philby writes: 'Since 1973 the absolutely vital NEC [of the Labour Party] has seldom been out of the hands of a hard-left majority and it has been through skilful use of this tool that the constitution of the party and its composition at the higher levels have been changed out of all recognition.'[11]

The essence of the plot of Forsyth's novel was a Soviet scheme to put Labour back into power in Britain by means of a mini-atomic explosion. A basic atomic bomb was to be constructed, small enough to fit into a suitcase and simple enough to be assembled from a dozen or so prefabricated components. Plan Aurora was to infiltrate such a bomb into the United Kingdom and to cause enough damage to appear like a nuclear accident close to a US air force base in East Anglia. The idea was to 'panic the ten per cent floating vote into unilateralism and support at the polls the only party pledged to uni-lateralism, the Labour Party.'[12]

Damage would be limited to the air base itself, which would be vaporized, part of a forest, a village, the foreshore and a bird sanctuary – enough to cause a wave of resentment against America and the British government of the day.

To put such an idea into fiction would, of course, help to destroy the effectiveness of any such plot which the Russians might put into operation in the future. If they had such a plot in mind, this might well be a means of warning them that news of it had leaked and that counter-measures were being prepared. It might cause them to scrap their project. But if such a scheme should be put into operation, the fact that the story had already been told in fiction might destroy the desired psychological effect on the floating voters.

Psychological warfare, or psycho-politics, can be waged as easily in fiction as in fact – sometimes more effectively and cheaply.

Perhaps the worst example of truth-twisting in psycho-politics today is to be found among left-wingers everywhere who suppress any suggestion or evidence that there are vital links between genetics, intelligence and race. Pressure has repeatedly been put upon scientists who wish to investigate these links more thoroughly. Often this pressure comes directly from bureau-cratic organizations, but it is also to be found in the whole of the race relations industry. Few realize how freedom of speech in many universities, Western and Eastern alike, is savagely denied to those who wish to pursue researches into the whole question of genetics. 'Left-wingers in all these countries [he is referring to the Western world] have taken care to deny these freedoms to those who do not share their unsupported belief in the equality of intellectual endowment, whether between people within a given country, or between different races,' declared Professor Hans Eysenck, of the London Institute of Psychiatry.'[13]

Professor Eysenck went on to assert that 'by every means within their power – breaking up scientific meetings or lectures, beating up their opponents, boycotting their public appear-ances, threatening arson and violence to booksellers who dare to stock books of which they disapprove – these enemies of freedom have enforced a virtual embargo on factual discussion in these fields.'

Those are serious allegations, though they may be somewhat exaggerated. The psycho-politics of the Left dislikes élitism or any suggestion of the possibility that one collection of human beings could be superior to most others. The reason is, of course, quite easy to define: in Marxist-Leninism the genetic factor would easily become something beyond the control of the psycho-politicians. Marxist-Leninism depends upon the acceptance of one view only: that intelligence can be controlled solely by a person's environment. The fact that people may inherit a higher or lower basic intelligence through their parents is totally ignored. It is also a doctrine which is absolutely forbidden.

The cynical thinking behind such taboos requires controlling or 'improving' people through their environment, which not only means providing them with reasonable living conditions, ample food and housing, but keeping them in conditions of apathy and ignorance as to how they might lead freer or better lives.

The British National Union of Students actually laid down a rule that students should not be given talks or lessons by Professor Eysenck. When the professor was asked to give a talk to the Statistical Society at Leeds University on the topic of 'Statistical and experimental methods of model construction in the social science', the meeting was broken up by a small group of agitators. Similar treatment was meted out to Dr W. Schlegel, another genetical researcher, when he tried to address students at Hamburg University.

Professor Eysenck also recalls a case of frustration in the United States, when some friends of his applied to a government grant-giving agency for funds to support an investigation into the relation between race and intelligence. 'They were told that while the proposal was scientifically acceptable, it was "too hot to handle politically". Would they agree to carry out their work in Hawaii instead of the mainland United States? They reframed their proposal; it was accepted, but with a proviso that they must not publish the intelligence test scores.' [14]

UFOLOGY
AND THE PARANORMAL

Research into the paranormal has become increasingly respectable even in the scientific world over the past forty years. While this is welcomed by most open-minded and truth-seeking people, it nevertheless has been accompanied by a disturbing increase in disinformation on the subject.

Probably this has been most marked concerning the subject of unidentified flying objects, or to give it an up-to-date name, ufology. I notice that in *Pears Cyclopaedia*, an admirably accurate and highly reputable reference book since 1897, the entry for 'Flying Saucers' is listed in its section on 'Ideas and Beliefs'.[1] It takes its place alongside Feedback Cult, Fascism, Feudalism, Freemasonry and Fundamentalism, not without good reason, for in some circles the very conception of UFOs has been elevated to a semi-religious belief. 'To an increasing number of people, many of whom feel a desperate need for spiritual guidance . . . Western religions seem unsatisfactory . . . Many therefore turn to cults and splinter groups which use ideas and terminology which to them seem more at home in the twentieth century than those that sprang to life thousands of years ago. To members of the Aetherius Society, for example, the idea that Jesus Christ lives on Venus and rides around in a flying saucer is neither blasphemous nor ludicrous,' states the *Cyclopaedia*. [2]

This dangerous trend had led indirectly to new pseudo-religious cults, including Scientology, discussed in an earlier chapter. Since World War II there have been literally hundreds of thousands of reports of people seeing unidentified flying objects and even, in many cases, claiming to have had contact with alien people inside them. The unhealthy hysteria in some circles has led, one suspects, to deliberate disinformation.

If the cult of ufology could be written off as entirely the creation of unstable or masquerading individuals in various parts of the world, it would present no difficulty, and indeed, would not be worth a chapter in this book. What worries many sane, highly educated and dedicated people in all parts of the world, Western and Eastern, is that amidst all the lies, inventions and folk tales of flying saucers some reports are sufficiently factual that they require careful study by some national defence ministries. This applies to the United States and the Soviet Union, some other Eastern European countries, and France, though little appears to have been done to get at the truth in the United Kingdom.

Unfortunately the result of official inquiries and research into such reports has failed to counter any disinformation tactics. If anything, the official attitude everywhere has left everybody even more mystified. If these ufological reports are the result of demented people seeing visions, or simply downright lies to gain notoriety, then officialdom should be able to dispose of them once and for all. But on the contrary, officialdom tends to be increasingly secretive on the whole subject. Indeed, they treat the whole affair as 'an official secret'.

Here are some statements on UFOs which will justify my allegations:

In a top secret Canadian government memorandum of 21 November 1950, it was stated that; 'The matter [UFOs] is the most highly classified subject in the United States Government, rating higher even than the H-bomb.'

Vice-Admiral Hillenkoetter, a former CIA executive, stated in 1960 that: 'It is time for the truth to be brought out . . . Behind the scenes high-ranking Air Force officers are soberly concerned about the UFOs. But through official secrecy and ridicule many citizens are led to believe that unknown flying objects are nonsense.'

Speaking on television to a Russian audience, Dr Felix Zigel, Moscow Aviation Institute, declared that 'unidentified flying objects are a very serious subject which we must study fully. We appeal to all viewers to send us details of any observations of strange flying craft seen over the territories of the Soviet Union. This is a serious challenge to science, and we need the help of all Soviet citizens.'[3]

Even the former President James Carter, during his election campaign in November 1976, vowed: 'If I become President, I'll make every piece of information this country has about UFO sightings available to the public, and the scientists. I am convinced that UFOs exist, because I have seen one . . . '

Yet that promise has only been half-kept. Very many reports on UFOs remain top secret and unavailable to the general public in the USA. Nonetheless, it is possible to establish that over the past forty years, there have been very many official reports by the US Defense Department, the CIA and other official organizations into sightings of UFOs. Declassified Defense, NASA and CIA papers reveal this only too clearly. The trouble is that hardly any of the ones now available for inspection tell us what we want to know.

One such report from the CIA states that 'the Air Force denies that UFOs are either US or Soviet secret weapons or extraterrestrial in origin: it contends that all sightings are of well-known objects (balloons, aircraft, meteors, clouds, etc.), or poorly understood atmospheric phenomena. The Air Force's primary concerns are with the psychological warfare aspects of the sighting craze; that there is no mention of "saucers" in the Soviet press; and the effect such sightings might have in an actual attack on the US.'[4]

Yet another memorandum from the Office of the Director, Planning and Coordination Staff, tells of the 'CIA responsibility and action in the field of UFO studies' in relation to possible new aircraft designs by the USSR and even a 'joint British-Canadian saucer-type'.[5]

These two messages alone raise all manner of thoughts. Are UFOs something conjured up by one power to baffle and frighten another? If so, what powers practise this form of deception? Are both the superpowers of America and the

USSR indulging in this game – tentatively, if not on a positive scale? Does this explain the secrecy of officialdom? Alternatively, do some powers believe that the UFO is the ultimate weapon of the future, once it is perfected? If no satisfactory answer can be given to any of these questions, then only one further query can be put: do some powers have sufficient evidence of an earth-probe by beings from outer space that they feel they dare not reveal their findings to their own people?

Declassified CIA papers show that in a memorandum of 1952 H. Marshall Chadwell, Assistant Director of the Office of Scientific Intelligence, wrote to Walter Bedell Smith, then Director of the CIA, asking what research was needed to determine whether the problem of UFOs had national security implications. Concern was expressed that the Research and Development Board of the Air Force was not doing much about this, and urging that the National Security Council should 'establish the UFO problem as a priority'.

Obviously at various stages in earlier years there has been something approaching consternation in some Defence Ministries around the world. M. Robert Galley, a former French Minister of Defence, stated on French radio that 'if listeners could see for themselves the mass of reports coming in from the airborne gendarmerie charged with the job of conducting investigations, all of which reports are forwarded by us to the National Centre for Space Studies, then they would see that it is all pretty disturbing.'[6]

The French set up an organization named GEPAN under President Giscard d'Estaing, exclusively to monitor reports on UFOs. GEPAN worked closely with some 15,000 police stations to which it delivered advisory manuals. As a result of this GEPAN actually exposed two hoaxes concerning UFOs in 1979: The Mitterand Government decided to close down GEPAN, but transferred the monitoring chores to the military.

GEPAN did have the effect of reducing the number of fake claims by people who swore they had seen UFOs; their links with the police helped in this respect. But even GEPAN's team of scientists were baffled by a sighting in the Gard region of France when they examined the terrain afterwards. Their report stated that 'we are in the presence of traces for which there is no satisfactory explanation and we can find no reason to suspect that the eyewitness is deliberately lying. For the first time we found a combination of factors which leads us to accept that something similar to what the eyewitness described actually did happen.'[7]

Remarkably enough, while the USSR keeps as silent as most other nations on UFOs, Dr Felix Zigel, who is highly regarded by many in the West, goes so far as to say that 'of all the offered hypotheses the most probable is that the UFO is an extra-terrestrial probe.' That is quite an exceptional statement coming from a scientist of repute. At the same time he admits that it is 'a hard nut to crack, even for a scientist of the highest rank' and that 'we are still a long way from understanding the true nature of UFOs'.[8]

Dr J. Allen Hynek, who for twenty years was scientific consultant to the US Air Force's investigation team studying UFOs, has stated that 'there's no doubt that the US Air Force has not played clean pool with the public. There's not a Machiavellian plot, perhaps, but the UFO reports have been played down.' Having taken this view, Dr Hynek set up the Centre for UFO Studies in 1973, and he claims he has collected 75,000 UFO reports from 133 countries. While admitting that many of the reports can be discounted as disinformation or worse, he insists there is still much to investigate further. Certainly all the evidence suggests a policy of evasion and truth-twisting both in the USA and the United Kingdom on this subject. The Earl of Kimberley, an active member of the House of Lords All Party UFO Study Group, said: 'I think the general public should be encouraged to come forward with evidence. Many do not, for fear of being ridiculed . . . let them badger their Member of Parliament and the Government to be open with them and to cease what I am convinced is a cover-up.'[9]

Now the truth is, whether or not the powers-that-be in Britain try to deny it, that the Official Secrets Act, and the D-Notice system of requesting non-publication can be applied to UFO reports, especially when they are monitored by the Air Force. Such reports have been kept secret in the UK just as much as in the USA. There exists a memorandum in which the former Director of the FBI, J. Edgar Hoover, referred to the fact that the US Army had retrieved a crashed disc in 1947 and that the FBI had been denied access to it, or to the report thereon.[10]

Despite the fact that some documents on UFO reports in the USA have been released to the public, unfortunately at least 135 such documents, to my knowledge, remain classified and with-held by the National Security Agency. UFO research in the USA is now officially handled mainly by the UFO Reporting Center, US Coast and Geodetic Survey, Rockville, Maryland, and their findings are still classified 'top secret'.

The British are even more secretive than the Americans about a subject upon which the public should be informed as to what is nonsense and what is not. Undoubtedly there have been some spoof books on the subject of UFOs, some of them written anonymously by scientists who should know better, but who cannot resist the money such fictitious rubbish brings them. But there is one fairly recent UFO report in the United Kingdom, involving both British officialdom and the US Air Force, which does deserve some attention.

In October 1983 the *News of the World* reported:

'A UFO has landed in Britain – and that staggering fact has been officially confirmed. Despite a massive cover-up, *News of the World* investigators have proof that the mysterious craft came to earth in a red ball of light at 3 am on December 27 1980 [*NB this was reported nearly three years later*]. It happened in a pine forest called Tangham Wood just half a mile from the United States Air Force base at RAF Woodbridge in Suffolk. An American airman who was there told us there were three beings in silver space suits aboard the craft. Farm cattle and forest animals ran berserk as the spacecraft, a sloping silver dish about twenty feet across its base, silently glided to land in a blinding explosion of light. About 200 military and civilian personnel, British and American, witnessed the astonishing event . . . '[11]

Why was this incident kept a secret for so long? Even after this newspaper report there was still silence. Questions raised in Parliament brought no adequate response from the Defence Minister. Indeed, there were some attempts to play down the story by suggesting that 'an unexplained light seen by a USAF colonel at RAF Woodbridge could only have been the rotating beam of the Orford Ness Lighthouse five miles away.'[12]

Was this an attempt at disinformation? I have copies of two letters which suggest that it could be and that the *News of the World* story was substantially true. In the first letter Colonel Peter W. Bent, USAF, of the Department of the Air Force HQ 513th Combat Support Group, informed the Citizens

Against UFO Secrecy that a vital report on this subject, dated 13 January 1981, written by Lt-Colonel Charles I. Halt, 'had been properly disposed of in accordance with Air Force Regulations'. But, added the letter, 'fortunately, through diligent inquiry and the gracious consent of Her Majesty's Government, the British Ministry of Defence and the Royal Air Force' a copy of it had been provided.

This report compiled by Lt-Colonel Halt, the deputy base commander at the USAF base at Woodbridge, was headed 'UNEXPLAINED LIGHTS', and it read as follows:

'Early in the morning of 27 December 1980 (approximately 0300), two USAF security police patrolmen saw unusual lights outside the back gate at RAF Woodbridge. Thinking an aircraft might have crashed or been forced down, they called for permission to go outside the gate to investigate. The on-duty flight chief responded and allowed three patrolmen to proceed on foot. The individuals reported seeing a strange glowing object in the forest. The object itself had a pulsing red light on top and a bank(s) of blue lights underneath. The object was hovering or on legs. As the patrolmen approached the object, it manoeuvred through the trees and disappeared. At this time the animals on a nearby farm went into a frenzy. The object was briefly sighted approximately an hour later near the back gate.

'The next day three depressions 1½ in deep and 7 in in diameter were found where the object had been sighted on the ground. The following night the area was checked for radiation. Beta/gamma readings of 0.1 milliroentgens were recorded with peak readings in the three depressions and near the centre of the triangle formed by the depressions. A nearby tree had moderate readings on the side of the tree toward the depressions.

'Later in the night a red sun-like light was seen through the trees. It moved about and pulsed. At one point it appeared to throw off glowing particles and then broke into five separate white objects and then disappeared. Immediately thereafter three star-like objects were noticed in the sky, two objects to the north and one to the south, all of which were about —— [indecipherable] off the horizon. The objects moved rapidly in sharp angular movements and displayed red, green and blue lights. The objects to the north appeared to be elliptical through an 8-12 power lens. They then turned in full circles. The objects to the north remained in the sky for an hour or more. The object to the south was visible for two or three hours and beamed down a stream of light from time to time. Numerous individuals, including the undersigned, witnessed the activities in paragraphs 2 and 3.'[13]

What is interesting about these disclosures is that the report from Lt-Colonel Halt to the British Ministry of Defence was belatedly obtained through the *American* Freedom of Information Act. Unfortunately various witnesses to this incident in this country are not prepared to allow their real names quoted as they are subject to the Official Secrets Act.

However sceptical and cynical people may be about UFOs, it cannot be denied that, if such reports amount to nothing but imagination, hysteria and poor judgement, it should surely be easy for officialdom everywhere to demonstrate this openly and positively. Therefore one must try to keep the balance between the nonsensical and lunatic on the one hand, the false rumours on the other and the extremely disinformative attitude of some governments. For example, what is one to make of a statement like this:

'One of America's best UFO investigators had the following information leaked to him by a CIA informant. UFOs originate from an Earth-type planet in a system whose Sun is dying. This Sun will either go cold and the population freeze, or it will nova and they will be incinerated: either way they need another home. Are the various governments in on the secret? ''Only some of them,'' says the CIA man. ''Others are told only if and when they need to be.'' Presumably this means when UFO activity gets near to panic proportions and we all become so disheartened at the prospect of war with another world that civilization collapses on itself.'[14]

My own inquiries have not revealed any positive source for these suggestions, so that, once again, one may suspect an element of disinformation somewhere along the line. So far there has been no firm scientific evidence for the existence of any human or humanoid life outside this planet. And in listening to any of these reports, whether leaked by seemingly responsible officials or persons of repute, or from the general public, it is as well to bear in mind that even enthusiastic UFO researchers admit that nine out of ten photographs of alleged UFOs are misinterpreted pictures of everyday events, or the work of hoaxers. In 1962 Alex Birch, then fourteen years old, faked a photograph of flying saucers as (so he claimed) they flew over Sheffield. The shapes were actually painted on the windowpane through which he took the photograph, which for ten years, after which he made a confession, was regarded as genuine. [15]

Then there is the story that aliens from another planet could be sending UFOs to Earth in a desperate bid to prevent a nuclear war. This unlikely proposition was seriously considered by a private meeting of members of the House of Lords in 1983, following the Woodbridge revelations. Sir Patrick Wall, MP, a member of the House of Commons Select Committee on Defence, who attended this meeting, said afterwards that 'the theory about aliens trying to warn us seems feasible to me. And, if that's the case, then we should listen to them.' [16]

It is, however, in the sphere of what can perhaps be broadly termed as PSI-espionage and intelligence that a great deal of disinformation has been going on for the past twenty years. The PSI factor ranges from psychic warfare to ESP and 'brain manipulation' and from psychokinesis to long-distance hypnotism. Reports of alarming developments of this kind have leaked from both Eastern and Western countries, with both America and Russia anxious to deceive one another as to the progress each has made.

Any nation, or group of nations, which managed to obtain a commanding lead in exploitation of such techniques, could achieve something like total superiority. By that time a whole arsenal of paranormal weapons could exist, ranging from the destruction of conventional weapons by psychokinesis and subliminal propaganda by telepathy to psychotronic signals which destroyed human brainwaves and a whole range of psychotronic weapons.

Exchange of information on paranormal or paraphysical developments between East and West has inevitably produced some misleading episodes and even hoaxes. Some of these hoaxes have been deliberately conducted with a view to getting the other side to reveal more. In 1968 an international conference on parapsychology was organized in Moscow by Eduard Naumov, a Soviet expert in studies of the paranormal. At the same time the impression was given in the Soviet press that, on an official level, such matters were condemned as being irrelevant and decadent. Some Westerners believed that this attack was in itself a piece of disinformation. Yet out of that conference came two clues as to the manner in which the USSR was using paraphysical techniques for intelligence work. Naumov incurred the wrath of the Soviet authorities by revealing that Russian Naval Intelligence had experimented in telepathy between a submarine and the shore and that Military Intelligence had developed means of intercepting telepathy between two human beings.

The question arises as to whether this was a genuine revelation to encourage the Americans to be more forthcoming on their own researches in this area, or whether it was, as some Westerners believed, pure disinformation. It is not possible to say whether or not there was any connection between what came out of that conference and Naumov's fate a few years later. In 1974 he was sentenced to two years' imprisonment and forced labour for what were termed 'financial irregularities'.

In 1959 a story appeared in a French magazine to the effect that the US Navy had carried out secret telepathy tests with the atomic submarine *Nautilus*, sending out messages to agents on land. 'Is telepathy the new secret weapon?' asked the French journalists. 'Has the American military learned the secret of mind power?'[17]

This story has never been confirmed by the US Navy either at that time or since, and most defence correspondents thought it was untrue. Only the Russians appeared to take the report seriously, with Dr Leonid Vasiliev, a Soviet scientist specializing in telepathy research, telling a scientists' conference in Leningrad that what the American Navy was putting into practice today was what Soviet scientists had been working on a quarter of a century ago. 'It's urgent that we throw off our prejudices,' he said. 'We must go back and explore this vital field.'[18]

The *Nautilus* story is now generally recognized by both scientists and some intelligence services as having been cleverly planted on the French. Some suspect that it may well have originated from the Russians, who have certainly carried out similar tests largely, so it is said, because a submerged submarine cannot communicate with land by radio. To cover up these experiments some Soviet scientists have suggested they were trying to apply telepathic guidance to chess games!

A vital informant on Russian experiments in PSI espionage has been Nikolai Khokhlov, a former KGB agent who defected to the West. He testified that a Soviet 'mind-control' programme had been backed by the military as well as the scientists and that the Russians have also experimented with psychotronic weapons. A clandestine report of success in a submarine-to-shore ESP transmission by a special section of Soviet Bio-Information Research led Douglas Dean, of the US College of Engineering, to demand the cooperation of the US Navy in ESP experiments. A few years ago Dean revealed at a parascience conference that two fellow psychologists, Hal Puthoff and Russell Targ, had actually been successful in such an experiment.[19]

Probably where Western scientists have the edge on the Soviet camp in matters of the paranormal is that a long tradition of psychical research has made them less liable to be exploited by clever hoaxers and tricksters. On the other hand the Eastern bloc probably has produced, certainly in the past fifty years, more genuine and effective psychic practitioners than are to be found in any other part of the world. What, however, is more important is that such people (and they are to be found in Bulgaria, Czechoslovakia and Rumania as well as in the USSR) are generally given employment by the State and are not free agents.

East and West play a game with one another in this paranormal field. Each in turn pours scorn on psychic experiments and each surreptitiously indulges in them. Naumov's status was seriously questioned by an inspired article in the Soviet journal, *Problems of Philosophy*, by four leading Soviet psychologists some six months before his arrest. The attack on Naumov was contained in an article entitled 'Parapsychology: Fiction or Reality?' Without naming Naumov, but clearly indicating to whom they were pointing, the authors denounced 'so-called "specialists", who declare themselves leaders and participants in organizations which never even existed in our country, for example, the Institute of Technical Parapsychology.'[20]

They went on to describe the parapsychologists as giving lectures which were 'irresponsible mixtures of mythology and reality'. Yet, despite repeated denials of psychological warfare research or other paranormal experiments linked to Army or Navy, the *New York Times* revealed on 19 June 1977 that parapsychology research was undertaken by the Soviet military in a special laboratory at Siberia's Science City, a town that serves as a centre for studies in a variety of subjects. One of the researchers was Dr August Stern, now living in Paris, who identified the centre as a branch of the Institute of Automation and Electrometry. Established in 1966, it was usually called 'Special Department No. 8.' and was under the direction of a naval officer, Vitaly Perov.

Dr Stern believed that the Institute was inspected by KGB officers, and he estimated that the facilities 'cost many millions' and were staffed by some sixty researchers from various parts of the USSR. His own work, Stern said, was in theoretical physics concerning PSI particles. In 1969 the laboratory was unexpectedly shut down, but Dr Stern thought it had been re-opened as a KGB-controlled laboratory in Moscow. [21]

New Realities, the Californian daily which has taken a keen interest in this whole subject, asks: 'What about the so-called "exchange" of parapsychological information that has been going on between East and West and the détente that many in this country – including this magazine – tried to encourage and foster? It now seems certain that the material so freely given by the West was "exchanged" for outdated and obscure parapsychological experimental data. So the Russians have had the best of both worlds: they have freely monitored American (and other) parapsychological findings published freely in parapsychological journals and other publications in this country.' [22]

This view was expressed in 1977 and possibly as a result of this and similar complaints from the West, someone behind the Iron Curtain decided to leak rather more material in the hope of maintaining the illusion of an absolutely free exchange of information. For in 1979 J. Billingham and R. Pesek produced *Communication with Extraterrestrial Intelligence*[23], a work based on the hypothesis that intelligent species may be widely distributed in the solar system and that attention should be paid to the possibility of interstellar communications. Now Rudolf Pesek, one of the authors, was the man who helped in the founding of CETI, an organization for studying this theme, in Czechoslovakia, and the book contained papers presented by thirty-eight authors from the Eastern bloc (thirty-one of these from the USSR) and nine from the USA. Associated with CETI is SETI (Search for Extraterrestrial Intelligence), which concentrates on the strategy of how the search should be carried out. The mastermind behind SETI is Professor N.S. Kardashev, of the Institute for Space Research, the USSR Academy of Sciences.

Outside official circles there is still some cautious exchange of information on paranormal research between the Russians and the rest of the world. The *International Journal of Paraphysics*, edited from the Paraphysical Laboratory at Downton in Wiltshire, has contributors in the USSR, Bulgaria, Poland, Hungary, Rumania and Czechoslovakia. It contains regular reports from all those countries. But the subject which has latterly attracted most interest both in Russia and at the privately-run Stanford Research Institute (SRI) in California is a concept called remote viewing.

Remote viewing has been called all manner of things from 'a vital part of the psychic arms race' by its supporters to 'drivel and hocus-pocus' by its opponents.[24] It was largely developed by Russell Targ, a laser physicist who has claimed to have carried out a series of joint experiments with Soviet scientists. These are based on the idea that remote viewing is the ability of a person to describe locations, events and objects from which he is separated by space and time, and conducting this to the extent of being able to 'see' inside buildings and filing-cabinets. However, many scientists condemn this as a waste of time and nothing more than a plot to keep the other side involved in research which leads to nothing worthwhile.

Certainly the Russians would be very interested indeed if Targ's concept could bring results. Martin Ebon, a parapsychologist and student of Soviet interest in such matters, claims that 'the Russians are curious about what Targ knows. Their whole intelligence operation is a gigantic vacuum cleaner. Russell Targ is caught up in that vacuum.'[25]

This viewpoint is supported by Larissa Vilenskaya, formerly of Moscow, but now conducting psychic research and arranging seminars on parapsychology in Israel. She worked at the bioinformation laboratory of the Popov Institute in the Soviet Union until it was closed in 1975, so she can be regarded as an authoritative witness. She claims that Russian scientists are interested in using psychic powers 'primarily to develop extended means for mental influence at a distance'. [26]

Arguments for and against the Targ remote viewing concept will doubtless continue for a long time to come, with each side accusing the other of disinformation. One of Targ's most interesting claims was a remote viewing experiment that is said to have spanned 16,000 kilometres. This involved the Soviet psychic healer, Djuna Davitashvili, who from her home in Russia is said to have described in detail events on pier 39 in San Francisco. Targ claims that a testimonial verifying the experiment was obtained from a member of the Soviet Academy of Sciences.

But the Committee for the Scientific Investigation of Claims of the Paranormal was not impressed. Paul Kurtz, the chairman of this Committee, said afterwards that 'you cannot conclude anything on the basis of one experiment. To know if this woman had precognitive powers would require many tests.' [27]

Misconceptions will doubtless continue to narrow the credibility gap on all these matters, and investigators will continue to be led up blind alleys. Yet sometimes a false and misleading premise can actually lead to the truth. Not so many years ago it was suggested that a psychic navigation system could have evolved in the rudimentary brain of the homing pigeon. Ultimately this led to the discovery that, while the theory was discredited, microscopic magnetic particles embedded in the sensory systems of birds, humans and even bacteria provided directional guidance within the natural magnetic flux fields of the Earth. Then again, when it was suggested that 'psychic mishandling' (whatever that might mean) could have caused a series of bomb explosions in the US Navy carriers in the Gulf of Tonkin during the Vietnam War, subsequent research showed these were probably brought about by an electrostatic phenomenon.

13

INFORMERS
OR DISINFORMERS?

One of the seemingly eternal problems in assessing the truth in international affairs over the past forty years has been that of arriving at a satisfactory conclusion as to who is a reliable informant and who is a disinformer. Many of the latter, often under the guise of genuine informers, have maintained an unjustified reputation for reliability for far too long.

The person concerned may not necessarily be a deliberate disinformer posing as an informer. This type usually gets found out in the long run, though the damage he has done may be incalculable. But at least he enables those he has misinformed to be more careful in future. A much more difficult problem is that of the unconscious disinformer, quite often an informer who, initially, has been invaluable, but who ultimately begins to lose his sense of what is real and what is fantasy. How genuine his revelations are becomes a matter for the intelligence service's psychiatrists to assess, and even they cannot always decide accurately what the problem is, as inevitably they lack the detailed political and intelligence background to do so.

The late Sir Maurice Oldfield, when he was head of MI 6, used to say that 'the very first offerings from the defector were far and away the best', but that, as time passed by, the defector tended to become increasingly unreliable. There are many reasons for this. One, obviously, is that the longer he is away from the country of his origin, the less up-to-date his knowledge. Yet he will have become so used to being interrogated, and presumably so anxious to help, that he may make guesses and even invent material. Some will become frightened that if they don't come up with some new information, they may be cast off or even disowned by the intelligence service which is protecting them. Others, having been used for so long to the stresses and strains of life under an authoritarian regime, find it difficult to come to terms with a new life in a democracy: fear makes them prey to all kinds of fantasies.

An admirable attempt to try and remedy this problem has been made by the Jamestown Foundation of the United States. This organization's objective is, by its own definition, 'to improve Western understanding of the Soviet Union', adding that what makes its programme 'unique is the method employed to achieve this goal – the cultivation and utilization of defectors from key positions in the Soviet government and society. For those selected defectors who choose to live openly under their own names, and to write and speak on international affairs, the Jamestown Foundation provides a private sector support system to enable them to lead a productive public life. The foundation also conducts research on the subject of defection.'[1]

The Jamestown Foundation came into existence largely because of a realization that defectors have not always been handled either intelligently or tactfully by the people who are supposed to be looking after them. There have, of course, been serious blunders by authority; when such well known defectors as Stalin's daughter, Svetlana, and Oleg Bitov return to the Soviet Union, the Eastern bloc can claim an enormous propaganda victory which discourages other would-be defectors.

Arkady Shevchenko has written of his own experiences as a defector that, 'looking back, I feel fortunate that the period of stress, confusion and bad judgement was relatively brief. The presence of steadying friends and strong support ameliorated the anger and humiliation I felt. I do not believe that what I went through during this period is all that different from other defectors' experiences. The important thing is that a person in this situation should never be left to fend for himself or to keep his feelings and emotions pent up inside. I know this is easier said than done, for friends who will go through such an ordeal with one are hard to find. Government officials, with all their good intentions and assistance in the settlement process, simply cannot replace someone personally close to you. I think that this is the reason why some Soviet defectors who have had no financial problems or difficulties in finding suitable jobs have still been unable to adjust to life in the West, and in a moment of desperate loneliness and despair have thrown their hopes away by returning to the Soviet Union.' [2]

The Jamestown Foundation has discussed its policy with senior officials of the CIA, the FBI and the National Security Council and has achieved a cooperative relationship with the US government. Already the Foundation has scored some successes – for example a typical case in which they were able to help a defector from a Soviet bloc country who had spent most of his career in a high post in Moscow. This man and his sister had, since defecting, worked seven days a week operating a laundromat in a rough section of Brooklyn. He told the Foundation that his business was about to go bankrupt, that agents of his former country were terrorizing him, and that as a result of his woes his sister was suffering severe psychological distress. Fortunately the Foundation was able to discover that most of the man's business problems had been caused by lawyers, lenders and suppliers who had taken advantage of his unfamiliarity with normal US business practices. So arrangements were made to stabilize and sell the defector's business and for him to move to Washington to begin a new career in research and writing.

One of the risks an intelligence service runs with any fairly highly-placed defectors from the Soviet bloc is that, however valuable their early information may be, in due course they may well become too zealous in their quest for the truth. In short, they see villainy where it doesn't exist and the long arm of Moscow having influence in places where it is, if not non-existent, at least only slightly so. Sometimes this tendency to be compulsively suspicious can be harmful, and it should always be remembered that obsessive suspicion is the chief vice of the Russians.

In this respect it is interesting to study the views of Anatoli Golitsyn, the KGB officer who defected to the CIA in December

1961, and who has earned for himself the reputation of being an invaluable informer. Golitsyn has declared that 'tactical forms of disinformation are intended to divert attention from the onset of the communist offensive in the final phase of policy. Strategic disinformation is a root cause of the current crisis in Western foreign policies. Even those who recognize the dangers of disinformation cannot conceive that it can be practised on so grand a scale and with a subtlety so disarming . . . They fail to take into account that communist penetration of Western governments and intelligence services provides an accurate early warning and monitoring service of Western reactions to disinformation.'[3]

Now I would not for one moment deny the truth of this as a useful warning to the Western powers. To support it there is the story which Shevchenko tells of a talk he had with Andrei Gromyko in which the latter was asked what he thought was the greatest weakness of US foreign policy towards the Soviet Union. 'They don't comprehend our final goals,' replied Gromyko, 'and they mistake tactics for strategy.'[4]

But the very greatest caution should be taken in assessing Golitsyn's views and allegations. In particular I refer to his theme that any reports of a Sino-Soviet split over the past twenty-five years amount to disinformation. To accept this view, as some intelligence officers in the West have done, would be a grave disservice to the Western cause and to the much improved relations between China and the West.

Golitsyn says that 'the unreality of the dispute [i.e. between China and the USSR] is clear when the record of the two sides is examined . . . There is nothing to choose between the two sides in practice.' Then he goes on to assert that 'it can be predicted that the communist bloc will go further in its exploitation of the fictitious Sino-Soviet split, carrying it to a formal (but fictitious) break in diplomatic relations and more impressive hostilities than have so far occurred on the Sino-Soviet borders . . . The spurious notion of a common interest between the US and the Soviet Union against China in the 1960s was deliberately contrived and successfully exploited in the interests of communist strategy.'[5]

Now Golitsyn's great fallacy lies in equating Soviet communism with the Chinese variety and assuming a logical progression of communism in China on the Soviet pattern, whereas nothing could be further from the truth. Chinese communism has always been influenced by the ancient Chinese philosophers: even its application of the technique of disinformation has owed more to Sun-tzu than to Moscow. Similarly, whereas the Soviet revolution was an industrial one that largely ignored the peasants and is still suffering from this error, Chinese communism owed its strength to the fact that it was an agricultural revolution in favour of the peasants. And under China's present leader the peasants are encouraged to produce more in their own interest, the government practically instilling into them Thatcherite virtues of self-help. Apart from all that, it was abundantly clear even by the early 1970s that the Chinese intelligence services, admirably low-profiled as they are, had the deepest misgivings of Soviet chicanery, and not least of the fact that Russian policy was to sow seeds of mistrust of China among Western diplomats and intelligence officers.

Naturally, Golitsyn's views are eagerly sought by those right-wingers who see Reds under every conceivable bed, from MI 5 to MI 6, inside the CIA and the FBI, and in many of the leading statesmen of the West. His book, *New Lies for Old*, was sponsored for its translation into English by two former members of the British intelligence services, Arthur Martin and Stephen de Mowbray. In a foreword to the English translation these two state that 'despite the rejection of his [Golitsyn's] views by many of our former colleagues, we continue to believe that the contents of this book are of the greatest importance and relevance to a proper understanding of contemporary events.'[6]

Golitsyn tersely dismisses the fact that the Chinese and the Russians took diametrically opposed policies on the Sino-Indian conflict in 1959, the Cuban crisis and on disputes concerning the borders of the USSR and China, which can hardly be explained away as an exercise in disinformation. It is also worth recording that in 1981 it was reported from Washington that 'under a secret and highly unusual arrangement China and the United States have been sharing very sensitive intelligence for the past year on nuclear tests and missile launches in the Soviet Union. The source of this intelligence is two listening posts equipped with sophisticated American technology and manned by Chinese specialists, according to the National Broadcasting Corporation.'[7]

The arrangement began in February 1979, when the Ayatollah Khomeini came to power in Iran and closed down a CIA listening post in the north-east of that country. A few months later five United States senators went to Peking and talked with the Chinese leader, Deng Hsiao-Ping, who allowed the Americans to set up similar listening posts in China. Could this conceivably have happened if the Sino-Russian split was solely disinformation?

Then there was the case of Oleg Bitov. This former editor of the *Moscow Literary Gazette* defected to Britain in 1983, spending his time for several months writing articles for the *Sunday Telegraph* and a book which had been commissioned by a British publishing house. The indications were that this would reveal Soviet Russia in an unfavourable light. Among other things that Bitov told officers of Western intelligence services was that he knew how the Soviets had invented an account of a supposed Western attempt on the life of Pope John-Paul II.

In August 1984, Bitov disappeared while in London. A month later he resurfaced in Moscow where he told a specially convened press conference how he had been kidnapped, taken to Britain, and held there against his will, by use of drugs, by British Intelligence.

Now it was shortly before Bitov defected to the West (and he was almost certainly a false defector, carrying out orders from the KGB) that the Western press began speculating that the Kremlin might have had a hand in the attempted assassination of the Pope. There might be a Russian as well as a Bulgarian connection, it was argued. What is interesting is that Bitov was the editor of the very Soviet magazine which published the Soviet version of this crime. Bitov's return to Russia came some weeks before an Italian judge was expected to release a report implicating the Kremlin, even if only indirectly, in the attempted assassination. This was something which Bitov could, if necessary, exploit in a variety of ways, one of which was that Western intelligence services had plotted the shooting of the Pope as one means of framing the Soviet Union and so stirring up a revolt in the Pope's native Poland.

There is a parallel here to the arrival of Yuri Nosenko in the West shortly after the assassination of President Kennedy, and his efforts to persuade the Americans that Russia had no hand in the killing of John Kennedy. Yet, as has already been indicated earlier in this book, the links between Lee Harvey Oswald and the de Mohrenschildts and the Cubans and Russians are only too well established. It might all be coincidence, but the CIA has traced the various strands back to the immediate postwar period. [8]

Who informs? Who disinforms? Can one trust the informants and officers of one's own side any more than those of a potential enemy? These questions are as relevant today as when the Romans used to ask '*Quis custodiet ipsos custodes*?' when emperor after emperor was murdered by the Praetorian Guard formed to protect them. Two examples will perhaps suffice as to the almost paranoid mistrust some leading statesmen in recent years have shown regarding their own officials and civil servants. It has been reported in a new book on the Kennedy family that soon after President John Kennedy had been shot in Dallas in 1963, his brother, Robert, the Attorney-General at that time, actually asked the CIA: 'Did the Agency kill my brother?' As Robert Kennedy is himself long since assassinated and official reports on this subject have not been revealed, one cannot for certain confirm this report. But it is an astonishing question by any standards, especially when one recalls how the CIA had been a powerful weapon in the armoury of the Kennedy administration.

Yet is this any more fantastic than Lord Wilson's belief that, when he was Prime Minister, a right-wing faction in MI 5 was deliberately plotting his downfall and seeking evidence against him? What is more, Harold Wilson, as he then was, believed that agents of the South African Secret Service (BOSS) were also involved in this plot. [9]

There were inquiries on at least three occasions between 1963 and 1974 when MI 5 did probe into matters associated with Wilson. But most of these inquiries centred upon contacts of his and some who had been given honours rather than the Prime Minister himself. I do know that MI 5 was highly suspicious of some of those who had been knighted or given peerages by Wilson.

However, one vital question remains unanswered. Was Wilson disinformed and so caused to suspect an MI 5 plot against him? Or was the right-wing faction in MI 5 disinformed and thus came unnecessarily to suspect Wilson? Having looked carefully into the whole affair as far as possible, I am inclined to think that there was widescale disinformation on both sides.

Having stressed at great length the details of Soviet deception techniques, I should also pinpoint the peacetime use of such tactics in the Western world. When studying declassified papers of the CIA I came across an item which in the volume of records released in 1983 (no. 9) referred to 'an instruction manual on the techniques and applications of the art of deception'. But some of the worst examples of the abuse of disinformation in peacetime came out of the Canadian government's McDonald Commission of Inquiry into the Royal Canadian Mounted Police/Security Service in the 1970s.

This Commission soon found it had to untangle an extraordinary mixture of misdeeds, lies, deception and scandal. Its full title was the Royal Commission of Inquiry Concerning Certain Activities of the Royal Canadian Mounted Police, and it operated under the chairmanship of the Honourable Mr Justice D.C. McDonald. The RCMP has always had a deceptive title: few people outside of Canada realize that for years it has fulfilled the role of counter-intelligency agency and security agency for the whole country. The McDonald Agency summed up its findings as: 'Effective security within a democratic framework – that is the fundamental precept which has guided our diagnosis of past failures and wrong doings in Canada's security system, as well as our prescription for reform of the system.'[10]

The report resulted in the establishment of the Canadian Security Intelligence Service in May 1983.

More detailed findings of the Royal Commission included a number of charges of irregular practices. It was found that there was a willingness on the part of some members of the RCMP to 'deceive those outside the Force who have some sort of constitutional authority . . . over them or their activities'; that electronic surveillance has been carried out while at the same time 'assuring Parliamentary committees that there was no wiretapping'.

But the most consistently practised of all improper activities was the willingness of the RCMP to lie to and deceive their governmental superiors 'and thus the people of Canada'. The

Commission's report also noted that 'extreme loyalty . . . has contributed to . . . the practice of deception.'[11]

Quite often when the life stories or revelations of defectors appear in the press or in books released to the Western world, there is an immediate attempt by some of the critics to dub such work as 'fabricated'. This inevitably casts doubts on the author and his or her credibility. In effect it means handing a ready-made propaganda trick to the Russians.

For a very long time the credibility of that most outstandingly valuable of defectors, Colonel Oleg Penkovsky, was in doubt in some intelligence circles, even after the Cuban missiles crisis in which he played such an important role, simply because of criticism of the *Penkovsky Papers*. Critics were cynical about this book, which was a bestseller all over the world. Some of this criticism was based on hostility to the CIA, alleging that some of the material was more CIA-inspired fantasy than Penkovsky's own story; others were impressed by Soviet scholars who denounced the book as bogus. Victor Zorza, the Soviet expert of the *Guardian* and the *Washington Post*, wrote that 'the book could have been compiled only by the Central Intelligence Agency', adding that Penkovsky had neither the time, nor the opportunity to have produced such a manuscript.[12]

While it would seem that there are some grounds for such criticism, not least because both Doubleday, the book's publishers and Peter Deriabin, a KGB defector to the CIA, declined to produce the original Russian manuscript for inspection, this in no way should be allowed to hide the fact that Penkovsky was a first-rate and accurate informant.

Similarly, when Shevchenko's book, *Breaking with Moscow*, was published and serialized by various papers on both sides of the Atlantic, it was denounced as 'a CIA fabrication'. Edward Jay Epstein, writing in the *New Republic* magazine, stated that 'what is fabricated here are not just car chases, meetings, conversations, reports, but a spy who never was.' 'The spy who came in to be sold' was the title of Epstein's article, a snide reference to the fact that the rights for the book were sold for £380,000, and Shevchenko was appearing on the lecture circuit at £7645 a time.[13]

Such allegations need to be heeded because Mr Epstein is a diligent and persevering writer whose investigations in journalism have scored many triumphs, not least his book *Legend: the Secret World of Lee Harvey Oswald*, in which he questioned the reliability of Yuri Nosenko's testimony, and suggested not only that he was a disinformer planted by the Russians, but that he had possibly been sent to cover the tracks of a high-ranking double-agent in the CIA. By this time there was a total split in the CIA ranks between those who supported Nosenko and others, like the astute James Angleton, who questioned his real motives for defecting.

Alas, the full truth about the Nosenko case may never be known, as a 106-page report prepared by Angleton's staff on the defector in 1965 was found to have vanished from its file within two years of the sacking of some, including Angleton himself, of the anti-Nosenko lobby in the CIA.

It is perhaps also worth recalling that when Yuri Nosenko defected to the Americans in 1964, the Russians suddenly reacted with a highly artificial and suspicious degree of indignation. Mr Tsarapkin, leader of the Soviet disarmament delegation at Geneva, accused the Americans of kidnapping Nosenko, and the Swiss authorities of 'clear lack of desire to grant effective assistance' in finding him. [14]

Shortly afterwards the KGB dismissed more than fifty officers after an investigation and then leaked the information that this was a result of the Nosenko defection.

Every technological development today is liable to trigger an ever-increasing output of disinformation, much of it originally being intended as real information. Indeed, the rapid progress of the technological revolution since World War II has in many respects made a great deal of espionage both outdated, futile and, even worse, counter-productive.

It has also resulted in scientists themselves being suspected, or accused of fraud. Since Mr Gorbachev became the head of the Soviet state there have been a number of accusations of this nature made against Russian scientists and scientific institutions. The Kirgiz Academy of Sciences was accused of 'reporting research which had not been done at all' and publicizing routine and insignificant developments as if they were major breakthroughs early in 1986. Mr Abaamat Masaliev, first secretary of the Kirgiz Communist Party, alleged that the academy had made claims which were 'wishful thinking', based on experiments which had not been performed. About the same time the Uzbek Academy of Sciences was accused of nepotism and general slackness.

One wonders whether a clue to these criticisms does not exist in a paper produced in Russia by one N.P. Vashchekin in 1982. Starting with a quotation from Marx and Engels, this examined the content of scientific information work. Its conclusion was that 'one of the most important tasks of scientific information work is to help to recognize bourgeois tendencies in an information system.'[15]

Sometimes the intelligence services, whether of East or West, take the law into their own hands and carry out operations about which their governments know nothing. Certainly in its earlier 'cowboy' days the infant CIA indulged in some tactics which were not far removed from those of a gangster, even if in a good cause. The CIA has tried to destabilize left-wing governments in Latin America and elsewhere and sometimes used intimidation. The French secret service arranged the blowing up of the Greenpeace vessel *Rainbow Warrior* without the knowledge of the French government, and even the coy British secret service has organized quite a few trips by frogmen beneath Soviet warships. Most honest of the lot is probably Israel's Mossad, which, without denying it, sends out hit squads to remove terrorists who have acted against their nation.

The Cyprus spy trial was a stupid waste of time and money. Above all the evidence which was built up by the prosecution was based on positive disinformation in several instances. One of the defendants was said to have handed over documents emanating from the Cyprus Signals Centre *at a time when he wasn't in Cyprus*; even the confessions appear to have been disinformation.

My own inquiries into the Cyprus RAF trial revealed that the real spy was almost certainly not in Cyprus – indeed he may have been inside GCHQ in Cheltenham. In the view of intelligence officers with whom I have talked, both American and British, Gordievsky, the senior KGB officer alleged to have provided Britain with vital information for several years before he defected, may on this occasion have unwittingly blundered.

It is a practice in Russian intelligence circles as in those of other countries to use all manner of bogus cover stories to protect against inter-departmental leakages. Thus, if the Russians had a mole inside GCHQ at Cheltenham, or elsewhere, they might well seek to protect him by inventing a source in Cyprus allegedly inside the Composite Signals Unit. Possibly this misleading titbit of information was picked up by Gordievsky, or someone else leaking intelligence to the British, and repeated to the SIS.

Someone took this report far too seriously and so a full-scale investigation was ordered on the flimsiest of evidence. Yet they should have realized these vital facts: first, that CSU in Cyprus garners raw SIGINT, which it passes back to Cheltenham where it is analysed; secondly, CSU may know who it is monitoring, but not what it is monitoring. So a spy at CSU would not be all that useful. Now if the Russians wanted to know how much of these signals can be read and what they mean, they would need to turn to a mole in either Cheltenham (GCHQ) or Fort Meade (the US National Security Agency). Once one has considered these facts it becomes obvious that the story of a spy in Cyprus, except for a small-time character, was highly suspect.

At the same time I must stress the whole point of this chapter which is that often genuine information can result in disinformation. If Gordievsky, or any other defector or mole inside the Soviet camp, provided this intelligence to the British, I do not doubt that it was with good intent. But a genuine informant is just as likely to pick up disinformation and not recognize it. As Maurice Oldfield commented, 'the passage of time makes the defector careless. He becomes too anxious to please and so he becomes less critical in analysing new material.'

14

SOME WESTERN WILES

One of the most uproariously amusing, if highly dangerous, exercises in disinformation was Operation Chonkin, carried out by two intrepid characters with an abnormal love of adventure, Vincenzo Sparagna and Savik Shuster.

One Saturday morning about two years ago this remarkable pair called on me and related a story which at first was hard to believe. The essence of it was that they had been to Afghanistan during the fighting between Soviet troops and Afghan guerrillas and had managed to distribute to the Russian soldiers thousands of copies of a faked edition of the Soviet Army newspaper containing all manner of false and demoralizing news and appealing to the Soviet 'comrades' to lay down their arms and desert.

The man who sent them to call on me was none other than that brave fighter against all attacks on personal freedom and friend of oppressed peoples everywhere, the late Josef Josten, secretary of the UK Committee for the Defence of the Unjustly Prosecuted. I felt certain that Josef was the last person to be taken in by a fictitious story, yet only when the two men unpacked their cases in front of me was I ultimately convinced. They handed out to me photographs of themselves taken in the mountains of Afghanistan, in Kabul, the capital, and in the company of Russian soldiers who had deserted. One Russian soldier was actually holding up a copy of the faked newspaper. Final proof was provided by copies of the actual faked newspaper, a satirical poster and their detailed account of the whole exercise. The two men had subsequently had printed French and Italian editions of their newspaper, containing simply the title and headings in Russian, so that people in Europe could see and read what they had done.

One night when there was a massive distribution of the faked *Red Star* in Kabul both in the bazaars and streets, some of the Russian sentries turned a blind eye. Soviet officers became extremely agitated when it was discovered what was going on and ordered instant reprisals. Afghans opposed to the Russians helped considerably in suggesting the best methods of distributing the clandestine publication, indicating where copies might be left on the walls of houses as well as using mendicants to put them into Russian hands. [1]

Quite brazenly the paper announced that 'the war is finished in Afghanistan . . . Russians and moudjahidines fraternize . . . the Soviet soldiers sent to defend the regime of Babrak Karmal and to occupy the country are deserting and mutinying . . . the government of Babrak Karmal is in flight.'

The paper also announced that 'this number of *Red Star* that you have in your hands is absolutely without precedent. Previously the paper has been directed totally on the orders of officers of the Party. Today it is a group of soldiers, coming from all the principal garrisons of the Soviet Union, who direct this paper. For the first time then *Red Star* is the veritable organ of expression of opinion of the ordinary Soviet soldier . . . In effect, from today, *Red Star* is no longer the paper of an army at war, but of an army which refuses to continue the battle.'

It is, of course, extremely difficult to judge the results of this disinformation operation, especially as it could not be sustained for longer than a single day, or two at the most. But from independent sources it would seem that quite a few desertions resulted from Operation Chonkin and that it greatly heartened the Afghans opposing the Soviet army of occupation. The skilful propaganda in the text of the paper, with faked letters from soldiers, complaining of chaos in the delivery of mails and of the appalling conditions under which they were living, all played a part in undermining morale among at least some hundreds of Soviet personnel out of the thousands who must have had a glimpse of the paper, or at least heard of its contents second-hand.

Can disinformation, expertly used, actually stop a war? This is a worthwhile question to ask in the light of Operation Chonkin. True, the activities of two men were not enough to end the occupation of Afghanistan by Soviet troops, but had their mission been carefully coordinated with the tactics of a secret service or some larger organization, anything could have happened. Of course such tactics could be used against one's own side in what a Western country regarded as a justified war, or war could even be started by the manipulation of false news.

Some disinformation perpetrated by Western nations even in recent years has been feckless, ridiculous and in many cases without the excuse of a rational point. Curiously (possibly an astute psychologist could explain why) this has on occasions been most marked in Anglo-French relations. It showed itself in the persistent hostility to General de Gaulle by some British diplomats from the end of the war right up to his last days as President of the Republic, and it has been evident in a great deal of falsification of Common Market issues in which both sides have been guilty. In 1968, when Christopher Soames was the British Ambassador in Paris, the Foreign Office broke all the rules of diplomatic etiquette by leaking a highly coloured and distorted version of a private talk between Soames and de Gaulle. The aim of this truth-twisting was to discredit the General in the eyes of his Common Market partners, but it was a stupid ruse which badly misfired.

Then came the extraordinarily foolish French blunder in the episode of the bomb attack which sank the Greenpeace organization ship, *Rainbow Warrior*, in Auckland Harbour in July 1985. Secret agents of the French government were caught out in an act of manslaughter and sabotage when frogmen were sent on an espionage mission, presumably with the aim of stopping Greenpeace from making their usual futile gesture of opposition against France's nuclear testing in the Pacific Ocean. As a result the ship was sunk and one of the crew members killed. New Zealand protested against this 'sordid act of international State-backed terrorism' and ordered the arrest of the two French secret service agents. The latter were sentenced to ten years' imprisonment.

All that the sinking of the *Rainbow Warrior* achieved was to make the Greenpeace movement more militant. It had been largely an environmental and preservation group started in opposition to American nuclear testing in the Aleutian Islands in 1971. But by early October 1985, it was reported that the 'high command of the Greenpeace movement, whose ships are confronting the French at their nuclear test site in the Pacific, has decided on a big expansion of its campaign to include nuclear disarmament. The decision, taken in great secrecy at a Sussex hideaway, marks the biggest departure in the pressure group's history. Up to now it has confined its campaigning to environmental issues mainly on ecological grounds. It now plans to campaign against nuclear arms in general.'[2]

The operation against the *Rainbow Warrior* still seems to have been a quite untypical French blunder, because even if the agents had not been caught it hardly helped their cause one iota. They may, and they probably did, underestimate the competence of New Zealand's security service, but it also seems possible that some form of disinformation given to the French secret service caused them to embark on such a futile project.

In the early days after the sinking of the ship the French denied all knowledge of the affair, or that they had anything to do with it. Almost immediately afterwards they started to blame the British. There was a huge disinformation campaign in the French media, claiming that the Greenpeace ship was sunk by agents of British intelligence. There was the report that a dinghy and diving equipment bought at Barnet Marine Centre in London were found abandoned alongside the sinking *Rainbow Warrior*. Then on 27 September 1985, General René Izbot, the new chief of the *Sécurité Extérieure*, stated on French television that he had discovered 'an operation to destabilize and destroy the French secret services'.[3]

Sir Geoffrey Howe, the British Foreign Secretary, immediately described French press and television reports about a British involvement as 'patently absurd' and based on 'disinformation'. Some of these reports suggested that the bombing of the *Rainbow Warrior* was retaliation by the British for the supply of French Exocet missiles to Argentina during the Falklands War. Yet at the very same time, in low key informal exchanges with British diplomats, their French counterparts were expressing regret at these 'unfortunate innuendoes'. If the *Rainbow Warrior* sinking had been carried out by British agents or American CIA officers, governments would have fallen and howls of 'another Watergate' would have gone up. But the French as a people are not hypocritically minded in the same way as the Anglo-Saxons: indeed, it is British hypocrisy which raises French hackles. Hardly anyone in France was embarrassed by their secret service's actions, only disappointed that they failed. France has no serious anti-nuclear movement, nor, for that matter, a 'Green' Party or ecological organization of any real importance. France believes in nuclear energy and intends to keep its independent deterrent. Only one newspaper in France put the Greenpeace episode in proportion and seriously aimed at obtaining the truth – 'too beautiful to believe' was how *Le Monde* described the official report of Bernard Tricot on the affair.

One can be sure that the Soviet intelligence services monitored the *Rainbow Warrior* affair closely from beginning to end, and the fact that the KGB could have been indirectly implicated in it seems to have been overlooked. Doubtless the Greenpeace movement has been infiltrated by the KGB: this would be relatively easy to do in view of their earlier experience of worming their way into other peace and environmental groups around the world. Greenpeace would give the Russians excellent opportunities for studying French nuclear technology once they had penetrated the movement and gained access to some of its ships. It may well have been that Russian agents supplied the vital information which led to the arrest of the French saboteurs.

By the end of 1985 there was a feeling in a number of capitals of the world that disinformation had caught them out and that their defences against this kind of thing were vulnerable. For 1985 was a year of confusion when nation misled nation. The West German magazine *Der Spiegel* published an interview with Vasil Bilak, a member of the Central Committee Secretariat of Czechoslovakia, in which he asserted that he and Alexander Dubcek, the deposed Czech leader, had signed a document before Warsaw Pact troops invaded the country, stating that the country was 'under the threat of a counter-revolutionary coup'. This caused Dubcek, now a forestry clerk in Slovakia, to end his self-enforced silence to refute this statement and deny allegations of misrule and that he had prepared concentration camps in Czechoslovakia. The Dubcek denials were published in the Italian newspaper *L'Unita.*

Then there was the Great Spy-Dust Thriller which was unravelled in August 1985, two months before the scheduled summit meeting in Moscow of Ronald Reagan and Mikhail Gorbachev. In three surprisingly hastily arranged meetings in a ballroom of the US Ambassador's mansion in Moscow members of the American community in that city were informed that embassy officials had discovered 'a potential health problem' being inflicted on them by the Soviets. It was all rather clumsily, if melodramatically, suggested that the Russians were spraying doorknobs, automobile seats and even the clothing of Moscow-resident Americans with a chemical known as NPPD, or nitrophenylpentadienal.

But the embassy staff making this claim declined to give any details of the dangers which this chemical or dust involved, or at that stage where it was found. 'All I can tell you is there is no doubt that the KGB is using the substance,' said *chargé d'affaires* Richard Combs. 'I can't go beyond that.'[4]

Later in Washington, however, CIA spokesmen were rather more forthcoming, adding that Americans' movements in Moscow could be monitored and their contacts noted by the tiny traces of the powder they left behind after having had clothes or car seats sprayed with it. Was it a powder or a liquid chemical, official spokesmen were asked? They were singularly divided on the answers they gave to their question. They countered by saying that large doses of NPPD could cause impotence, nerve damage and even cancer. Then Senator David Durenberger, chairman of the Senate Select Committee on Intelligence, declared that the CIA first discovered the Russians were using a chemical on Americans as long ago as the mid-1970s, but they had seemed to stop until about eighteen months ago.

Even the US Embassy in Moscow alleged that the 'spy-dust' powder could cause cancer.

Naturally, the Russians indignantly denied having indulged in any such tactics and they accused the Americans of trying to ruin the summit talks, or make them impossible. No doubt the KGB has always kept the closest watch on all foreign diplomats, especially the Americans, but one cannot help feeling they would be much more likely to use sophisticated means for such surveillance: electronic systems offer far better results than powder.

It is likely that it was highly exaggerated to the point of being classified as misleading. Strangely, officials of the US National Institution of Health and other government research organizations were suddenly ordered to refer all questions about NPPD back to the State Department. But this did not stop members of the scientific community giving their own view that very little was as yet known about NPPD, but that what was known fell 'well short of substantiating Washington's alarm', and going on to add that 'the chemical is one of several related compounds that were studied fifteen years ago in a search for improved antibacterial agents – and found to be both essentially useless and not particularly toxic.'[5]

When the State Department suggested that NPPD was a substance capable of causing genetic changes and therefore possibly cancer, Dr Frederick Oehme, a medical researcher at Kansas State University, said that this would only apply to bacteria or other one-celled organisms. As to whether it could be used as a tracking agent, opinions differed widely, some saying that to identify it a laboratory spectograph would be essential. Finally in February 1986 the American Embassy in Moscow withdrew its charge that this substance could cause cancer, the Ambassador, Mr Arthur Hartman, saying that tests of the substance in America had shown it did not pose a health hazard.

Moscow must have been much more worried by the news that one of the KGB senior officers, Oleg Gordievsky, had defected to the British, and he had been plying them with information for ten years as a double-agent. But it was Washington's turn to be worried when Vitaly Yurchenko, the so-called 'high-ranking KGB officer' reported as having defected to the West in September 1985, returned home to Moscow to give a press conference two months later, alleging that he had been kidnapped and ill-treated by the CIA.

There is little doubt that Yurchenko was the key figure in a massive disinformation exercise on several counts. It has been suggested that one of his aims was to discredit Gordievsky, who had defected only four months earlier, and to warn the Americans to be doubtful of accepting any information from the British which might come from this source. For during his debriefing in Britain Gordievsky had revealed that the Russians had a highly placed mole inside the CIA. 'Yurchenko told us there were no moles in the CIA,' stated one US counter-intelligence expert in Washington, adding that 'we can build a fairly solid case that Yurchenko was conceived, created and set in motion because of Gordievsky. When you put it up to a suspicious optic, a lot of pieces fall into place.' [6]

Until that statement was made in Washington many in the intelligence world had believed that Yurchenko had been unfortunately mismanaged when he was in the hands of the CIA. It was thought that he had slipped through their net and escaped to Moscow because of a nervous depression following a broken love affair. At his press conference Yurchenko had stated that he had been 'abducted on the steps of St Peter's Basilica in Rome and flown, drugged, to a CIA safe-house'. [7]

He denied totally that he had ever defected to the Americans, and in reply to a question about an alleged affair with the wife of another Soviet diplomat in Canada whom he was said to have visited with the permission of the CIA, he replied: 'The story of the woman in Canada was invented by the CIA to compromise me. It was their last slim chance because their earlier efforts had failed.' [8]

Despite all this American intelligence experts remained divided on the question of whether Yurchenko came over to the West as a genuine defector, or was a KGB plant all the time. There can, however, be no doubt that, especially in the light of this division of opinion, the CIA and FBI 'handlers' of the man were remarkably inefficient. He was allowed to wander around unattended on occasions and it is now believed that his first contact with the Russians prior to his decision to return to Moscow came when he visited a bowling alley. One report stated that Yurchenko's lover was Mrs Valentina Yereskovsky, wife of the Soviet Consul-General in Montreal, and that the CIA and Canada's security and intelligence service arranged a rendezvous for the pair in Canada. The story goes that she refused to defect and that this rejection of Yurchenko's proposal caused him to become acutely depressed so that he made up his mind to go back to Russia. [9]

Whatever the full truth of this remarkable story it reeks of disinformation on both sides and in the long term neither the Americans nor the Russians can be said to have gained much from it. On the other hand, where disinformation is concerned the Russians, having a dictatorial system of government and the ability to impose total secrecy, must be expected to gain most from their policy of 'active measures'. One disadvantage for the West is that the freedom of expression in the media may well upset disinformation tactics, good and bad. Every time the media show up Western disinformation which has visibly failed, or been a disastrous blunder, the clamour for greater access to information breaks loose. The harm done by the Watergate affair opened the floodgates of information so that many matters which should have remained secret became common knowledge to friend and foe alike.

Meanwhile the Russians are seeking still further means of making their own active measures more foolproof and less easy to detect. Worldwide direction of such plans is now made by Service A of the First Chief Directorate, which has doubled in size over the past fifteen years. From all reports its officers are among the most brilliant and imaginative in the whole service of the KGB. One of the most important aspects of the way that Service A functions now is the steady increase in numbers of professional disinformation experts who leave the Soviet Union for the West under the guise of defectors, a marked trend in the past few years.[10]

More disturbing is the manner in which other terrorist organizations, including some in Latin America and especially those of some Arab countries, have started using their own disinformation tactics with considerable success in the diplomatic sphere. For the past few years in diplomatic circles, especially those of the British Foreign Office, it has become established policy to regard the notorious Yasser Arafat as the leader of a modern democratic Palestinian Liberation group and to encourage talks with the man. Certainly Arafat poses as a moderate, but Brigadier Ehud Barak, head of Israel's Military Intelligence Service, stresses that there has been an increase of terrorist attacks against Israel in the past eighteen months: in 1985-6 over 660 such attacks compared with 383 for the whole of 1984. He attributes this to the presence of a PLO headquarters in Jordan, which provides training for individuals and is controlled by Abu Johad, Arafat's deputy. In the case of the Italian liner hijacked by terrorists, Israeli Military Intelligence insists that this was an operation in which the PLO was really negotiating with itself, and that the Arafat pattern was to pretend to be moderate while indulging in terrorism without having to pay any political price.

To turn aside from the eternal game of disinformation in the field of international relations, an increase in truth-twisting in everyday life and the domestic politics and life of each nation must be noted. Much of it is in common parlance an ever-growing habit of passing the buck. Modern bank officials, for example – especially in Britain – are notorious for blaming all errors on 'the computer' when in fact an individual is at fault. Another area in which the British citizen is most likely to be misinformed without having any chance of discovering the fact is in matters of health and hygiene. Two of the worst examples have been the immunity of state hospitals from prosecution, until recently, and the fact that the Data Protection Act of 1986 does not give the individual the right to examine any of the information stored on his medical files. Indeed, the great fallacy of this ill-designed Act is that it only covers records stored on computers, so that old-fashioned manual files are outside the Act's requirements.

There has been a lamentable lack of information on many of the drugs prescribed by doctors and the person taking them is frequently not told of the risks, nor of any of the precautions that should be taken concerning them. It is a national scandal that if a Briton wishes to know these things, his only hope of enlightenment lies in the United States of America. A vast amount of information, from hygiene to foodstuffs, is freely available to the public under America's Freedom of Information Act. Yet many reports affecting the health and well-being of British citizens can sometimes only be found out by an application made under this Act. Some of these reports reveal appalling neglect in matters of hygiene in the United Kingdom, as well as detailed laboratory tests on food additives – tests which have led to their being banished in the United States, though still being used over here. One report available under the American Freedom of Information Act concerns British meat processing plants. The latter must be inspected before they are allowed to export to the USA, but the same strictures do not apply to meat sold in the UK.

On the subject of food and hygiene there is a vast amount of

217

concealment of the truth in the United Kingdom. Recently an independent group of scientists claimed that a number of chemical additives used in food were suspected of causing cancer. The author of the report, Melanie Miller, stated that there were more than 3500 additives used in food in Britain, forty per cent of which could provoke allergic reactions and that certain common compounds in most kinds of processed food were cancer-inducing.[11]

In 1985 the British government intervened to censor advice given in an independent report on healthy eating because of demands by the Department of Health. Advice had been submitted with a view to reducing the number of deaths from heart disease by a change of diet, but pressure was put upon Dr John Gatrow, chairman of the Joint Advisory Committee on Nutrition Education, to make cuts and changes in the report. This was due to complaints from food industry and farming organizations that such advice could lead to a drastic reduction in the sales of butter, milk and meat. In a letter of protest which Dr Gatrow wrote on behalf of the Committee he said: 'We resent this treatment by the DHSS, which we regard as insulting and quite contrary to the terms on which members of the committee undertook the work of preparing the leaflet. JACNE (Joint Advisory Committee on Nutrition Education) was constituted so that it would be seen to operate without pressure from the government or the food industry.'[12]

In probing for examples of disinformation in various spheres of life I have discovered that in the United Kingdom the frequency of such malpractice is more to be found in hospitals, medical services and health policies than anywhere else. Much of the disinformation is, in fact, a direct result of the setting up of area health authorities where more often than not the ignorant are in command. The ineptness of many of these health authorities is almost unbelievable, but it is nearly always masked from the general public. Only since the government belatedly came round to the idea of ending the criminal farce of granting Crown immunity to state hospitals have some of the appalling facts about hospital hygiene become known. Not ending Crown immunity years ago (for which all governments are to blame) has provided a splendid excuse for covering up the dreadful standards of hospital cleanliness and the 211 outbreaks of food poisoning in hospitals over the past six years.

A survey by the Institute of Environmental Health Officers revealed that several million pounds would have to be spent by health authorities in bringing kitchen equipment up to modern hygiene standards once Crown immunity was abolished. The survey also found that 600 of the 1002 hospital kitchens broke health regulations and 97 would have been liable to prosecution except for Crown immunity. [13]

It has become a habit of British life to blame whoever is in power for almost everything that goes wrong, regardless of whether it is something they directly control or not. Nobody should shirk from criticizing a government where the responsibility is obviously in its domain, but much criticism of this type is mindless and ill-informed, actually enabling the real culprits to go unnoticed. A typical example of this has been the constant blaming of the government of the day, Tory or Labour, for the lengthy waiting lists for hospital beds. 'It's the government's fault,' goes the parrot cry. 'They won't hand out enough money.' The public takes up this call from the prompting of local MPs, councillors and especially health authorities. But to put the blame on the government of the day has been a tactic of disinformation by very many health authorities for several years.

'Inefficiency, not lack of resources, is the major cause of hospital waiting lists,' declared Mr John Yates, a health services management expert. 'Assuming that lack of money causes waiting lists to grow does not tally with the facts,' he added, having studied the problem for the National Association of Health Authorities. Some districts which are short of money manage to keep their waiting lists as short as, and sometimes shorter than, those which are well funded. Some well-funded districts still had long waiting lists. [14]

It was estimated that one million people were waiting for operations in Britain, 300,000 of whom had been waiting for more than a year. In some instances the facts uncovered by diligent research showed that a substantial minority of surgeons 'simply do not do enough operations . . . Fifty-three of the country's 191 health districts have half their beds empty at any one time.' [15]

Indeed, in ear, nose and throat departments the average number of empty beds has risen as high as forty-three per cent of those available.

In health and environmental matters, however, disinformation from both sides obscures the issues. This has been most marked regarding the curse of the 1980s – the appearance of AIDS, or Acquired Immune Deficiency Syndrome. What is fact and what is fiction? As this is a worldwide problem of growing seriousness, however, the dilemma must be faced.

The stark truth seems to be that the disease poses a far greater threat to the human race generally than the Black Death of the Middle Ages and that if it is not tackled fearlessly, many disasters lie ahead. Indeed, it might well happen that nobody will be sufficiently aware of the problem until populations everywhere drastically and rapidly decrease.

If anything I incline towards the pessimists' views on AIDS, but I would prefer to accept their exaggerations than the views of those who underplay the dangers. Needless to say the Russians were among the first to disinform people about the extent of AIDS in their country. In October 1985, Pyotr Burgasov, the Soviet Deputy Health Minister, told the Russian trade union newspaper *Trud* that there were no recorded cases of AIDS in Russia, giving as a major reason that homosexuality was illegal in the Soviet Union. [16]

Within three months the Soviet Union admitted for the first time in an article in *Sovietskaya Kultura* that some of its citizens had AIDS, but claimed there were fewer than ten victims and gave no indication as to whether any deaths had occurred. Even in making this somewhat reluctant admission a spokesman suggested that the disease resulted from 'Pentagon-inspired experiments', rather a quaint piece of disinformation in the style of old fashioned Bolsheviks!

This is almost as intriguing as the claim of a British consultant, Dr John Seale, that a mad scientist could be to blame for unleashing the AIDS virus after he had discovered links between AIDS and the lethal VISNA virus which attacks sheep. His theory was that a scientist could have created AIDS while experimenting with VISNA.

That remarkable journal, *Executive Intelligence Review*, went even further into the realms of fantasy when one of its editorials stated: 'A decade ago in 1975 *EIR*'s editors were warning, before the name of AIDS was known to the public, that the usurious debt-collection policies being forced by McNamara and Co on Africa in particular would lead to the outbreak of uncontrollable disease pandemics on the African continent and then spread to every corner of the globe. Then three years ago . . . *EIR*'s Medicine Editor, Dr John Grauerholz, predicted that AIDS, which originated as projected in the most impoverished regions of Africa, would soon spread beyond the most vulnerable "target" populations of homosexuals and drug addicts into wider and wider circles of the population.'[17]

To blame the World Bank and McNamara for AIDS is surely stretching the imagination somewhat, but certainly the world's bankers and some Western politicians have actually encouraged the impoverishment of Third World countries by failing to check environmental decay and the turning of agricultural land into desert while allowing industry to be developed at the expense of food-growing.

In Britain one district health officer issued a hospital circular which accused the media of scaremongering over AIDS. Circulated among staff at Hull Royal Infirmary it stated: 'Alarmist and inaccurate media coverage has created unfounded fears in health care workers about the possible risks when dealing with an actual or suspected AIDS case.'

A theatre technician at the hospital denounced the circular as 'irresponsible when experts are saying that the plague of AIDS could reach epidemic proportions'. As Dr Marion McEvoy of the government's Communicable Diseases Surveillance Centre has described AIDS as 'the greatest challenge to doctors this century' and declared that up to 250,000 people in England and Wales will have been infected by it within two years, the opinion of the theatre technician seems just about right. The British government has been ambivalent on the problem. Dr Peter Jones, of the Haemophilia Society, protested to Mr Norman Fowler, Health Minister, that the Department of Health should have issued guidance earlier to allay fears about the spread of AIDS.[18]

Earlier on doctors had protested that breaking up the fifty-two Public Health Service Laboratories and transferring them to the control of district health authorities would hamper the fight against AIDS. A minority report by two advisers to the Department of Health on this very vital point was somehow ignored. Belatedly, the Health Minister lifted his threat to break up the laboratories.

Dr Howard Stoate, of Bexleyheath in Kent, tends to think

that much of what has been said about AIDS are 'scare stories, often based on misconceptions about the illness, causing unnecessary fear and panic . . . AIDS is . . . of very low infectivity and requires special circumstances for it to be passed between people. There is virtually no known risk to the general public from AIDS sufferers.'[19]

This might sound reassuring until one reads on and learns – to quote Dr Stoate again – that 'the introduction of a routine screening test used by the Blood Transfusion Service has virtually eliminated this risk in Britain. A few haemophiliacs may have contracted AIDS from infected imported factor 8. This has now been avoided by the use of a heat treatment technique which destroys the virus.'[20]

However let us turn again to Dr Peter Jones, who is director of the Northern Haemophilia Centre at the Royal Victoria Infirmary, Newcastle-upon-Tyne. Dr Jones told a Newcastle conference organized by health care workers that 'on the scanty evidence we have it looks as if the [AIDS] virus can survive heat treatment. It would be misleading to guarantee 100 per cent safety . . . The problems facing the haemophiliac group are enormous. It is now virtually impossible for them to get life assurance.'[21]

Yet at the same time the Department of Health was stating that it had 'every reason to believe that heat-treating is effective in this country'.[22]

On the subject of AIDS the performance of the British Medical Association has been quite remarkable. It is often overlooked that the BMA is not only in effect a trade union, but in many respects a more reactionary, anti-social trade union than those of many ordinary workers. It has often been ambivalent on AIDS and certainly has given no positive lead on the question except in one most astonishing exception. In 1986 the BMA produced *The Long Term Environmental and Medical Effects of Nuclear War*. This included the remarkable prediction that an AIDS outbreak would follow nuclear war. It stated that: 'Animal studies have shown that radiation impairs the immune system, and there is much clinical evidence of immuno-suppression by X-irradiation in humans . . . a marked increase in AIDS-related diseases should be anticipated among such survivors [i.e. in a nuclear war].'

Disinformation in some of the cases cited in this chapter is perhaps technically outside the meaning of the word, yet it cannot be too strongly stressed that suppression of vital facts, or the putting over of only half the truth, is in effect misleading the public. It is no use arguing that some treatment which is safe in, say, fifty per cent of cases, is totally safe. As for the BMA's argument on the impairing of the immune system, there are other diseases of this kind quite apart from AIDS:

On this note I wish to end this book. Unless there are reasons which are vital to the security of the State and its protection, suppression of facts with the intention of misleading people amounts to truth-twisting as much as downright lies. The telling of a half-truth, evasion, pretence and unjustified assurances, or misleading theories are all part and parcel of the tactics of disinformation. They may be blatantly evident in the chicaneries of the USSR and its allies and therefore there is a danger of people getting a one-sided picture – i.e. that machinations of this kind are only to be found in the Eastern bloc. Nothing could be further from the truth: just as much vigilance is needed in some of the democracies.

CHAPTER NOTES

FOREWORD

    1 'Children's "illness" invented by mothers', *The Times*, 18 October 1985.
    2 *The Godfrey Papers: The Naval Memoirs of Admiral J.H. Godfrey,* vol. viii, Churchill College Archives, Cambridge University.
    3 *Ibid.*

CHAPTER 1

    1 The Godfrey Papers.
    2 SHAEF Intelligence report, 11 March 1945.
    3 *Crusade in Europe*, Dwight D. Eisenhower, page 434.
    4 *Patriot or Traitor: The Case of General Mihailovich,* David Martin, Hoover Institution Press, 1979.
    5 *One Man's Wars: the Story of Charles Sweeny, Soldier of Fortune*, Donald McCormick, Arthur Barker, London, 1972. The author's informant was Dr James Spark, of Austin, Texas, who provided details of Sweeny's Yugoslav project.
    6 *Ibid.*
    7 *The Victims of Yalta*, Count Nikolai Tolstoy, Hodder and Stoughton, London, 1977.
    8 Public Record Office, File FO 371/47897.
    9 *Tito's Flawed Legacy: Yugoslavia and the West: 1939-84, Nora* Beloff, Gollancz, 1985.
   10 *The Guardian*, London, 4 February 1980.
   11 US Senate Hearings, 63-061 0.
   12 *International Affairs*, an official Soviet publication, No. 10, 1983.
   13 'Einstein suspected by FBI of hatching Hollywood plot', report from New York, *Daily Telegraph*, 10 September 1983.
   14 *The KGB Lie Machine*, Robert Moss, *Daily Telegraph*, 1979.
   15 *The Guardian*, London, 18 February 1981.

CHAPTER 2

1   *Washington Post*, 15 November 1965.
2   *The Times*, 24 July 1954. See also 26 July.
3   *Ibid.*
4   'Clue to 30-year spy mystery revealed', Anthony Glees and Andrew Wilson, *The Observer*, 7 January 1985.
5   *Ibid.*
6   *Ibid.*
7   *The Service: The Memoirs of General Reinhard Gehlen,* Reinhard Gehlen, translated by David Irving, World Publishing, New York, 1972.
8   'Reinhard Gehlen: An Elusive Character', Dr Kenneth J. Campbell, *Intelligence Quarterly,* Weston, Vermont, April 1985.
9   In *The CIA and the Cult of Intelligence*, Victor Marchetti and John D. Marks, Jonathan Cape, London, 1974, the authors cite Stanley Karnow, *Washington Post* correspondent in Asia in 1972 as the source of this story.
10   *The Deception Game; Czechoslovak Intelligence in Soviet Political Warfare*, Ladislas Bittman, Syracuse University Research Corporation, 1972.
11   *Ibid.*
12   Interview with Ladislas Bittman in *Dezinformatsia: Active Measures in Soviet Strategy*, Shultz and Godson.
13   The prosecutor's statement, cited in the *Daily Telegraph* of 17 December 1953, stated that 'in 1920 Beria, then in Georgia, again committed an act of betrayal, having established secret contact with the Menshevik secret police (Ochrana) in Georgia, which was a branch of British Intelligence. He tried to use organs of the Ministry of Internal Affairs, both in the capital and in the provinces of the Soviet Union, against the Communist Party and the Soviet Government in the interests of foreign capitalists.' He further added that Beria and his associates 'had murdered people who they thought might expose them. They had killed M.S. Kedrov, a member of the Party since 1902, and a member of the GPU collegium under Dzerzhinsky.'
14   Gerald Brooke, the British teacher who was caught and imprisoned in Russia in the 1960s, was working for the NTS, which was a prime reason for his arrest even though the real aim was to have a hostage in order to negotiate for the release of the two Krogers, who had been arrested for espionage and sentenced in London to 20 years' imprisonment. In the end the Krogers were exchanged for Gerald Brooke – hardly a fair exchange, particularly as Brooke had merely been involved in distributing clandestine leaflets, not in spying.

CHAPTER 3

1   'The Soviet Britannica', Midstream, vol. xxvi, no. 2, February 1980.
2   *Encyclopaedia Britannica*: 'Armenian S.S. Republic', vol. 2, page 27.
3   *Encyclopaedia Britannica*: 'Soviet Union', vol. 17, page 352.
4   'The Style of Soviet Propaganda', Lev Navrozov, *Midstream*, February 1980, vol. xxvi, no. 2.

5 'Goldsmith hails "victory" as *Der Spiegel* spy action is settled', Terence Shaw, Legal Correspondent, *Daily Telegraph*, 8 October 1984.

6 *Ibid.*

7 *Synthesis*, 20 May 1977.

8 Cited by the Deputy-Director of the CIA in his report, *CIA Study: Soviet Covert Action and Propaganda*, presented to the Oversight Sub-Committee of the Permanent Select Committee on Intelligence, House of Representatives, 6 February 1986.

9 'Exposing the KGB', by Richard Cox, *Conflict Quarterly*, journal of the Centre for Conflict Studies, University of New Brunswick, winter 1982.

10 *Ibid.*

11 Report from John Miller in Moscow, entitled 'FO Mole named by Russians', *Daily Telegraph*, 30 March 1983.

12 *Daily Mail*, 2 October 1930.

13 'Exposing the KGB', Richard Cox, *Conflict Quarterly*, winter 1982.

14 *Ibid.*

15 *Ibid.*

16 'New School Text book praises the brave Mau Mau', *Sunday Express*, 2 April 1978.

17 *Sunday Telegraph*, 13 October 1985, article entitled 'Children's book shows Britain as cruelly racist.'

CHAPTER 4

1 Letter in the *Church Times* from the Bishop of Bristol, 7 September 1973.

2 Letter to *The Times*, from Chief Clemens Kapuuo, 31 December 1975.

3 *Church Times*, 18 July 1969.

4 *Daily Telegraph*, 24 April 1974.

5 *Beckenham Journal*, 22 June 1978.

6 Published by Keston College, Kent, England, a centre for the study of religion and communism. The documentation was edited by the Rev. Michael Bourdeaux.

7 US Senate Sub-Committee to investigate the administration of internal security in the light of Communist Bloc Intelligence Activities in the US, 18 November 1975, US Govt Printing Office, Washington, DC., 63-061-0.

8 Office of National Estimates memo to CIA, declassified 7 October 1977.

9 *Moscow News*, no. 51. Zabirov even went further in this article. He added that 'many senior church leaders in the West and the Third World have come to recognize the growing force of Marxism and are ready to make common cause with it.'

10 London *Standard*, 20 March 1981.

11 *Daily Telegraph*, 25 August 1981: '"Army" quit churches council.'

12 *The Fraudulent Gospel*, Foreign Affairs Publishing Co., 1977. Letter to the author from Mr Bernard Smith, 20 August 1979.

13   CSCI – 316/04249-67, from James Angleton, Deputy Director of Plans and Operations, CIA, to J. Edgar Hoover, Director, FBI.
14   *Vancouver Sun*, 5 August 1983.
15   Document No. 2-11, page 10, World Council of Churches' Sixth Assembly report.
16   *Canvas*, WCC Assembly newspaper, 10 August 1983.
17   'Atrocities of Soviet Occupation', Michael Field, *Daily Telegraph*, 16 November 1985.
18   'Russian Church campaign against NATO Missiles', R. Barry O'Brien, *Daily Telegraph*, 17 January 1983.

CHAPTER 5

1   *Daily Telegraph*, 11 November 1985.
2   Statement by Mrs Patricia Rose to the author.
3   *Ibid.* Also tape-recordings by Sydney Knowles.
4   *Ibid.*
5   Cited by Chapman Pincher in '"Buster" Crabb's Last Dive', *Unsolved*, vol. 2, issue 24, 1984.
6   *Ibid.*
7   Statement by Mrs Rose to the author.
8   *Ibid.*
9   Statement made to the author.
10   *Ibid.*
11   *The Times*, 11 February 1964.
12   *The Oswald File*, by Michael Eddowes, Clarkson N. Potter, Inc, New York, 1977.
13   *Ibid.*

CHAPTER 6

1   'Mind Games', an article by Oliver Cambren, *Prediction,* November 1983.
2   *Datalink*, 3 October 1977.
3   *Ibid.*
4   *US Naval Institute Proceedings*, July 1985. Published by the US Naval Institute, Annapolis, Maryland 21402.
5   'Computer era crisis time in Russia', Ian Ball from New York, *Daily Telegraph*,   1985.
6   *Fortune* magazine, 1985.
7   *The Threat: Inside the Soviet Military Machine*, Andrew Cockburn.
8   See also *The Israeli Secret Service*, Richard Deacon, Hamish Hamilton, London, 1977.
9   Engineering Information Monthly, No. E1850907658.

CHAPTER 7

1   'Reagan's Space Plans Threaten Planet', David Millward, *Daily Telegraph*, 31 August 1985.

2 'Will SDI work and is it moral, scientists ask', by Ian Brodie, in Livermore, California, *Daily Telegraph*, 30 September 1985.

3 *How to Make Nuclear Weapons Obsolete*, Robert Jastrow, Sidgwick and Jackson, London, 1985.

4 *New York Times Magazine* and *International Herald-Tribune*, 28 January 1985.

5 *The Environmental Consequences of Nuclear War*, John Wiley and Sons, Chichester, 1985.

6 Letter to the *Daily Telegraph*, Miles Copeland, 3 August 1985.

7 CIA De-classified Papers, telegram from the American Ambassador in Moscow, No. 1204, 3 December 1958.

8 'Stonewalling on Star Wars', Theo Sommer, *Newsweek*, 30 September 1985.

9 Statement by Lord Carver in a discussion on the British deterrent, sponsored by the Royal United Services Institute and the British Atlantic Committee, 30 April 1980.

10 'Star Wars tests are a sham, says scientists', Ian Mather, Defence Correspondent, *Observer*, London, 29 December 1985.

11 *Morning Star*, London, 5 February 1983.

12 'Labour Threat to NATO, says Reagan Aide', *Daily Telegraph*, 7 February 1986.

CHAPTER 8

1 Report No. 11 of the Royal Commission on Environmental Pollution Cmnd 9675, Stationery Office, London, 1985.

2 *Ibid.*

3 Investigation by the USA General Accounting Office, 1984-5.

4 *The Times*, 6 December 1985.

5 *Ibid.*

6 *Ibid.*

7 *Nuclear Disaster in the Urals*, Zhores A. Medvedev, Norton, New York, 1979.

8 *The Guardian*, 9 December 1985.

9 *Ibid.*

10 'Stop This Nonsense, nuclear energy is safe!', article by Professor Sir Fred Hoyle, *Daily Mail*, 17 June 1980.

11 *Ibid.*

12 *Ibid.*

13 '60,000 "Back Scargill" on Windscale', *Daily Telegraph*, 16 September 1977.

14 'The Folly in Breeding Deceit', Professor Joseph Rotblat, *The Guardian*, 29 May 1980.

15 Cited in *Killing Our Own*, Harvey Wasserman and Norman Solomon, Delacorte, New York, 1982.

16 'Acid Rain Scourge Hits Oaks', *Daily Telegraph*, 19 October 1985.

17 'Acid Rain will turn Alps into treeless wilderness', *Sunday Telegraph*, 19 January 1986.

18 'Chest Ills Linked to Acid Rain', *Daily Telegraph*, 25 October 1985.

19 Survey of straw and stubble burning by the National Society for Clean Air Report, *Daily Telegraph*, 30 December 1985.

20 'Dounreay Letters Faked', *Sunday Telegraph*, 11 August 1985.

21 'A Threat worse than any nuclear attack', letter by Dr Kitty Little in the *Daily Telegraph*, 2 January 1981.

22 Royal Commission on Environmental Pollution report, No. 11, Cmnd. 9675, 1985.

CHAPTER 9

1 Statement by John McMahon, deputy director for Operations, CIA, to the Subcommittee on Oversight of the Permanent Select Committee on Intelligence, House of Representatives, 96th Congress, 2nd session, 19 February 1980.

2 Hearings before the Permanent Select Committee on Intelligence, House of Representatives, 97th Congress, 2nd session, 13, 14 July 1982.

3 *Ibid.*

4 *Ibid.* Also Special Report No. 101, 'Soviet Active Measures: An Update', July 1982, US Department of State.

5 *Ibid.*

6 Danish Ministry of Justice statement, issued 17 April 1982. See also House of Representatives Permanent Select Committee on Intelligence, 13 July 1982.

7 *Republica* (Lisbon), 15-20 July 1975. *Diario de Lisboa, Diario de Noticias, O Seculo* and *Diario Popular* for the same period.

8 MPLA claims of FNLA atrocities and cannibalism were published in *Le Monde*, 26 August 1975. The author is also obliged to Professor Douglas L. Wheeler, of the University of New Hampshire, for information on this subject.

9 See Special Report No. 88, US Department of State, Bureau of Public Affairs, October 1981. This report records a number of forged documents in this period, including a memorandum allegedly prepared by the CIA, criticizing Islamic groups as a barrier to US goals in the Middle East, and suggesting tactics to suppress, divide and eliminate these groups. This report was published in the January 1979 issue of the Cairo magazine, *Al-Dawa*.

10 Foreign Affairs Note, US Department of State, 'Soviet Active Measures: Focus on Forgeries', April 1983.

11 *Jeune Afrique*, 17 November 1982, and *Times of Zambia*, 10 January 1983.

12 Golitsyn's comments were published in the *New York Times*, 17 December 1982, in an article by Henry Kamm. Golitsyn also made the point that this assassination did not fit into the rationale of assassination as practised by the KGB and that poison, not shooting, was much more likely in such a case, as the Soviet Service had special poisons to inflict mortal diseases without leaving traces of poisons, so that death could be attributed to natural causes.

13 *The Dove and Bear*, Luigi Forni, Midas/Umbrella, 1985.

14 *Morning Star*, 21 September 1984.

15 'Soviet Active Measures': Special Report No. 110, US Department of State, Bureau of Public Affairs, September 1983.

16 *Ibid.* It is worth noting that in the summer of 1982 Moscow's Radio Peace and Progress made much of the allegations by an American citizen, Scott Barnes, who falsely claimed he had been asked by US Special Forces in March 1982 to assist in the use of chemical and biological weapons against El Salvador rebels. Barnes, who has been an occasional mouthpiece for Soviet disinformation, also incorrectly stated that he was a former Green Beret, FBI agent and CIA officer.

17 *Ibid.*

18 *Executive Intelligence Review*, 19 February 1985.

19 *Ibid.*

20 *Daily Mail*, London, 8 January 1986.

21 *Simerini*, Nicosia, 28 November 1985.

22 'Tory is victim of KGB Plot', *Daily Telegraph,* 25 January 1986.

CHAPTER 10

1 *Secrecy and Democracy: The CIA in Transition,* Admiral Stansfield Turner, Houghton Mifflin, Boston, 1985.

2 *Calvi, the cult and the Masons*, Lorana Sullivan, *Observer*, London, 3 October 1982.

3 *Ibid.*

4 *Ibid.*

5 *A History of the Chinese Secret Service*, Richard Deacon, Muller, London 1974.

6 Article entitled 'Henry Kissinger Named as Soviet Agent': *Confidential Intelligence Report of the Herald of Freedom,* New Jersey, April 1974.

7 Article entitled 'The Deadly Weapon of the Secret World: Disinformation', *Double Eagle*, New York, May 1978.

8 *Ibid.*

9 *Confidential Intelligence Report*, April 1974.

10 *Who Should Not be Who in the Reagan Administration*, New Benjamin Franklin Publishing Co., New York, 1985.

11 *EIR*, 26 February 1985.

12 *EIR*, 26 February 1985: 'Kissinger Watch', M.T. Upharsin.

13 New York *Daily Mirror*, 11 June 1971.

14 *Ibid.*

15 Various claims have been made as to the 'moles' inside the British, American, German and Israeli Services whom Goleniewski unmasked both to the FBI and the CIA, including Heinz Felfe and Hans Clemens (West Germany), Gordon Lonsdale (alias Konon Molody), Henry Houghton and John Vassall (British Admiralty), George Blake (MI 6), Colonel Israel Beer (Israel) and Colonel Stig Wennerstrom (Sweden). Goleniewski himself claimed that between 12 January 1961, when he arrived in the USA, and December 14 1963, he 'briefed US authorities on the reports and microfilms already sent through' and 'also brought with him complete data on 240 persons who were intelligence agents of the industrial, scientific and

technical bureau of the Polish Secret Service who were located in Western Europe and the USA.'

16   'HR 5507, a Prize Defector, Now the Boomerang' by David Wise, New York *Herald Tribune*, 8 March 1964.

17   Goleniewski's claims to be the Tsarevich have never been accepted by any of the US Intelligence and Counter-Intelligence Services.

18   GRODZISK's statement was made on deposition and given to the CIA and the FBI, though the material has not been released under the Freedom of Information Act to the best of the author's knowledge.

19   *Ibid.*

20   *Double Eagle*, vol. iv, No. 5, May 1978.

21   Cited from a subscription application form, giving the address of HIH Aleksei Nicholaevich Romanoff, PO Box 281, Murray Hill Station, New York 10016.

CHAPTER 11

1   *Brain-Washing: A Synthesis of the Communist Textbook on Psychopolitics*, published by New Times Ltd, and distributed by the Victorian League of Rights, Melbourne, Victoria.

2   *Ibid.*

3   *Daily Telegraph*, 29 January 1986.

4   *Ibid.*

5   See also Jean-Paul Sartre's 'Preface' to *The Wretched of the Earth*, Grove Press, New York, 1966.

6   'Socialism with Two Faces', by C.L. Sulzberger, *International Herald Tribune*, 3 April 1976.

7   *Ibid.*

8   'I spy a new discipline', *The Times* Diary, *The Times*, London, 19 December 1975.

9   Article in the *Neue Berliner Illustrierte,* No. 2, January 1976, by Dr Julius Mader.

10   *Ibid.*

11   *The Fourth Protocol*, Frederick Forsyth, Hutchinson, London, 1984.

12   *Ibid.*

13   'How the Left has science by the throat', by Professor Hans Eysenck, *Daily Mail*, 2 September 1977.

14   *Ibid.*

CHAPTER 12

1   *Pears Cyclopaedia*, 85th edition, 1976, Pelham Books, London.

2   *Ibid.*

3   Dr Zigel was speaking on Soviet TV on 10 November 1967.

4   CIA memorandum of 22 August 1952, declassified in 1979.

5   CIA memorandum ER-9-4255, 11 June 1957, declassified in 1979.

6   M. Galley was speaking on French radio on 21 February 1974.

7   '"Flying Saucer" has the boffins baffled', by David Paskov, report-

ing from Paris in the *Sunday Express*, 24 July 1983. The GEPAN report, supported by scientist Alain Esterle, indicated that analyses of the ground where the alleged spacecraft had landed produced startling results. Chlorophyll and other substances in the plants had been reduced by between thirty and sixty per cent.

8   Dr Zigel made this statement to Henry Gris and William Dick and it was quoted in *The National Inquirer* of the USA. But he was careful to add that 'the majority of Soviet scientists are still taking a sceptical stand on the problems of UFOs.' In the Russian magazine *Smena*, in April 1967, Dr Zigel wrote that 'Soviet radar has picked up unidentified flying objects for twenty years.'

9   The Earl of Kimberley, former Liberal spokesman on Aerospace, speaking in a UFO debate in the House of Lords, 18 January 1979.

10   Cited under the Freedom of Information Act, obtained through Mr Timothy Good, Britain's foremost lecturer on UFOs.

11   'UFO Lands in Suffolk', *News of the World*, 2 October 1983.

12   Adrian Berry, writing in the *Sunday Telegraph*, 17 October 1983, suggested that the sighting of the UFO was a misreading of the rotating beam of the Orford Ness lighthouse. Incidentally, Mr Berry in the same article also suggested that President Carter's UFO sighting in October 1969 was a 'misrepresentation of the planet Venus'. This seems highly unlikely as Carter, who graduated in nuclear physics, served as an officer on nuclear submarines and one of his duties would have been taking navigational fixes from the stars. Carter's original sighting report does not bear any similarity to the planet Venus, which would have been a familiar object to any US Navy officer.

13   This report was made on Department of the US Air Force headed paper and addressed to 'RAF/CC', so that clearly the British authorities were kept in the picture.

14   'The Greatest UFO of them All', Oliver Cambren, *Prediction*, August 1985.

15   *Unexplained* (Orbis Press, London), 1982-83, published photographs of the faked 'flying objects'. The British UFO Research Association has modern methods of image-processing by computer to analyse UFO photographs submitted to them for testing.

16   'UFOs "Trying to warn us of nuclear war" ', Keith Beabey, *News of the World*, 13 November 1985.

17   *'Du Nautilus'*, by G. Messadie, *Science et Vie*, No. 509, February 1960.

18   *Soviet Review*, vol. 2, no. 6, June 1961.

19   *Alpha*, issue no. 5, Nov.-Dec., 1979: see article on Submarine ESP.

20   *Problems of Philosophy*, September 1973: article by W.F. Zinchenko, A.N. Leontiev, B.M. Lomov and A.R. Luria.

21   Cited in an article entitled *Moscow: Behind the ESP Enigma*, by Martin Ebon and the editors, *New Realities*, California, 16 June 1977.

22   *New Realities*, 16 June 1977.

23   *Communications with Extraterrestrial Intelligence*, by J. Billingham and R. Resek, NASA, Ames Research Center, Moffett Field, California.

24   In a letter to the *New Scientist*, 20 December 1984, Thomas J. Best,

of the Royal Australasian College of Surgeons, Melbourne, alleged that 'the hocus-pocus of Targ and Harary and SRI has, several times, been comprehensively exposed for the superstitious clap-trap that it is.'

25 *Psychic Warfare: Threat or Illusion*?, by Martin Ebon.

26 Cited in the *New Scientist*, 22 November 1984, in an article entitled 'Strange Case of the psychic "spy" '.

27 *Ibid.*

CHAPTER 13

1 The Jamestown Foundation of Washington, DC: extract from its *Project Description*.

2 *Breaking With Moscow*, by Arkady Shevchenko, Alfred A. Knopf, New York.

3 *New Lies for Old: The Communist Strategy of Deception and Disinformation*, by Anatoli Golitsyn, the Bodley Head, London, 1984.

4 *Ibid.*

5 *Ibid.*

6 *Ibid.*

7 Report from Jeremy Campbell in Washington entitled 'Chinese spy on Russians for the US', The *New Standard*, London, 18 June 1981.

8 CIA declassified papers show that as long ago as 1946 George and Jeanne de Mohrenschildt, close contacts of Oswald, were found to have had links to the Soviet diplomat and undercover agent, Feodor Aleksevich Garanin in Washington.

9 'How Sir Harold's claims were blown apart', Chapman Pincher, *Daily Express*, 20 October 1977: 'He [Sir Harold] seriously suspected that "right-wing elements" were plotting to overthrow democracy in Britain and that South African agents were involved. This fear was at the root of his attack on MI 5.'

10 Royal Commission of Inquiry Concerning Certain Activities of the Royal Canadian Mounted Police: 2nd Report: 'Freedom and Security Under the Law', August 1981.

11 *Ibid.*

12 Cited in *The CIA and the Cult of Intelligence*, Victor Marchetti and John D. Marks, Jonathan Cape, London, 1974.

13 'Defector's Spy Story a "CIA fabrication" ', Richard Beeston, from Washington, *Daily Telegraph*, June 1985.

14 'Russia accuses Americans of kidnapping', *The Times*, London, 12 February 1964.

15 'Socio-Philosophical Problems of Scientific Information Work' by N.P. Vashchekin, Nauchno-Tekh. Information Service, Moscow, no. 3, 1982.

CHAPTER 14

1 *Actuel*, no. 50, December 1953, Paris, and *Frigidaire*, Primo Carnera srl, Milan.

2 'Greenpeace takes on Star Wars', *Observer*, 6 October 1985.

3 ' "Plot" against French spy service', Michael Field, from Paris, *Daily Telegraph*, 28 September 1985.

4 *Newsweek*, 2 September 1985.

5 *Ibid.*

6 'Double Defector's Secret Orders', Erskine McCullough, in Los Angeles, *The Standard*, London, 19 November 1985.

7 'Moscow Laughs over Defector's tales of the CIA', Nigel Wade, Diplomatic Staff, *Daily Telegraph,* 15 November 1985.

8 *Ibid.*

9 *Los Angeles Times*, 10 November 1985.

10 *Les Russes Sont Arrivés*, by Cyril Chenkin, Scarabée et Compagnie, Paris. Chenkin was a former member of the NKVD and a friend of Rudolph Abel, who defected to the West in 1973.

11 *Danger: Additives at Work*, a report by the London Food Commission.

12 'Guide to Healthy Eating Blocked', Oliver Gillie, Medical Correspondent, *Sunday Times*, 4 August 1985.

13 'Clean-Up in Hospitals "Will Cost Millions" ', *Daily Telegraph*, 8 February 1986.

14 ' "Wasted Beds" Behind Hospital Waiting Lists', *Daily Telegraph*, 28 October 1985.

15 *Ibid.*

16 *Trud*, Moscow, 6 October 1985.

17 *EIR*, 6 September 1985.

18 *Guardian*, London, 23 September 1985.

19 *Beckenham Times*, 13 February 1986: 'Putting AIDS in Perspective'.

20 *Ibid.*

21 *Daily Telegraph*, 13 February 1986.

22 *Ibid.*

Index

Abakumov, Viktor 46
ABM (Anti-Ballistic Missiles) Treaty of
    1972 115
Acid rain 135-138
Adenauer, Dr Konrad 38,39
Afghanistan War 76-78, 208-210
'Agent Smrk' 70
Ahnenerbe Occult Bureau 18
AIDS 8, 107, 220-223
Ainstain, Reuben 29
Anderson, Anna 167
Andropov, Yuri 47, 113, 143, 152
Angleton, James 76, 91, 92, 159, 205
Angolan Civil War 148
Arafat, Yasser 51, 216
Arbatov, Georgi 176
Arbatov American Institute 176
Arnold-Forster, Mark 27
Ashley, Jack, MP 126
Atomic Energy Authority 131
Attlee, Clement 25, 128
AWTSC (Atomic Weapons Tests Safety
    Committee) 128

Baader, Andreas 176
Baader-Meinhof organization 176
Baker, Dr David 114
Barak, Brigadier Ehud 216
Barrington-Ward, R. McG. 9 ·
Barry, Michael 77
Bartlett, Dr 114
BBC's Overseas Services 22, 36
Beloff, Nora 26, 224
Benn, Anthony Wedgwood 130
Bennett, Sir Frederick 157
Bent, Colonel Peter W. 187
Beria, Lavrenti 45, 46, 171-173, 225

Berrill, Sir Kenneth 130
Bethell, Lord 156, 157, 162
Beves, Donald 82, 83
Bevin, Ernest 25, 34
Bezimensky, Lev 29
Biddle, General Drexel 37
Biddle, Margaret 36, 37
Bilak, Vasil 212
Billingham, J. 193
Birch, Alexander 189
Biryuzov, Marshal 118
Bitov, Oleg 152, 197, 201
Bittman, Ladislas 44, 225
Blake, George 44, 168, 178
Blunt, Anthony 83
B'Nai B'rith 161, 162
Boldyrev, K. 47
Borberg, Colonel P.H.J. 178
Bormann, Martin 40, 41
BOSS (Bureau of State Security,
    South Africa) 202
Bourdeaux, Rev. Michael 70, 76, 226
Brezhnev, Leonid 153
British Council of Churches 67, 74,
    75
British Medical Association 222, 223
British Nuclear Fuels 131
Brzezinski, Dr Zbiganiew 115, 154
Bulganin, Marshal 84, 117
Burdick, Eugene 42
Burgasov, Pyotr 220
Burgess, Guy 57, 82, 87
Butler, Lord 141

Campbell, Dr Kenneth 41
Campagne Anti-Outspan 67
Capell, Frank A. 165

Carter, President James 154, 184
Carter, Peers 77
Carver, Field-Marshal Lord 121, 228
Catholic University of America 110
Castro, Fidel 154, 156
CETI (Communications with Extra-
    terrestrial Intelligence) 193, 194
Chadwell, H. Marshall 185
Chalfont, Lord 162
Chandra, Romesh 31
Chauhan, Jagit Singh 156
Cherneyeni, Mrs V. 62
Chetniks, the 21-23
Childers, Erskine 58
Chou En-lai 151
Christian Peace Council Conference
    31, 74, 76
Churchill, Sir Winston 10, 20, 21, 25,
    128
Churchill, Winston, MP 60
CIA 35, 36, 42, 72, 75, 76, 90-92/116,
    143-147, 151, 153, 155, 156, 159, 160,
    163, 167-169, 177, 183-185, 189, 198,
    200-206, 212-215
CIA (303 Committee of) 35
Clark, Judge William 145
Clark-Kerr, Sir Archibald (Lord
    Inverchapel) 20
Clason, Anders 179
Clemitson, Ivor 12
Clifton, Father Michael 74
CND (Campaign for Nuclear
    Disarmament) 112, 113, 119, 120
Coates, Rev. Peter 68, 70
COCOM (Co-ordinating Committee
    for Export Control) 106
Cohen, Rose 54
Colby, William 92
Combs, Richard 213
Cominform, the 31
Computers 95-110
Composite Signals Unit 207
Confederation of British Industries 105
Copeland, Miles 116, 228
COSDEGUA (Confederation of
    Diocesan Priests of Guatemala) 73
Cox, Baroness 61
Cox, Richard 56, 59, 60, 226
CPRS (Central Policy Planning Review
    Staff) 130
Crabb, Commander Lionel 84-89, 227
Cranston, Senator Alan 127
Cuban Missiles Crisis 45, 118, 200, 204
Cyprus Signals Centre 206, 207

Dalai Lama 116
Davidson, Basil 60

Davitashvili, Djuna 195
Dean, Douglas 192
Dedijer, Professor Stefan 176-179
Dedijer, Vladimir 176
De Gaulle, General Charles 156, 210
De Mohrenschildt, George 93, 95, 202,
    233
De Mowbray, Stephen 200
Deng Hsiao-Ping 201
Department 8 (Disinformation Dept of
    the Czech Intelligence Service) 44
Department D of the KGB 143
Deriabin, Peter 204
D'Estaing, Giscard 185
Deutsche Volksunion 29
Djuretic, Veselin 23
Doenitz, Admiral Karl 17
'Double Cross' Committee 10
Dozier, Brigadier-General James 151
Dubcek, Alexander 43, 212
Durenberger, Senator David 213

Ebon, Martin 194, 232
EDC (European Defence Community)
    37, 38
Eddowes, Michael 92, 227
Eden, Sir Anthony (Lord Avon) 25, 39,
    85
Eilts, Herman F. 146
Einstein, Dr Albert 30, 31
EIR (Executive Intelligence Review)
    52, 156, 161, 162, 165, 166, 220, 221
Eisenhower, General Dwight D. 19
Elektronorgtechnika 106
ELINT (Electronic Intelligence) 107
Elliot, Kenneth 88
Elorg 106
Encyclopaedia Britannica 48-50, 225
Epstein, Edward Jay 204, 205
Eysenck, Professor Hans 180, 181, 231

Fanon, Franz 175
FBI (Federal Bureau of Investigation)
    30, 31, 91, 167, 186, 198, 200, 215
Federal Communications Commission
    of the USA 103
Felfe, Heinz 38
Felman, General Richard 22
Fleming, Ian 58, 59, 164
FNLA (National Front for Liberation
    of Angola) 148
Forgeries by the KGB and others 142-158
Forni, Luigi 153
Forsyth, Frederick 179, 231
Fowler, Norman 221
Freedom of Information Act (USA)
    189, 217

Index

FRELIMO 67
Fremde Heere Ost (West German Military Intelligence) 40
Friends of the Earth 130, 132, 139, 140
Frolik, Major Josef 28, 70

Gaddafi, President Muamur 156
Gagarin, Alexis 167
Galley, Robert 185, 231
Gamov, Prokopy 56
Gandhi, Indira 155, 156
Gandhi, Rajiv 157
Gatrow, Dr John 218
GCHQ 207
Gehlen, General Reinhard 22, 38, 40, 41, 225
Generals for Peace 121
GEPAN 185
Gloucester, Duke of 162
Godfrey, Admiral J.H. 10, 15, 224
Goebbels, Josef 46, 90
Goldsmith, Sir James 52-53, 226
Goleniewski, Lieutenant-Colonel Michal 164-170, 230, 231
Golitsyn, Anatoli 89, 92, 152, 198-200, 233
Gorbachev, Mikhail 205, 213
Gordievsky, Oleg 206, 207, 214, 215
Grauehr, Colonel 15, 17
Grauerholz, Dr John 221
Graves, Philip 51
Greenpeace organization 131, 140, 206, 210, 211
GRODZISK 169-170, 230, 231
Gromyko, Andrei 199
GRU (Soviet Military Intelligence) 44, 55
Gulyashki, Andrei 58, 59

Haig, General Alexander 123
Hallstein, Professor Walter 39
Halt, Lieutenant-Colonel, USAF 188, 189
Hammarskjold, Dag 89, 90
Harris, William 119
Hartman, Arthur 214
Hebditch, David 104
Henderson, Arthur 58
Hess, Rudolf 41
Highland Regional Council 132, 139
Hill, Sir John 131
Hillenkoetter, Vice-Admiral 183
Hitler, Adolf 17, 20, 39, 41, 51
Hollis, Sir Roger 57
Hook, Professor Sidney 48
Hoover, Edgar G. 30, 31, 76, 91, 186, 227

Howe, Sir Geoffrey 211
Howe, Marcus 67
Hoyle, Sir Fred 130, 133, 134, 228
Hubbard, L. Ron 173, 175
Humphrey, Senator Hubert 117
Hynek, Dr J. Allen 186

Iacoveves, Sazzas 158
Indian Brotherhood of the North-West Territories 67
IRA (Irish Republican Army) 176
International Council of Scientific Unions 116
International Technological Collaboration Unit 130
International Trading Corporation 106
Investroic Group 106
Izbot, General René 211

Jagdverbaende, the 17
Jamestown Foundation 197, 198
Jastrow, Professor Robert 115
Jesuit Order, the 71, 72
Johad, Abu 216
John, Dr Otto 37-40
John XXIII, Pope 72, 75, 76
John-Paul I, Pope 65
John-Paul II, Pope 75, 151-153, 201
Johnson, Rev. Dr Hewlett 65, 66
Johnston, Senator Olin D. 167
Jones, Dr Peter 221, 222
Jones, Professor R.V. 178
Josten, Josef 208
Juan-Carlos, King of Spain 145
Justice Commandos of the Armenian Genocide 176

Kampelman, Max 115
Kapuuo, Chief Clemens 67, 226
Kardashev, Professor N.S. 194
Kennedy, President John F. 89, 90, 91-93, 201, 202
Kennedy, Robert 93, 202
Kent, Monsignor Bruce 113
Kerans, Commander John 88
Keston College 70, 75, 226
KGB, forgeries of 142-158
Khokhlov, Nikolai 192
Khomeini, Ayatollah 201
Khrushchev, Nikita 84, 117, 118
Kilgallen, Dorothy 93, 95
Kimberley, Early of 186
Kimsey, Herman E. 166
Kinnock, Neil 179
Kirkpatrick, Jeanne 151
Kissinger, Henry 162, 163-165, 230
Klugmann, James 21

Knowles, S.J. 86, 227
Kotyepov, General 47
Kuznetsov, Valentin 123
Kyrill, Archbishiop 77, 78

Lagerfelt, Dr Johnson 77
Lansdale, Colonel Edward 42, 43
Large and Associates 132
LaRouche, Helga Zepp 161
LaRouche, Lyndon 52, 156, 161, 162, 165
Latey, Mr Justice 173, 175
Lawrence Livermore Laboratory 114, 121
Lawrence, T.E. 13
Lederer, William J. 42
Lenin University 71, 171
Lenin, V.I. 16
Lekhi, Pran Nath 157
Levchenko, Stanislas 151
Little, Dr Kitty 139
Livingstone, Dr David 61
Lodge, P-2, Italian 162
Lumumba, Patrice 90, 155
Lund University 176-179
Luns, Dr Josef 135, 148

Maclean, Donald 57, 82, 87
MAD (Mutually Assured Destruction) 121, 122
Mader, Dr Julius 144, 178
Malenkov, Georgi 45, 117
Malik, Bishop Alexander 77, 78
Marshall, Lord 140
Martin, Arthur 200
Martin, Kingsley 54
Marx, Karl 65, 206
Masaliev, Abaamat 206
Masaryk, Jan 43
Mather, Ian 121
Mau Mau terrorist campaign 60, 61
M'Bow, Amadou Mahter 61
McCarthy, Senator Joseph 30, 37
McDonald, Mr Justice D.C. 203
McDonald Royal Commission of Inquiry into the RCMP 203, 204
McEvoy, Dr Marion 221
McMahon, John 143, 229
McNamara, Robert 220, 221
Medvedev, Zhores 129, 228
Melkov, Captain R. 88, 89
Mendès-France, Pierre 36-38
Menzies, Sir Robert 128
Merkulov, Vladimir, 123, 147
MI 5 57, 82, 83, 88, 202
MI 6 44, 177, 196, 200
Mihailovic, Draza 21-23, 40, 48, 224

Millar, Sir Frederick (now Lord Inchyra) 39
Miller, General Eugene 47
Miller, Melanie 218
Montagu, Ewen 87
Moslem Brotherhood 146, 147
Mossad, the 29, 206
MPLA (Popular Movement for Liberation of Angola) 67, 148
Mugabe, Robert 66
Muller, Lieutenant-General 149
Mulley, Fred 24, 130
Mussolini, Benito 71

National Centre for Space Studies (France) 185
National Council of Civil Liberties 105
National Security Council (USA) 153, 185, 187, 198, 207
National Society for Clean Air 138
National Union of Seamen 132
NATO (North Atlantic Treaty Organization) 28, 31, 79, 121, 123, 135, 144, 145, 148, 178
Naumov, Eduard 190-192
Nautilus, USS 191
Navrozov, Lev 50, 225
Nazi-Soviet Pact 9
Ne'eman, Dr Yuval 107-108
Nehru University 179
Nel, Louis 81
Nemchenko, Major General 56
Nicholas II, Tsar of Russia 164, 166, 168
Nikodim, Archbishop Metropolitan 65, 68
Nkomo, Joshua 66, 90
Noel-Baker, Philip 58
Norman, Rev. Dr Edward 69
Northrop Corporation 149, 150
Nosenko, Yuri 90-92, 167, 201, 205
NTS (*Natsionelno-Trudovoy-Soyuz*) 46, 47

Oehme, Dr Frederick 214
Oestreicher, Canon Paul 79
Official Secrets Act 186, 189
Office of Scientific Intelligence (USA) 185
Oldfield, Sir Maurice 196, 207
Operation Chonkin 208-210
Orwell, George 11, 12
OSS (Office of Strategic Services) 35
Oswald, Lee Harvey 90-93, 202, 205

Palestine Liberation Organization 61, 146, 176, 216

Panitza, John Dimi 152
Papandreou, Andreas 146
Paraphysical Laboratory (UK) 194
Parnell, Charles S. 142
Parker, Lord Chief Justice 134
Pathé, Charles 55
Patton, General George 19, 20
Paul VI, Pope 66, 71
Payne, Rev. Dr Ernest 68, 69
Penkovsky, Oleg 118, 204
Perle, Richard 124
Perov, Vitaly 193
Pesek, Rudolf 193
Petersen, Arne Herlov 147
Petrovsky, D. 54
Philaret, Archbishop 79
Philby, Kim (H.A.R.) 57, 82, 179
Pigott, Richard 142
Pilsudski, Marshal 23
Ping Fa 10
Ponomarev, Boris 63
Popov Institure 194
Pound, Admiral of the Fleet Sir Dudley 10
Protocols of the Elders of Zion 51
Pruetzmann, Hans 17
PSI 190-195
Puerto Rico Solidarity Committee 67
Puznetsov, Alexandrovich 55

Rabb, Maxwell 153
Radio Free Europe 36, 41
Radio Liberty 36, 41
Rainbow Warrior 206, 210, 211
'Rand, Michael' 43, 44
Rawlinson, Lord 52, 53
RCMP (Royal Canadian Mounted Police) 203, 204
Reagan, President Ronald 111-112, 120, 145, 154, 213
Red Brigades, Italian 144
René, President Albert 147
Roosevelt, President F.D. 20, 25
Rose, Mrs P. 85, 88, 89, 227
Rotblat, Professor J. 135
Royal Commission on Environmental Pollution 126, 141
Royal Commission of Inquiry into British nuclear tests in Australia 127, 128
Rutter, Dr Nicholas 8

Sadat, President Anwar 146, 147, 149
Sakharov, Andrei 130
SALT (Strategic Arms Limitation Talks) 119, 120
Salvation Army 74

Sartre, Jean-Paul 175, 231
Scargill, Arthur 136
Schmidt, Wulf 11
Schwartz, Professor Richard 30
Schweitzer, Albert 90
Scientology organization 171, 175, 183
Scricciolo, Luigi 151
SDI (Strategic Defence Initiative) 111-124, 165, 228
Seale, Dr John 220
Sejna, General Jan 53
Semichastny, Vladimir 59
Service A 27, 53, 216
Service Five (*Komitet Informatsii*) 15-17
SETI (Search for Extra-terrestrial Intelligence) 194
SHAEF (Supreme Headquarters Allied Expeditionary Forces) 18, 224
Sharma, Dhirendra 179
Shevchenko, Arkady 197, 199, 204
Shuster, Savik 208
SIGINT (Signals Intelligence) 107, 207
Sillitoe, Sir Percy 88
Sinclair, Major General Sir John 86
Smith, Bernard 75, 226
Smith, Walter Bedell 185
Soames, Christopher (now Lord Soames) 210
Socialist Workers' Party 162
SOE (Special Operations Executive) 21-24, 177
Solidarity 153
Solzhenitsyn, Alexander 66
Sommer, Theo 120
Southwood, Professor Sir Richard 126, 141
Spaak, Paul-Henri 34
Sparagna, Vincenzo 208
SRI (Stanford Research Institute) 97, 194
SRI International 104
Stalin, Josef 16, 21, 25, 34, 45, 117
'Star Wars' 111-124, 228
Stearns, Monteagle 145
Stern, Dr August 193
Stickley, Charles 171, 174
Stoate, Dr Howard 221, 222
Strauss, Dr Franz Josef 52, 53, 148
Sun Tzu 10, 16, 200
SWAPO 67
Sweeny, Colonel Charles 23, 224
Sykes, Greta 62

Targ, Russell 192, 194, 195
'TATE' 11
Thatcher, Margaret 147, 154, 162
Thompson, E.P. 32